Mimesis and Sacrifice

Violence, Desire, and the Sacred

Series Editors
Scott Cowdell, Chris Fleming, and Joel Hodge

Volumes in the series:
Vol. 1. *Girard's Mimetic Theory Across the Disciplines*,
edited by Scott Cowdell, Chris Fleming, and Joel Hodge
Vol. 2. *René Girard and Sacrifice in Life, Love, and Literature*,
edited by Scott Cowdell, Chris Fleming, and Joel Hodge
Vol. 3. *Mimesis, Movies, and Media*, edited by Scott Cowdell,
Chris Fleming, and Joel Hodge
Vol. 4. *René Girard and Raymund Schwager: Correspondence 1974-1991*,
edited by Scott Cowdell, Chris Fleming, Joel Hodge,
and Mathias Moosbrugger
Vol. 5. *Mimesis and Atonement: Rene Girard and the Doctrine of Salvation*,
edited by Michael Kirwan and Sheelah Treflé Hidden
Vol. 6. *Möbian Nights: Literary Reading in a Time of Crisis*,
by Sandor Goodhart
Vol 7. *Does Religion Cause Violence?: Multidisciplinary Perspectives on
Violence and Religion in the Modern World*, edited by Scott Cowdell,
Chris Fleming, Joel Hodge, and Carly Osborn
Vol 8. *Mimetic Theory and Film*, edited by Paolo Diego Bubbio and
Chris Fleming
Vol. 9 *Mimesis and Sacrifice*, edited by Marcia Pally

Mimesis and Sacrifice

Applying Girard's Mimetic Theory Across the Disciplines

Edited by
Marcia Pally

BLOOMSBURY ACADEMIC
LONDON • NEW YORK • OXFORD • NEW DELHI • SYDNEY

BLOOMSBURY ACADEMIC
Bloomsbury Publishing Plc
50 Bedford Square, London, WC1B 3DP, UK
1385 Broadway, New York, NY 10018, USA
29 Earlsfort Terrace, Dublin 2, Ireland

BLOOMSBURY, BLOOMSBURY ACADEMIC and the Diana logo are trademarks of
Bloomsbury Publishing Plc

First published in Great Britain 2020
This paperback edition published in 2021

Copyright © Marcia Pally and Contributors, 2020

Marcia Pally has asserted her right under the Copyright, Designs and
Patents Act, 1988, to be identified as Editor of this work.

For legal purposes the Acknowledgments on p. vii constitute an extension
of this copyright page.

All rights reserved. No part of this publication may be reproduced or transmitted
in any form or by any means, electronic or mechanical, including photocopying,
recording, or any information storage or retrieval system, without prior
permission in writing from the publishers.

Bloomsbury Publishing Plc does not have any control over, or responsibility for, any
third-party websites referred to or in this book. All internet addresses given in this
book were correct at the time of going to press. The author and publisher regret any
inconvenience caused if addresses have changed or sites have ceased to exist,
but can accept no responsibility for any such changes.

A catalogue record for this book is available from the British Library.

A catalog record for this book is available from the Library of Congress.

ISBN: HB: 978-1-3500-5741-8
PB: 978-1-3502-5404-6
ePDF: 978-1-3500-5742-5
eBook: 978-1-3500-5744-9

Series: Violence, Desire, and the Sacred

Typeset by Deanta Global Publishing Services, Chennai, India

To find out more about our authors and books visit www.bloomsbury.com and
sign up for our newsletters.

Contents

Acknowledgments · vii

Introduction *Marcia Pally* · 1

Part One Our Understanding of Sacrifice, Expanded:
Origins, Development, Types, and Valence

1 A Comparative and Evolutionary Perspective on
Sacrifice and Cooperation
Peter M. Kappeler · 37

2 Sacrifice Between West and East:
René Girard, Simone Weil, and Mahatma Gandhi
on Violence and Nonviolence
Wolfgang Palaver · 51

3 Patterns of Sacrifice and Power Structure
Hassan Rachik · 64

4 Rabbinic Reflections on Intentional Sacrifice and Sanctification
Tsvi Blanchard · 77

5 Kant on Sacrifice and Morality
David Pan · 90

6 Sacrifice amid Covenant: From Abuse to Gift
Marcia Pally · 103

7 Generative Sacrifice: Girard, Feminism, and Christ
Anna Mercedes · 118

8 Sacrifice and Liberation: A Reading by the *Magisterium*
of the Catholic Church in Latin America
Francisco Canzani · 130

Part Two Is the "Problem" of Sacrifice a Problem of
Conceptualizing Masculinity?

9 Between Victim and Perpetrator:
Constructions of Heroic Masculinity and the Religion of Death
Ulrike Brunotte · 147

10 The Ambiguity of Sacrifice in a Post-Heroic Nation:
    A Military Perspective
    Rolf von Uslar   161

Part Three An Expanded Understanding of Sacrifice
            Applied to the Economic, the Political, and the Future

11 Gift or Sacrifice? History, Politics, and Religion
    John Milbank   177
12 Strategy, Spectacle, or Self-emptying?
    Sacrifice and the Search for Business Ethics
    Philip Roscoe   190
13 Common Good Economy:
    Capitalism, Sacrifice, and Humanity
    Adrian Pabst   203
14 Suffering and Sacrifice in an Unfinished Universe
    Ilia Delio, OSF   216

Concluding Thoughts
    Marcia Pally   228

Notes on Contributors   245
Index of Names and Concepts   248

Acknowledgments

My first thanks go to the contributors to this volume, who have, from their many perches and disciplines, brought much to our understanding of sacrifice and the thinking of Rene Girard. I have learned a great deal from each of them through their chapters and through the many conversations we have had in working on the book. Their research in different schools and traditions has made it possible not only to see this wide-ranging topic through a variety of priorities and research tools but also to look at sacrifice in one arena *in light* of work done in another—to look, for instance, at sacrifice in the military in light of Christian theology and gender studies or sacrifice in gender studies in light of the sociology of business.

This project began with an international, interdisciplinary conference in June of 2016. We are deeply grateful to the Fritz Thyssen Foundation and the Telos Paul/Piccone Institute for their generous funding of that conference. Equally are we grateful to the Theology Faculty at Humboldt University-Berlin, the conference site, for the welcoming provision of space, administrative assistance, and other in-kind services. Our welcome at the Theology Faculty would not have been possible without the leadership of Prof. Dr. Rolf Schieder, organizational assistance from Julia Dietrich and Anika Tobaben, and administrative assistance from Petra Haupt—to them, many thanks.

Our gratitude goes also to Prof. Dr. Wolfgang Palaver, who brought the idea of the project for consideration to the editors of the series on Rene Girard at Bloomsbury Academic, Scott Cowdell, Chris Fleming, and Joel Hodge. Much appreciation to them for their advice at all stages of the book and to Wolfgang Palaver for his generous insights on the important through-lines of the volume.

We are indebted to our publisher, Bloomsbury Academic, and to all the people at Bloomsbury for their help in bringing this manuscript to the public: Colleen Coalter, Becky Holland and the team at Deanta, among others.

For her support throughout the many stages of research, writing, and editing this volume, I thank Pamela Parker, who has vetted so many ideas with good cheer. I would like to express my gratitude also to my teachers at the Solomon Schechter School, who were my first guides to giving, sacrifice, community, and thinking. Sending me to this school was a great gift from my parents, Nettie Rose Pally and Sidney Pally, and from my grandfather, Isaac Schachter, who insisted on this sort of education, even for girls.

—Marcia Pally, editor, November 22, 2018

Introduction

Marcia Pally

In the neo-hardball of much public discourse today, "sacrifice" sounds like a bad thing. It seems either like sentimental nostalgia for a "simpler time" of "supportive communities" inapplicable to present economics and geo-politics. Or it is the call of the suicide bomber. In either case, "sacrifice" is not what one wants to be doing. Yet the concept of sacrifice has played a foundational, organizing role in nearly all human cultures. Central to theology, to the political and military imaginaries, to economic systems, and to personal identity and responsibility, it has inspired, disturbed, and abused. This is no less so at present, as Julia Meszaros and Johannes Zachhuber write, "Sacrifice without a doubt has been an obsession of modernity. There is no other period in Western history, with the possible exception of late antiquity, that has seen a comparably sustained, critical engagement with this religious ritual, its theoretical underpinnings, and the problem of its theological, ethical, and social justification" (Meszaros and Zachhuber 2013: 1).

This book emerges from an international, interdisciplinary conference, "Sacrifice: Biological and Theological Investigations for Economic and Military/Political Praxis," funded by the Fritz Thyssen Stiftung and the Paul Piccone/Telos Foundation and held at the Theology Department of Humboldt University-Berlin in June 2016. Both the conference and the present volume are concerned with the meanings, practices, and valence of sacrifice in present societal arenas from the military and business to politics and gender relations. Why and how do our ideas about sacrifice motivate us, to do what, under what conditions is sacrifice productive and when, abusive? The book is also concerned with the resources that inform our understanding of sacrifice (and thus its valence and practice), among them philosophy, political and military theory, evolutionary biology, economics, gender studies, and theology.

In this endeavor, the book shares a basic intention with the work of Rene Girard, whose writings on sacrifice have over the last half century contributed so much to our understanding. By saying it "shares a basic intention," I mean that Girard explored the historical and cultural conditions from which sacrifice emerged (why we do it) and how sacrifice works (its societal function, what it moves us to do). That is, he had a primary engagement with the act and institution of sacrifice, investigating the phenomenon itself rather than discussing about it. This is the endeavor also of this volume. It dives into the primary questions about sacrifice's foundations and functions that occupied Girard for much of his life.

This is not accidental as many of the book's authors work outside "guild approved" (Meek 2011: xiv) Girardian studies but deeply inside the investigation of sacrifice in particular societal arenas. In focusing specifically on the understanding and practices of sacrifice, this volume distinguishes itself from recent works on mimesis that we recommend to our readers (among them, Cowdell, Fleming, and Hodge 2014, 2015; Goodhart et al. 2009). Moreover, the idea of bringing a broadly interdisciplinary approach to the study of sacrifice was precisely to get at the "outsider" perspective, to cull from areas in which Girard worked (literary and religious studies, for instance) but also from those which Girard did not plumb (evolutionary biology, sociology of business, and gender studies). This volume thus builds on recent efforts by Girardian scholars to expand the reach of his ideas into such fields as cultural anthropology, archaeology, and cognitive psychology (Antonello and Gifford 2015); the cognitive, developmental, and neuro sciences (Garrels 2011); political violence (Dumouchel 2015); movies and other media (Cowdell, Fleming, and Hodge 2016); and theology (Dawson 2013; Heim 2006; Goodhart 2014; Kirwan and Hidden 2016). The hope is that our interdisciplinary approach allows for research grounded in the premises, investigational categories, and research tools (fieldwork, biblical exegesis, among others) of a wide range of inquiry to illuminate our understanding of contemporary sacrifice and so to remark directly and indirectly on the positions taken by Girard.

The contributors' common interest in sacrifice's foundations, motivational power, and outcomes has yielded considerable agreement with Girard. All contributors, for instance, share Girard's view of humanity as social. This is our "catholiticity," as contributor Ilia Delio puts it (Delio 2015: Kindle Locations 441–43). Human persons develop through relationships, acculturation, and what Pierre Bourdieu called *habitus*—the network of dispositions, or "conductorless orchestra" in Bourdieu's charmed phrase (Bourdieu 1990: 58–59), that is formed by categories of perception, language, worldview, values, and individual experience and so guide people to think and act in certain ways and not others (Bourdieu 1984: 170, 471). This understanding of the person as societally embedded runs counter to reductionist readings of the Lockian social contract.

Indeed, Locke's theory of mind supposed an impressionable infant who develops through input from its sensory and relational milieu. It runs counter as well to neoliberal conceptions of the person as separable from relations and community to move or be moved through positions in the economy.

Yet this agreement between our contributors and Girard has also raised questions. A brief recap of Girard's classic theory of sacrifice may be helpful in understanding them.

In brief: Girard's theory of sacrifice

As a first tenet, Girard held that to understand the goings-on of the world and promote human flourishing, one needs an understanding of our foundational condition, what biologist Darcia Narvaez calls our "baseline": "To approach eudaimonia or human flourishing, one must have a concept of human nature, a realization of what constitutes a normal baseline, and an understanding of where humans are" (Narvaez 2014: 438). The Girardian "baseline," the foundational person-in-society, is not the hunter-gatherer, cooperatively minded within her group and often across primary bands (Seyfarth and Cheney 2012; Silk and House 2011; Trivers 1971; Waal 2014; Wilson 2013; see below for a more extended discussion). She is not the participant in the Aristotelian *polis*, the biblical person-in-covenant, or the citizen of modern covenantal political theory based on the *pacta* and common good (Althusius 1603/1964: chapters 1, 3–4). She is not liberalism's "individual" possessed of rights nor is she a member of liberal democracy, a working together of *polis*, *pacta*, and liberal regard for the individual.

While all these presume commitment to not only self-betterment but societal flourishing, the Girardian archaic human is enmeshed in competition-prodded aggression *within* her own primary group, a fallenness begun "with Cain" and much like Hobbes's short, brutish world. This competition and aggression are, on Girard's account, the unavoidable outcomes of living among others. For as groups cultivate shared values, individuals inevitably compete over them, or as Hobbes wrote, "If any two men desire the same thing, which nevertheless they cannot both enjoy, they become enemies; and in the way to their End, . . . endeavour to destroy, or subdue one another" (Hobbes 1651: ch. 13, par. 3).

Girard acknowledges the absence of competition in, for instance, parental love. But he finds that our very acculturation and internalization of *common* values yield within groups the desire for similar material and honorific gains. "Our neighbor," Girard writes, "is the model for our desires" (Girard 2001: 10). What we want mimics what others want. From shared desires and goals comes competition for these wanted items. "Conflictual mimesis" unavoidably emerges except in the rare case of limitless resources (Girard 1977: 187). From mounting competition comes an agonistic view of neighbor and potentially society-rending tensions. "The principal source of violence between human beings," Girard concludes, "is mimetic rivalry" (2001: 11).

In short, as contributor Wolfgang Palaver insightfully notes (Palaver 2013: 37), the Girardian person is far from Aquinas's cheerful *homo homini amicus* (man is friend to man) and more Hobbes's *homo homini lupus* (man is wolf to man). But perhaps the Girardian person is most like Augustine's synthesis: "For there is nothing so social by nature, so unsocial by its corruption, as this race" (Augustine 426/2014: 520). Kant too observed this paradox of the human condition, our "ungesellige Geselligkeit" (unsociable sociability) emerging from our autonomy and individual striving amid our unavoidable life with others (Kant 1784/2009: 13, 14).

In light of this paradoxical *un*social sociability, Girard held that to transform our competitive, unsocial tendencies, metanoia is needed, a change in heart inspired not by modernity's rationalism or science but by Christ's love and invitation to "non-violent imitation" (Heim 2006: 220). "The scientific spirit," Girard wrote, "like the spirit of enterprise in an economy, is a by-product of the profound action of the Gospel text" (1986: 204–05). This compassion, so great that Jesus was willing to die for humanity, shows suffering from the perspective of the victim, who is never deserving of such a lot. Yet, this love determines also to forgive the perpetrator, indeed to love all humanity, and so a cycle of retaliatory violence is preempted. Elias Canetti (1984: 143–45), Moshe Halbertal (2012), Palaver (2018: 267–68) and Charles Taylor (2004: 36) among others have described the self-righteous fury that may erupt where victimhood is not tempered by forgiveness—what Canetti calls "religions of lament." But together, the perspective of the downtrodden, forgiveness and love can transform worldview and world. In his last work, *Battling to the End*, Girard concludes, "Humans have only to adopt the behavior recommended by Christ: abstain completely from retaliation, and renounce the escalation to extremes" (Girard 2010: Kindle Location 181).

Absent this love and forgiveness, humanity finds solution to mimesis-prodded competition and aggression in the selection of a scapegoat who is labeled as the source of accumulating societal tensions. These tensions may be the violence and injustice that the group itself calls sin (Girard 1987, 2011). "The community," Girard explains, "unites against a victim in an act of spontaneous killing. This act unites rivals and restores peace and leaves a powerful impression that results in the establishment of sacrificial religion" (McDonald 2003).

In such sacrifice, Girard finds the origin of the sacred, from which religious and other societal institutions develop. Religion, Girard held, is "part of human nature" (Vattimo and Girard 2010: 31). Owing to its salvific function in rescuing the group from mimesis-induced violence, the act of sacrifice acquires something of the transformative sacred. The victim, as it has "given" itself for the group, too takes on a sacred aura. Girard thus writes of a "double transference," where the group sees its scapegoated victim as source of both society-rending violence and sin *and* salvific societal bonding (Girard 1987: 37). "The peoples of the world," Girard continues, "don't invent their gods. They deify their victims" (2001: 70).

While the original sacrifice is always one of real violence (Girard 1986: 25), its repetition, ritualization, and incorporation into the culture bring about a "mythological crystallization" (Girard 1987: 247). The resulting myth-narrative, submerging the original brutality and making it irretrievable to societal memory, generally includes four features: a moment of primordial crisis (threat to the group); a "sin," wrongdoing or violence that has brought the crisis about; a perpetrator who has committed this wrong; and a ritual whereby society rids itself of the wrong-doer by murder or exile. From this ritual arises the panoply of archaic religious practices, their calendar of ritual recurrence (sacred time), ritual/sacred spaces, myths, and taboos (prohibitions against whatever "sin" ostensibly provoked the original tensions; see also, Eliade 1998: 20–65). Throughout these secondary religious practices and myths, the scapegoating mechanism is preserved sub rosa, as part of the culture to be ritually repeated until—Girard's final step—society embraces Jesus's offer of love and its "non-violent imitation."

Considerations arising in the book: Competitive aggression—as old as "Cain" but not as old as "Adam"

Contributors to this volume agree with Girard on humanity's mimetic nature and our at least initial acquisition of values through acculturation. There is further probing, however, of the idea that shared values—because of their very *sharedness*, because they are learned through mimesis within societies—inevitably bring on society-rending competition and aggression. Thus, primary questions running through this volume are as follows:

- Might mimesis lead to a different end, even to cooperativity and reciprocal concern?
- Might competition and aggression be brought about by something other than mimesis and shared values?
- Could sacrifice have had a function other than as a steam valve for mimetic competition?
- Are there sorts of sacrifice that benefit human living and societal flourishing?

One line of inquiry (Kappeler and others, this volume) follows evolutionary biology in its explorations of hunter-gatherer societies (95 percent of our evolutionary development). These societies preceded the development of agriculture, private property concentrations, population densities, and significant sociopolitical hierarchies, and they may well precede the archaic period of Girard's focus. Without written languages, they certainly predate the many literary examples and recorded histories used to illustrate Girard's theory of an original scapegoating violence that is suppressed and yet emerges covertly in later literature and myth. The premise of such suppression is that the original violence took place earlier, before the writing of its literary chrysalis.

But we might also look to even earlier, hunter-gatherer forms of living that preceded unequal property distribution and competition—ways of living that appear to have been more cooperative and less violent. Girardian theory itself suggests that there likely were such earlier forms. After all, his archaic societies *already* had a commitment to containing competitive aggression. They already held to the value of societal peace though this is by no means necessary, and our closest relatives, the chimpanzees, do not share it (Schmid-Hempel 2015). The practice of scapegoating sacrifice was an endeavor, however misguided, to preserve peace among the many by forfeiting the few (Girard 1986, 2004: 13). Absent such a violence-reducing goal, archaic societies could have let mayhem take over. Given that preferences against violence are not automatic or necessary but rather evolve over extended periods of time, it appears that evolutionary pressures for relatively harmonious living had long been in play. Studying communal hunter-gatherer societies may illuminate the substantial portion of human evolution that preceded the competitiveness, hierarchies, and violence of agrarianism. Because the nature of human life—what portion of our makeup is competitive/aggressive and what portion, cooperative—concerns many of this book's chapters, I'll take a moment to very briefly sketch the argument from evolution.

What do we learn from early humanity? Even before the *Homo sapiens*, the *Homo erectus*, to sustain the cooperation of hunts, group protection, and the care of offspring with long, vulnerable childhoods, evolved "an entirely new level of social organization beyond anything seen in nonhuman primates" (Bellah 2011: Kindle Location 2019). The later hunter-gatherer *Homo sapiens* were mimetic and shared group values, yet this mimesis did not provoke high levels of competition and aggression but rather substantial solidarity, egalitarianism, and sharing within groups. Beginning with the repetition of facial expression and gestures, mimesis likely emerged, Sarah Hrdy notes, several hundred thousand years ago owing to the long period of childcare and close adult-child interaction required by relatively unformed human infants. As childcare was performed not only by mothers but by many (even nonkin) adults, it eventually yielded what Hrdy calls "emotional modernity," the human capacities to "read" and relate to the emotions of others, to sustain relationships and to generalize this relating to those one hasn't met before, even to strangers (Hrdy 2009: 204–06, 282)—that is, to sustain joint intention, attention, and care.

Looking at humans today, developmental psychology too notes the importance of relationship to child development (Gilligan and Snider 2018) and of mimesis to our relationality. Human infants develop through continuing interaction and nexes of relationships with kin, community, and all that impinges on them—the opportunities and stresses that bear on each child's milieu. In Darcia Narvaez's summary, "Whom a person becomes is a co-construction of genes, gene expression from environmental effects . . . and the ecological and cultural surroundings . . . . There is no being without shared social relations" (2014: 15, 103). In this developmental process, mimesis is a mechanism of relationship. From birth onwards, we mimic facial expressions and gestures (Gallagher 2005: 244–45), thus creating a "shared space," a "unified common intersubjective space" (Gallese 2005: 105, 111). To mimic is to participate in the world of the other, whom even infants know is different from themselves (Reddy 2008: 19–21). Relationality is the ability of distinct, unique persons to relate to and share in the world of others. "There is a sense in which one 'participates' in the other person's state, yet maintains awareness of 'otherness' in the persons with whom one is sharing" (Hobson and Hobson 2012: 120–21). This likeness with *different* others grounds the capacity to recognize human-ness in strangers, to relate to and work with them.

In sum, mimesis bridges otherness; it is the stuff of bonding and empathy. It tells us that others, however different, are also like ourselves, creating conditions for cooperation and commitment. This is part of our "deep enculturation," Merlin Donald writers, returning to humanity's early development (2001: 264). Absent these mimetic and relational capacities, coordinated, cooperative activities are very difficult. Thus, mimesis—along with long, relatively protected childhoods—was one of the prime factors undergirding *Homo sapien* development of both play activities and the transmission of complex knowledge, from toolmaking and proto-language to celebrations and cooperative work. "All the processes of change, imagination, and learning," Alison Gopnik concludes, "ultimately depend on love. We can learn from the discoveries of earlier generations because those same loving caregivers invest in teaching us. It isn't just that without mothering humans would lack nurturance, warmth, and emotional security. They would also lack culture, history, morality, science, and literature" (Gopnik 2009: 15).

Mimesis teaches us mime, imitation, gesture, and importantly, the abstraction of sequences of behavior from the immediate context, allowing us to reenact the past, communicate future plans, and describe an imaginary world (Donald 2001: 263–65)—all requirements of play activities and learning complex skills for future use. In turn, play—as it conjures the imaginary and develops into repeating activity-patterns with agreed upon goals and rules—is possibly the origin of society-bonding ritual (predating language and sacrifice). Indeed, the very "fairness" requirement of play positions it (and any rituals emerging from it) as solidarity-building (Bellah 2011: Kindle Location 1579, 1602). Johan Huizinga, in his classic study of play, continues, "Now in myth and ritual the great instinctive forces of civilized life have their origin: law and order, commerce and profit, craft and art, poetry, wisdom and science. All are rooted in the primaeval soil of play" (Huizinga 1950 [1938]: 5).

To be sure, unplayful, uncooperative behavior and violence was not unknown within primary hunter-gatherer groups. To begin, scapegoating aggression is evident among certain nonhuman primates (de Waal 2005: 167–70). Paul Schmid-Hempel, noting humanity's "hyper-cooperativity," also notes that chimps are far more violent and demonstrate far less in-group cooperation (2015). Though in-group aggression (and the primate "alpha-male" ranking system associated with it) diminished markedly in hunter-gatherer humans, some form of it remained even within hunter-gatherer groups. Certain members may have become greedy and transgressed the group's norms of sharing and cooperativity. The group in turn developed ways of sanctioning such lack of fairness (Schaik and Michel 2016). These sanctions, however, served to uphold the egalitarianism of private-property-less hunter-gatherers—an egalitarianism which was not just a "gentlemen's handshake" or case of "reverse dominance," where each male agreed to not take the other men's food and women as long as they did not take his. Rather, egalitarianism resulted from long evolutionary pressures toward what Robert Bellah calls "the strong pull of social solidarity" (at least partially grounded in mimesis) and "community morality" (Bellah 2011: Kindle Location 2783), where not fear of sanction but desire for affection and belonging are the primary motivators. In something of an evolutionary virtuous circle, the desire for belonging yields a group ethos of fairness and sharing, and such groups select for cooperative, sharing behavior in its members.

The situation *between* groups is more complex, with both cooperativity and competition. Samuel Bowles, an economist relying on computer simulations and somewhat less on evolutionary anthropology, describes "parochial altruism." Here, altruism within the group is strengthened by a "parochial" preference for the in-group and hostility to outsiders (2008: 326; see also Palaver 2015: 153–56). Emile Durkheim and Henri Bergson had similar views, holding that fear of outsiders and animus against them serve to unite the in-group. "Who can help seeing," Bergson wrote, "that social cohesion is largely due to the necessity for a community to protect itself against others, and that it is primarily as against all other men that we love the men with whom we live? Such is the primitive instinct" (1935: 22).

Yet there is some question of whether preference for the in-group of necessity brings along hostility toward others, especially among hunter-gatherers. First, a consistent culture and practice of parochial altruism is more likely among early sedentary, agricultural societies with city-clusters, where alien tribes or nations were ever nearby and often in competition for resources. It is less likely in roving hunter-gatherer bands, where contact with outsiders was intermittent and bands were less frequently in resource competition as they continually moved around. Moreover, cooperation in hunts, mating, and other activities was not infrequent among individuals who were not kin and between hunter-gatherer groups when they did cross paths. Evidence for such "reciprocal"—not parochial—altruism (Trivers 1971) is not inconsiderable: "Natural selection," Dorothy Cheney and Robert Seyfarth write, "therefore appears to have favored individuals who are motivated to form long-term bonds *per se* not just bonds with kin" (Seyfarth and Cheney 2012: 170; see also, Bowles and Gintis 2013; Churchland 2012; Roca and Helbing 2012; Silk and House 2011). Reciprocal cooperativity, Edwin Scott Fruehwald finds, "appears to be hard-wired into human brains. In other words, there is a universal grammar of reciprocity just like there is a universal grammar of language" (2009). We are, Donald Pfaff writes, "wired for goodwill" (2014: 5).

David Barash (2013) notes that even intergroup war is not genetically hardwired but rather "historically recent," "erratic in worldwide distribution" and "a capacity." Capacities are "derivative traits that are unlikely to have been directly selected for but have developed through cultural processes ... capacities are neither universal nor mandatory" (see also, Ferguson 2013; Fry 2007). "There is presently no conclusive evidence for intergroup fighting in the early Pre-Pottery Neolithic," Clare, Dietrich, Gresky, Notroff, Peters, and Pöllath (2019, 101) write, and though they warn against ignoring evidence of violence where it did occur, they conclude, "Caution should nevertheless be exercised if we wish to avoid a situation which sees the 'bellicosification' of prehistory" (2019, 101). In his noteworthy overview of the literature, Bellah finds the emergence of war to be associated with the property concentrations and sociopolitical or religiopolitical hierarchies of later agrarian living: "War does seem to be correlated with economic intensification and to emerge in relatively recent prehistoric historic times ... organized warfare oriented to territorial conquest does seem to appear only where rich economic resources are locally concentrated" (2011: Kindle Location 3041–43).

The preference for cooperativity, especially within but also across groups, may be the human "baseline" as Narvaez put it. Evolutionary benefits included improved hunting and other activities among cooperative rather than competitive clans and the greater longevity (and longer time to reproduce) that comes with less frequent violent conflict. Importantly, however complex the situation may have been across groups, there is substantial agreement on the evolutionary preference for cooperativity as a "baseline" within groups. In present society, when violence is committed, we experience outrage and find aggression appalling as it violates our relational baseline. Were humanity "wired" for competitive abuse rather than cooperativity, violence would feel *comfortable*. Even if one allows that humanity became more competitive with the development of agriculture, population and property concentrations, and sociopolitical hierarchies, Nicholas Christakis and James Fowler (2009) find that, in modern capitalist economies and urban anonymity, generous acts prompt generous responses not only dyadically but exponentially, spreading through our relational networks. That is, it appears that our hunter-gatherer cooperativity, evolved over several hundred thousand years, has remained part of the human repertoire.

These findings suggest some tension with the Girardian archaic, where society-rending, competitive aggression arises *within* the group, precisely where evolutionary biology finds cooperativity and solidarity to be strong. Even in cases where a group selects an outsider as sacrificee (a captive of war, for instance), the aggressions to be defused are those within the group, emerging from shared group values. And on Girard's theory, sacrificial victims were often chosen from within the group, again where cooperativity and solidarity were substantial.

To resolve the apparent tension between evolutionary biology and mimetic theory, we might consider that they describe different episodes in human development, with biology offering insights into an earlier, long hunter-gatherer period of significant (if not perfect) cooperativity while mimetic theory offers insights into a later, shorter period of agrarianism, population and property concentrations, and greater competition and violence (see Bellah 2011: chapters 3–5 for an overview of the development of the agrarian archaic). The competitive aggression that emerges from the very shared-ness of values *within* groups may be precisely as old as "Cain," just as Girard said. But he did not say it is as old as Adam, as old as humanity itself. That is, competitive aggression may be only as old as the "Fall"—or as evolutionary biology would have it, as the long transition—from hunter-gatherer sharing and cooperativity to the greater competitiveness of propertied, hierarchical agrarianism. In this sense, the "Fall" marks the sin of substantial wealth gaps, unfair distribution of resources, the abuse of large portions of the populace, and insufficient regard for the welfare of the group as a whole.

If this is the case, Girard's insights about sacrifice as a response to societal competition also pertain to this later, more competitive phase. For if mimesis-prodded competition/aggression was not foundational or predominant within earlier hunter-gatherer societies, there would have been less need for a ritual steam valve (sacrifice) to defuse it and restore intragroup cooperation. Ritual among hunter-gatherers may have developed at first not from sacrifice but from play, as Bellah, Donald, and Huizinga, among others, hold. That is, hunter-gatherer ritual may have in the main served to build solidarity not because of mob-bonding against a scapegoat but because of a three-part outcome of evolution: we are a relational species; our "deeply enculturated" relationality emerges at least in part from the long period of childhood mimesis; so that *the activity of mimetically performing together ritual patterns that are fair and shared by all gives Homo sapiens the feelings of relatedness, belonging, and being cared for that we evolved to want and need.*

It's the evolution from mimesis to play patterns that gives feelings of belonging and care, and then from play patterns to ritual that Hrdy, Bellah, Donald, Huizinga, Whitehouse and Lanman (2014), and others explore. In a primary sense, play is a counterpoint to scapegoating violence, and I will dip just for a moment into the discussion of fictive worlds to flesh this out. Play "play-acts" that which troubles us; Girardian sacrifice enacts real violence against what troubles us, the scapegoat who, as the word denotes, is innocent. Drawing a picture of an animal, for instance, as part of a ceremony in which an upcoming hunt is theatrically invoked is a form of play or fiction formation. It anticipates the risks of the hunt without real danger or features of sacrifice. The hunt itself is not play. Murdering someone to beseech the gods for a good hunt too is not play but real violence.

Our fictive arenas—from "horsing around" (playing at fighting) to fairy tales, roller coasters and theater—provide opportunities for us to near and experience, or nearly experience, our fears, tensions, uncertainties, and greatest hopes in a relatively safe environment so as to better broker them in our emotional and psychological centers. We confront the fears and desires that threaten to overwhelm safety and the self, and the fictive confrontation assures us that we can survive *because* in every play-event, no matter how much it skirts danger, at the end, we are alive and endure. The lesson, no matter how many actors are dead on stage, is that when the game is over or the lights come up, we prevail. At a primal level, we are psychologically bolstered for the risky project of living. The purpose of our fictive arenas is to completely pull us into the drama and yet in the end, leave us completely out to endure intact.

This is not the scapegoating of a (real) innocent but a fictive mechanism to address fears and desires without real harm. Our first fictions, as Freud reminds us, are dreams, where we theatrically rehearse the unresolved issues of our lives to better deal with them when awake. This, the great film theorist Siegfried Kracauer explains, is what we do when we create awake-dreams in theater, film, and other ritualized reenactments of past or future events. We depend on them "for the reflection of happenings which would petrify us were we to encounter them in real life" (Kracauer 1960: 305). The point of fiction is that we aren't in "real life." When a hunger-gatherer band paints a picture of an animal as part of a pre-hunt ceremony, the band knows that the ritual is not the hunt. The animal has not been caught, but the group's hopes and trepidations have been emotionally rehearsed in ritual and art to lower fears and strengthen courage for the hunt itself. When we go to a horror movie, we do not hope that our throats are ripped open by undead ghouls; there is a difference between assault and a Halloween release. When we go on a roller coaster, we do not hope to plunge to a shattering death; there is a difference between a car crash and an amusement park ride. We give ourselves a bracketed encounter, a "reflection" of the fear, in order to experience ourselves not-crashing, as surviving. And if there is an accident with injuries or deaths, this is no longer play but real-life tragedy. Robert Sklar writes that fiction gives "viewers access to events that happened when they were not there, to the dangerous, the fantastic, the grotesque, the impossible, *at a close but safe remove*" (Sklar 1975: 21, emphasis mine).

We have not only personal, idiosyncratic fears and hopes. People share similar ones by dint of being human—by dint of the hundreds and thousands of years of evolution for relationship, belonging, harmony, and concomitant fear of death and chaos. Groups experience fears and desires particular to their milieu (fear of a specific flooding river, hope that a specific prey will be caught, dread of a specific invader). These, directly or encoded, are the raw material of our fictive worlds—from cave paintings and myths to the latest film—where we enact them "at a close but safe remove" without inflicting real harm. Genre films, John Cawelti writes, are modern myths that "enable people to reenact and temporarily resolve widely shared psychic conflicts" (1984: 12). Thus, Kracauer notes in *From Caligari to Hitler* (1957), one gains insight into a society's fears, hopes, and doubts—and our own—by examining its play arenas and fictions.

In short, we theatrically rehearse—without inflicting real violence—what threatens safety and self for the implicit, reassuring message that we are alive and intact, and so we shore up our ability to go on with the risky project of living. We do so *together* because of the three-part outcome of evolution: our relationality and mimetic natures, which make performing ritual activities together soothing to *Homo sapiens*, giving us the feelings of relatedness, belonging, and safety. From mimesis—mime, imitation, and the abstraction of behavioral sequences from the immediate context—we come to social play and then to fictive reenactments of past and future events, which develop into art, ritual, and myth. Describing the archaeological site at Göbekli Tepe (9000–7000 BCE), a ritual site shared by still small, roaming groups, Clare, Dietrich, Gresky, Notroff, Peters, and Pöllath (2019, 105) write that the "ritual enclosures, the T-pillars, and associated pictorial representations and sculptures could be understood as the stage and scenery for a late hunter-gatherer mythological narrative, one used by these communities for the conveyance of shared moral values, the documentation of group memories and histories, the formation of identities, and the promotion of intergroup cooperation and altruism." The gathering of many different groups at the site "would have fostered strong between-group bonds, enhanced by the shared emotions of participating in especially memorable acts" (2019, 122). There is no evidence, they add, of human or animal sacrifice—as a steam valve for accumulating competitive aggression or other reasons—at the Göbekli Tepe site.

Though the evolution from mimesis and play patterns to fictive enactments and then ritual occurred early in *Homo sapien* development, preceding the Girardian archaic, play enactments and ritual didn't stop there but rather continued to be primary human ways of dealing with fears and desires into the archaic period (and into modernity). With later agrarianism and the increasing societal tensions arising from property concentrations and significant hierarchies, Bellah and Schaik and Michel note, real-life violence became more frequent, stoking fears of future tensions and violence—just the raw material of dreams, art, and ritual of the sort described in Girard's archaic. That is, a rise in societal violence was accompanied by fictive forms and rituals to cope with it, much as we observe in survivors of war and other trauma today (persistent violence in dreams and a wide range of other coping mechanisms). Society running amok with gangs (or local chieftains) bludgeoning each other is real-life violence. A codified, repeating ritual of sacrifice as a (terrifyingly misguided) effort to contain the mayhem is part violence and partly on the road to fictive reenactment. Once the sacrifice is no longer performed but "crystallized" as myth, as Girard writes, we have a fictive world in which fear of society-rending tensions ritually "plays" itself out.

To be sure, any tensions within earlier hunter-gatherer societies that could not be resolved by the usual nonviolent means may also have ended in real violence. Yet the long evolution toward fairness, sharing, and cooperativity in hunter-gatherer groups (*contra* artificially imposed and enforced cooperation) makes real violence in this context the rarer case. Evolutionary biology finds both violations of cooperativity and violent punishments unusual in hunter-gatherer contexts because *these societies were not harboring foundationally competitive individuals straining to break free of cooperation norms but rather were comprised of people who had over hundreds of thousands of years evolved strong sharing and fairness norms* and nonviolent means of addressing occasional breaches that were in the main effective. This does not mean that hunter-gatherers had no daunting hopes (for belonging or a successful hunt) or terrifying fears (of injury or death). Surely they did, and at least some were expressed in play enactments, other rituals, and art. But it may be that the preponderance of these terrors and desires did not, among high-cooperative hunter-gatherers, emerge from the sorts of interpersonal competitiveness and violence found in later stratified agrarian societies. Again, given the long evolution toward fairness and cooperativity, tensions were not likely to become so society-rending that the usual nonviolent means of addressing them would fail.

In sum, there is an evolutionary argument that mimesis—imitation, the abstraction of behavioral sequences from the immediate context into the imaginary—enabled play activities, play enactments, and ritualized fictive forms in relatively cooperative hunter-gatherer societies. These ritualized forms in turn may have provided a basis for later archaic rituals that developed to deal with the societal stresses and violence emerging from the property concentrations, population densities, and hierarchies of agrarian living and early human city-clusters. Archaic ritual sacrifice, where violence against an innocent is not occasional but an integral, necessary part, is indeed real violence against the scapegoat but also ritual to preserve the peace among the many.

Archaeology finds evidence suggestive of this history at, for instance, Çatalhöyük, the site of a crowded Anatolian Neolithic community in existence as the radical shifts to agrarianism and concentrations of population and property were occurring (7500–5700 BCE; Clare, Dietrich, Gresky, Notroff, Peters, and Pöllath 2019). Some human remains show injuries to the head, which may indicate both real intragroup violence *and* ritualized fighting that developed as psychological rehearsals to cope with fear of violence "at a close but safe remove" (Sklar 1975: 21) but where injury might accidentally occur. Difficult initiation rituals, where injury may be sustained, are also fictive enactments of the dangers of future hunts and male adulthood. Evidence of injury may also suggest human sacrifice though one must be cautious in ascribing causality as injury and death may also result from falls, accidents (on the hunt or elsewhere), male-on-female abuse in the newly patriarchal social order, blows not within the group but against members of various out-groups (slaves or captives, for instance, as we don't know who the people in question were), etc. It is also difficult to know what percentage of the population sustained such injuries. In the case of rare "foundation burials," where a person is buried in the foundation of a house, caution must be exercised in labeling these sacrifices as it is difficult to determine whether such persons were sacrificed for the occasion or had died of other causes while a house was being constructed.

Art at Çatalhöyük shows numerous depictions of animals in positions of predator and prey, suggestive of pre-hunt images (Hodder 2019). In some, humans surround, tease, and overpower the animal, also suggestive of pre-hunt fictive forms where vulnerable, trepidatious humans together play-act power and victory over the wild animal. (A similar mechanism is in play in Mardi Gras/Carnival and the Jewish festival of Purim, where the vulnerable and powerless play-act superiority or victory over powerful elites.) Domesticated or tame animals are depicted hardly at all, suggesting that these images were cultural and psychological mechanisms for Çatalhöyük residents to cope, in relatively safe play arenas, with fear of life's dangers. Animal skulls, antlers, and boar tusks from former hunts were used as home decorations, talismans of power over wild animals, and success in high-risk endeavors. Several painted images depict very dangerous animals that were known but rare in the region, such as leopards, or animals in theatrical, highly stylized formations, further suggesting their function as "movies" to assuage fears of animal attack. Two leopards, for instance, are seen in symmetrical mirroring, a geometrical configuration that creates for the viewer a comforting sense of order and control over the scene (*contra* asymmetry, which creates imbalance and tension). In another image, two rows of people, also in soothing symmetry, are dressed in leopard skins, donning "costumes" of might and power and dancing as they face a line of animals to be caught, from small to the most risky, the large bull. These rows of costumed dancers prefigure the use of symmetrical patterns in fictive presentations from classical art and ballet to the films of Busby Berkeley.

It has been suggested that Çatalhöyük art and decorations reflect not hunts but sacrifice and that animals were domesticated first for sacrifice and only later for food (Hodder 2019). Yet the lack of images showing the moment of the animal's death, pyres, and other accoutrements of sacrifice make this difficult to determine. Moreover, as hunter-gatherers already used animals for food, it is somewhat strained to argue that later, more sedentary societies with the ability to keep animals would not continue to do so with the animals they kept. Benoit Chantre holds that food provision preceded symbolic sacrifice, noting that only when agrarianism and animal domestication were more firmly established in the middle of the Çatalhöyük period, "when the basic food supply was assured, around 6,500 BCE, and when domestic animals (sheep and goats at Çatalhöyük) provided a store of meat sufficient for the group's survival, that the sacrifice of wild animals could have acquired a 'memorial' value, in other words a ritual meaning" (Chantre 2019, 173). He continues, "Many clues lead one to think that the progress of the sacrificial institution is linked to that of urbanization" (2019, 183) that is, to the city-clusters that emerged with agrarianism, population density, property concentrations, and the Girardian archaic.

The details of the transition from hunter-gatherer to archaic living—how, when, and under what conditions violent, symbolic sacrifice occurred—remain open questions in this book. While the competitive stresses of agrarian, stratified societies may have prodded actual sacrificial violence, it's worth recalling that an earlier idea of sacrifice in cooperative hunter-gatherer societies consisted of forgoing resources for the sake of the common good, a "fairness" feature present in humans and even the more violent chimps. "Chimpanzees and humans," Frans de Waal writes, "go even further by moderating their share of joint rewards to prevent frustration in others. We owe our sense of fairness to a long history of mutualistic cooperation" (2014: 71)—pointedly, to giving up, sacrificing, what we might keep for ourselves for the sake of others and the group. This common-good sort of sacrifice is not the bane of civilization, as real violence is, but its constructive ground. Giving and sacrificing for fair distribution through the commons is a necessary and positive feature of society because it makes living with others work.

Thus, we come to the following questions: Is there a universal, foundational form of sacrifice? Need there be only one? If so, is it grounded in mimetic competition and scapegoating? And if mimetic competition is not the ground for all sacrifice, what are other grounds and what are sacrifice's other functions?

If one holds, as Schaik and Michel, Bellah and others do, that competition and aggression increased markedly with the development of agrarianism and property concentrations, then it is not social living or mimesis per se that prod competition and aggression—as hunter-gatherers were both social and mimetic but conspicuously less violent. It may be that inequality—or mimesis under conditions of inequality—is the spark for the mimesis-competition-violence conflagration. This is precisely what anthropology finds in archaic civilizations, which are described (*contra* hunter-gatherers) as having agriculture, private property, social classes which were "unequal in power, wealth, and social prestige" *and* high intragroup aggression. Governance was based not on kinship but "a tiny ruling group that used coercive powers to augment its authority was sustained by agricultural surpluses and labor systematically appropriated from a much larger number of agricultural producers" (Bellah 2011: Kindle Locations 3279–81).

Under such conditions, sentiments of protest against the violation of our evolution-bred cooperativity might well emerge as would resentment against unfair wealth and perhaps violence against those few who had it. "Upstarts," who try to take wealth and power from those who have them, may also appear. The old hunter-gatherer way of handling both resource-grabbing and upstarts no longer worked in these much larger archaic societies, where those with power and upstart-hopefuls could gather around themselves supporters of their own. As a result, violence erupted in an effort to gain resources and power. Bellah suggests that this rather straightforward resource-grab—not scapegoating sacrifice—was the "first killing" (Bellah 2011: Kindle Locations 3965). Add the militarization of archaic civilizations and the mayhem could be substantial. "Large, prosperous societies are almost always in danger from the havenots at their fringe, or from other prosperous groups who would like to become even more prosperous. In a situation of endemic warfare, the successful warrior emanates a sense of mana or charisma, and can use it to establish a following" to take as much power and wealth as he could (Bellah 2011: Kindle Locations 3974–76).

However, even if Bellah holds that this was the "first killing," he also notes, in support of Girard, that sacrifice, often human, was soon to follow in archaic societies. With the emergence of kings—identified as a god or god's son or the mediator between the gods and the people (who cannot communicate directly with the divine)—human sacrifice was "almost always" a feature of archaic religious ritual (Bellah 2011: Kindle Locations 3292, 3861).

This may be our recent past of the last 6,000 or so years. But this means that it is not only violent sacrifice that is "crystallized" and preserved sub rosa in ritual and myth. A prior (hunter-gatherer) cooperativity and sacrificial forgoing-for-the-commons would have earlier and already been submerged under agrarian property concentrations and their accompanying competitive violence. We labor under this double suppression. Moreover, our earlier cooperativity may be resurrected in narrative and symbol much as mimetic violence is. We labor also under these double narratives. Our art and religions are replete with tales of both mayhem and giving, sharing and sacrificing for others. That is, not only the dark aspects of the social psyche but also the wisdom about the best means for human flourishing is preserved.

Schaik and Michel propose something like this in noting that the last 7,000 to 10,000 years of agriculture and property concentrations are too short a time to have substantial influence on the sort of relational, cooperative creatures humans evolved to be over hundreds of thousands of years of hunter-gathering. Our competition and aggression, they suggest, appear to be responses to the "new," propertied, hierarchical way of life that violates our evolution-tested sense of equality, fairness, and cooperation.

On this view, primary cooperativity persists in the human condition as a palimpsest, pushing against the layers of gross inequality, unfairness, and sociopolitical hierarchies. Such foundational cooperativity has important consequences. It may make some difference to the possibility of present and future human relations if cooperative ones are foundational to the species and if competition-prodded violence is a later if terribly important matter. The prognosis for humanity is far more optimistic with a long hunter-gatherer history of cooperativity and reciprocal concern than if humanity to date has never lived amid such an ethos but only envisioned it, from under the woes of competitive aggression, as a religious or political ideal. If cooperativity, substantial within groups and present also across groups, is hundreds of thousands of years of foundation, it might be more ready-to-hand.

I'll suggest three examples of such a palimpsest, beginning with the Garden of Eden and Fall narrative. This is not to say that the authors of Genesis remembered more cooperative, egalitarian hunter-gatherer life or the transition to agrarian living that occurred perhaps 5,000 years earlier. Rather, our evolution-tested cooperativity, emerging over hundreds of thousands of years, remains in our DNA and neurological centers of emotion. The evolutionary expectation of sharing and cooperation (if not the memory of actual hunter-gatherer life) emerges in fictive forms just as other hopes, disappointments, and longings do. The Garden of Eden narrative tells of a bygone paradise where there is no conflict and food is not the product of exhausting subsistence farming and worse, unfairly distributed. Rather, it can be picked off the trees by all. The unavoidable contrast to the hierarchical, often violent conditions of the period in which Genesis was written too is given literary expression as the "Fall." What is captured is not the history from hunter-gathering to agrarianism but a sort of evolutionary grief and protest against conditions that violate our evolution-tested sense of equality, fairness, and reciprocal giving.

The crucifixion narrative too may be a trace or eruption of primary cooperativity and its importance to human flourishing. The narrative begins with violence against Jesus but turns in focus to Jesus, fully human, giving his life for humanity. Indeed, the prime import of the narrative is donative self-giving, which both saves humanity and reminds us of how we too may act should we follow Jesus. The narrative resurrects for us, amid brutality, the idea that loving, giving sacrifice is a possibility for humanity.

The Hebrew covenant is another remnant of reciprocal giving. It may be less a "breakthrough" (from the archaic to something new), as Bellah and others suggest (2011: Kindle Location 4761) and more a human possibility since our long, hunter-gatherer evolution. In narrative and as a theological tenet, it asserts a reciprocal commitment between humanity and God and among persons, where each party acts for the flourishing of the other (see Pally, this volume). That is, the theological language of both Testaments sets out as a belief system what we believe from evolution and (hunter-gatherer) experience. In theological voice: We, metaphorically in the image of a loving, giving God, are made to be loving and giving in the world in which we live. We, the recipients of God's love and donation, may follow Jesus's ways and act with love and generosity—we have the capacity to "adopt the behavior recommended by Christ," as Girard wrote. After all, if we were not capable of such behavior, it would be fruitless to recommend it.

This is what is meant by "witness," a person, narrative, or symbol that doesn't let us forget. Witnesses to our foundational reciprocity and commitment to the commons include the Passion, Eucharist, Ten Commandments (*luhot ha'brith*, tablets of *covenant*) and the biblical narratives of covenant. These are found not only in the prophets (which are often cited in support of our covenantal obligations to each other) but beginning with God's covenant with Adam, Noah, and the Genesis patriarchs "for the blessing of all humanity" (Genesis 12:3, 26:4, 28:14; see also Palaver 2015: 158–60). While Girardian theory holds that the violence of the original scapegoating sacrifice is submerged but preserved—witnessed—in ritual and narrative, our earlier hunter-gatherer cooperativity may *also* endure throughout the violence of later forms of living. It may be witnessed in narratives and symbols that grab us because they call up our primary nature.

The idea that the evolutionary preference for sharing, reciprocity, and cooperation is stated also in religious language does not suggest that religious tenets and narratives are ancillary to the "real" evolutionary science—that they are simplified stories to convey complex biology. Rather, it suggests that the world and humanity have developed in certain ways and that human observation makes some headway into understanding those ways in all the scientific and symbolic modalities in which humans think.

In short, the theology and evolutionary biology point to one ontology. Such an ontology confirms the importance of Girard's concern with aggression *because*, on an evolution and ontology of reciprocal giving, scapegoating sacrifice and related aggression violate the very nature of the species. And no good can come of transgressing our baseline. Indeed, Girard held that all religions seek the cessation of violence (1987: 401) and are undergirded by an "ontology of peace." The evoltionary biologist might add that this ontology is the outcome of the long period of adaptation to hunter-gatherer life. The pursuit of peace was, after all, already a priority among Girard's archaic societies and why they resorted to scapegoating sacrifice: it is an effort to preserve peace among the many even if misguidedly by forfeiting the few. That is, even the sacrificers were motivated by a primary preference for peace, which is not the case for our cousins, the chimps. If archaic humanity had no *a priori* desire to stop aggression, why did archaic groups develop a ritual to stop it? Why not have Hobbesian war?

One might say that Girard's work, its underpinning ethic, was to find a better way to peace and to locate the resources that would guide us there. This brings us to the question of whether all roads to such a better way lead through the cross. And this lands us in the thicket of Girard's relations to other faiths (Milbank, Palaver, Pally, this volume). It is an ambivalent story. On the one hand, Girard maintained that the crucifixion narrative uniquely reveals suffering from the victim's perspective and so offers a compassionate understanding of the world that is radically different from the worldview of the scapegoating mob. "All of my work," Girard noted in 2005, "has been an effort to show that Christianity is superior and not just another mythology.... This revelation of collective violence as a lie is the earmark of Christianity. This is what is unique about Christianity. And this uniqueness is true" (Girard and Gardels 2005: 46). In his last book, Girard reprised, "All of my books have been more or less explicit apologies of Christianity. I would like this one to be even more explicit" (Girard 2010: Kindle Location 182). Girardian scholars have noted much the same in his work and call for a more robust investigation of Girard's ideas in light of the ways other world religions teach love and donative self-sacrifice for the common good (Depoortere 2008: 147, among others).

Girard's emphasis on the crucifixion also set his work in tension with Judaism. In his early work, he described the First Testament as a mixed form with strains of both archaic, scapegoating violence and its rejection. Somewhat outside current intertestamental scholarship (Hamerton-Kelly and Scroggs 1976; Sanders 1983; Stendahl 1976; Wendel and Miller 2016; Wright 2012, 2013 among many others), Girard concluded that the mixed First Testament does not fully replace violence with donation and care. This, he held, "is brought to fruition by the New Testament where it is accomplished decisively and definitively" (Girard 1986: 103). Girard held this view at the end of his career as at the beginning (2010: Kindle Location 182–90). "We can thus see in Jesus," Palaver astutely writes,

> a confirmation of those Old Testament texts that stand in defense of persecuted victims and help to reveal the workings of the scapegoat mechanism. Meanwhile, the other line of development in the Old Testament—namely, that which displays a proximity to mythical narrative—is criticized and overcome in the New Testament.... For Girard, the only real and nonviolent means to overcoming mimetic rivalry is found in the New Testament. (Palaver 2013: 214, 218–19)

In Girard's work, the insufficiency of non-Christian faiths comes through more notably in his remarks about Islam, especially after the September 11, 2001, attacks against the United States. He identified mimetic competition at a global level as terrorism's root cause (Girard, Tincq and Hilde 2002) but he held also that "God is essentially power" in Islam and "non-power" or love and giving in the Christian faith (Girard and Gill 2005: 20). What Islam lacks, again, is the crucifixion narrative that moves humanity from power to love. "In Islam," Girard reprised in 2008, "the most important thing is missing: a Cross. As in Christianity, Islam rehabilitates the innocent victim, but it does so in a militant way. . . . The Cross is the symbol of the inversion of violence, of the resistance to lynching" (Girard and Meotti 2008: 184). As the God of Islam retains the "militant way," Islam "makes violence totally divine" (Girard and Doran 2008: 28). In his last work, *Battling to the End*, Girard concluded that Islam

> has used the Bible as a support to rebuild an archaic religion that is more powerful than all the others. It threatens to become an apocalyptic tool, the new face of the escalation to extremes. . . . Archaic religion collapsed in the face of Judeo-Christian revelation, but Islam resists. While Christianity eliminates sacrifice wherever it gains a foothold, Islam seems in many respects to situate itself prior to that rejection. (2010: 214)

This is not a substantive engagement with Islam on the part of the octogenarian Girard. Nonetheless, Girard's remark above about "Judeo-Christian revelation" testifies to a growing understanding of non-Christian faiths as also ones of compassion, donation, and the ontology of peace that he had held was universal to all faiths (Girard 2014: 43). He gradually saw rupture but also continuity between archaic myth and the crucifixion narrative (Girard 2010: xv) and more congruence of values between the First and Second Testaments. In an ironic complement, he held that Nietzsche correctly understood the Judeo-Christian heritage as speaking from and for the downtrodden whom Nietzschean ideal despises—even if Nietzsche despised the Judeo-Christian tradition for doing so (Girard 1996: 272).

Looking beyond the Abrahamic religions, Girard became interested in the renunciation of material goods, which led him to mysticism and Buddhism. Palaver and Schenk note that as early as 1979, in his correspondence with the theologian Raymund Schwager about *The Scapegoat*, Girard sought to bring mimetic theory into engagement with the eastern religions (2018: Kindle Location 490). At the time, Girard found the Hindi tradition to have "everything but the truth" in its failing to take the perspective of the scapegoated victim (Girard and Schwager 2016: 76–77). But by 2002, in lectures on sacrifice in the ancient Indian Vedas, he saw greater parallels between the Bible's overcoming archaic scapegoating and developments in Buddhism (Girard 2011).

Girard's engagement with non-Christian faiths is not the focus of the present volume (we recommend Palaver and Schenk 2018 to the interested reader). Our focus remains on the historical and cultural conditions for sacrifice (why and how it motivates us), on the types and valence of sacrificial practice (what it motivates us to do) and on the understanding of sacrifice undergirding various societal arenas today. This will emerge in the description of the chapters, to which we now turn.

A look at the book

This volume begins with Peter Kappeler's description of sacrifice as evolutionarily productive, as giving for the sake of others or the group—what evolutionary biology calls "cooperation." The evidence from early humans, their immediate ancestors and primate cousins, points to the uniqueness of human "hyper-cooperativity" within kin-groups and not infrequently across larger networks. Kappeler does not argue that humans start out competitive and learn to be cooperative for pragmatic advantage but that human society evolved in the first place for substantial cooperation/giving/sacrifice. The questions that this evolutionary trajectory poses for mimetic theory are not about the inarguable history of violence in the (evolutionarily) recent agrarian, hierarchical period but about the nature of human living in the earlier, long hunter-gatherer phase. Thus, it contributes to our understanding of what has been present and suppressed through human history—cooperativity, competition, both?—and the narratives and practices through which the suppressed returns.

In the next section of the book, several authors look at practices and conceptualizations of sacrifice that differ in some ways from early mimetic theory, beginning with Girard's own look at sacrifice as his work evolved. Chapters by Blanchard, Canzani, Mercedes, Milbank, Pabst, Palaver, Pan and von Uslar look at which understandings of self, group/society, survival, gain, and transcendent yield practices of sacrifice that are reciprocal, of the self (not another "scapegoated" party), voluntary and understood as gift for others and the common good.

Wolfgang Palaver notes two important developments in Girard's thought. While Girard had long held that all faiths seek a cessation of violence, his later works reveal a growing interest in the ways non-Christian faiths express such an ontology of peace. The second shift notes that the cross teaches us not only about the evils of sacrifice-as-murder but also about the productive possibilities of donation/sacrifice of the self. As these possibilities are developed in the works of Simone Weil and Mahatma Gandhi, Palaver explores their theories of oppression, resistance, and sacrifice. Weil in particular influenced Girard's growing appreciation of a universal ontology of peace and the need for donative (self-) sacrifice to realize a more just and less violent world.

Hassan Rachik and Tsvi Blanchard raise an empirical challenge to Girard's classic theory: Can all sacrifice be subsumed under one category or type? This question does not challenge Girard's ethics or his view that all faiths, even those that include ritual sacrifice, seek peace. Rather, it asks: Where ritual sacrifice does occur, is it always prodded by the same societal factors (mimesis) and is it always of the same type? Rachik's fieldwork on Islamic sacrifice in Morocco finds instances that resemble "crystallized" archaic sacrifice (with its placating of the gods etc.). But he also finds instances that appear to be grounded in different sorts of societal matters. The strict Girardian (stricter than Girard himself) might argue that the sacrifice described by Rachik originally followed the competition-scapegoating pattern but was later crystallized and subsumed into the form that Rachik encountered. Our strict Girardian would have to bring evidence of such a trajectory. Alternately, different forms of sacrifice may have emerged from different societal and historical conditions. Importantly, Rachik's call "to note that sacrifice has been adapted to a wide range of situations" lends support to Girard's growing efforts to explore forms of sacrifice that his early work had not considered as well as sacrifice in other faith traditions.

Tsvi Blanchard's study of sacrifice in the Hebrew Bible and rabbinic interpretation raises similar questions about the universality of a single type and genealogy of early sacrifice. The ritual actions and more importantly the *intentions* required by ancient Hebrew sacrifice aim not at placating an enraged god or at mob-bonding but rather at expressing a reciprocal, covenantal relationship with God, where both God and the people and the people among themselves are bonded by commitment and love. Again, the strict Girardian might assert that this sacrifice was originally of the scapegoating type but later subsumed into other ritual forms. And again, our strict Girardian would have to bring substantiating evidence. But Girard's later explorations into how non-Christian faiths express the universal ontology of peace may be the more productive path to follow. Blanchard's description of sacrifice as creating a space in which to better experience commitment to God and community illustrates the sort of ritual in which Girard was increasingly interested as he explored the cross's lessons in (self-) sacrifice for others.

Following this covenantal idea is David Pan's look at Kant's notion of sacrifice and the sublime. Here, (self-) sacrifice for a higher Good is a linchpin of moral conduct. Pan agrees that this is a positive and wanted form of sacrifice but takes issue with Kant on what exactly makes it moral. As Pan reads him, Kant identifies morality's *telos* not as the higher Good itself (external to the human actor) but rather as the human actor's *capacity* to sacrifice. The focus on the internal, human potential rather than on the consequences *to the world* of sacrifice/giving misidentifies, on Pan's view, what is societally and morally important about sacrifice. Pan's position has strong resonance with Girard's work on the cross's second lesson, the need for donative self-sacrifice in the world (not just in our capacities) to end violence and promote greater justice.

Drawing on covenantal theology in my own chapter, I build on Kappeler, Pan, and Blanchard to propose a donative (self-) sacrifice as both necessary to a just society and our natural proclivity, our cooperative ontology. I begin by exploring Girard's engagement with the First Testament to note that his early view of the text as a mixed, quasi-archaic form under-recognizes its perspective of the victim, its prohibitions against scapegoating, insistence on moral responsibility, and care for the needy. Expanding on Blanchard, I look at the *tanachic* covenant and the meaning of sacrifice in the covenantal context. As the brutal sacrifice of the crucifixion becomes divine love in the Christian understanding, sacrifice amid covenant is the symbolic, human voice in the conversation that sustains reciprocal giving and covenantal commitment. As with Blanchard and Pan, this is the sort of ritual increasingly of interest to Girard.

Anna Mercedes too seeks a broad understanding of sacrifice that notes not only its abusive but its donative forms. As she reads him, Girard holds that humanity will ever reject Christ-like love until we learn the lessons of the cross. That is, rejection of Christ is the human condition for the present. While Mercedes is quick to note that coerced sacrifice has been a mechanism of oppressive patriarchal and colonial systems, including Christian ones, she builds on the feminist theology of Traci C. West and Sarah Coakley to argue that sacrificial self-giving even under unjust circumstances is not evidence of only a fallen world, of only our rejection of Christ. Such a unifocal view risks the erasure of the very sacrificial acts and actors we deem to be moral—if not blaming the victims then under-valuing their actions. A finer investigation of sacrifice argues for the recognition of resistance strategies in the sacrificial actions of oppressed persons, which can serve also as means to social and personal transformation.

The chapter by Francisco Canzani is a companion piece to Mercedes as it draws on Christian theology to understand sacrifice in a continent with some of the world's largest income and wealth gaps. The theology looked to here is the reports of the Magisterium of the Catholic Church in Latin America 1955–2007. The chapter also recalls Rachik's anthropological approach as Canzani's work is something of a case study in Girardian theory: Does it describe human conduct in situ? Investigating both the Magisterium documents and their impact on church policy, Canzani finds that the sacrifice of today's poor to the gods of greed and power falls easily within Girard's descriptions of mimetic competition and the sacrifice of some for the benefit of others. But like Mercedes, Canzani echoes Girard's later understanding of the crucifixion as a lesson not only in the evils of sacrifice-as-murder but also in the productive possibilities of sacrifice-of-self. Canzani looks at how this productive application of sacrifice appears in the Magisterium reports.

Two chapters in our book, one, a military-historical account and the other, from military theory, look at the practice and conceptualizations of sacrifice as they inform masculinity. As many chapters in this volume find, sacrifice may be a constructive or destructive force, but when it is the latter, how much of the "problem" is a problem of "manliness"?

Ulrike Brunotte's account of sacrifice as constructed by the Weimar right wing and Nazi party describes a masculinity that lauds the willingness to self-immolation "for the nation." However, rather than the self-donation of the cross—the willingness to (self-) sacrifice for the world's downtrodden—this sacrifice is a perverse magnification of the archaic. That is, it sacralizes violence itself. The murder of others—the victims scapegoated for societal and geopolitical problems—is both permitted and encouraged to benefit the state. One's own death in the process of such murder is the highest of life's achievements. In her close reading of the Langemar(c)k-myth, the story of schoolboy soldiers who ostensibly went willingly to their deaths on the battlefields of the First World War, Brunotte reconstructs the Weimar/Nazi transformation of these young soldiers into self-immolating heroes and "living" brothers of the next generation, to sing and march with the young and so to inspire them to join the eternal "undead" brotherhood of those willing to murder and die in the next war. Brunotte then explores the extension of this sacrificial death cult from Weimar's male youth clubs to all of German society in the Nazi period.

Rolf von Uslar, a colonel in the Bundeswehr, looks at the problem of sacrifice from the other end of modern German history. To avoid the Nazi abuses of sacrifice, Germany now risks a pendulum swing to a "post-heroic" that would, on von Uslar's view, leave the country with no concept of sacrifice, no capacity to identify where (self-) sacrifice is the moral course. In addressing this, von Uslar follows Girard's understanding of the cross as teaching much-needed donative (self-) sacrifice. Such an understanding could ground a moral military. Von Uslar argues not for Germany's abstention from violence—as this leaves the world to those willing to perpetrate it—but for an understanding of military self-sacrifice as *katéchon*, "the one who restrains."

The chapter by John Milbank serves as a bridge to the book's final section on sacrifice as applied to the political, the economic, and a future run increasingly by a tandem of humanity and its "intelligent" machines. Milbank engages the work of Marcel Gauchet, Philippe Descola, and Moshe Halbertal to argue against the idea that the political is of necessity a move from the archaic religious toward the ostensibly more civilized secular. He holds instead (in agreement with Blanchard, Pally, and Pabst) that a gift-giving reciprocity grounded in religion is not only the first form of human living but the prevailing one. Sacrifice, Milbank concludes, is not constrained to murderous scapegoating but "retains . . . its primordial subordination to gift."

Milbank investigates the move from ancient tribal to monarchical forms of governance to argue that this "was not a shift to the political and secular but rather a mutation within a religious, gift-exchanging vision and practice" which preserved the "divine oikonomia of distributive care." Preserving a religiously framed, gift-giving ethos made monarchical politics subordinate to the gift-care economy and beholden to it. It should be noted that the shift Milbank describes from the tribal to the monarchical is not the same as the transition from hunter-gatherer to hierarchical agrarianism. Milbank discusses the turn of the ancient Hebrews from tribal to monarchical governance, and these tribes were already agricultural and governed by sociopolitical hierarchies. Milbank addresses the period *after* the shift to farming to hold that reciprocal gift remained robust in premodern monarchical systems (as it had been in tribal systems) as both faith tenet and societal foundation.

While Milbank sees some economy of distributive care in the premodern, Philip Roscoe is less sanguine about present economies (as Milbank too is). This iteration of capitalism, Roscoe holds, relies on an ethos of sacrifice-all-for-the-firm. This ethos structures the work environment, from hirings and firings and production-distribution schedules to the "masculinized" agonistic atmosphere that hobbles female employees. Roscoe adds to the Girardian model the observation that the present business version demands not only the sacrifice of others for the sake of profits (as businesses lay off workers and close factories in response to automation or the lure of low-wage countries) but also the sacrifice of oneself, from entry-level workers to CEOs. This is not the sacrifice of the cross, which aims at ending sacrificial violence, but self-donation that keeps the sacrificial cogs going. Yet Roscoe is critical also of a naïve Levinasian counter-model that proposes unending, unstructured, and "unquestioning self-abandonment to a proliferation of demanding Others and forbids a rational settlement of those demands."

From the perch of political theory and philosophy, Adrian Pabst too critiques the sacrifice of "useless" people that is endemic to neoliberal capitalism, which he describes as the "globalization of indifference" and neo-Promethean marriage of market to technological change with little regard for the aims and relationships that people actually live for. Yet on Pabst's account, it is not a foundational, competitive human nature that grounds this indifference but, echoing Roscoe, our particular form of capitalism that normalizes and prioritizes greed and competition. Pabst thus takes issue with what he sees as two Girardian presuppositions: one, that our most important resources are scarce so that people must compete for them and two, that humanity is by nature competitive. Referring to work done in the humanities and natural sciences, Pabst suggests instead that the most important aspects of life, friendship and beauty, are not scarce commodities for which people must compete. Moreover, human beings are not naturally competitive but desire mutual recognition for their contribution to the common good. This desire, common to all persons, seeks not the sacrifice of others but reciprocal, donative self-sacrifice. In Pabst's words, "Self-sacrifice and a commitment to reciprocity, relationships of give and receive."

Pabst thus serves as a summation of the many chapters in this book that share Girard's ethics and *telos* but which suggest a cooperative biology and ontology that precede the archaic. This is not inconsistent with Girard's work as he held that the archaic dates back to "Cain," post Fall, but not to the primary humanity of Adam. It's worth noting that such primary cooperativity may make a good deal of difference to our present sociopolitical policies. If such cooperativity is not a religious or political *ideal* to be one day fulfilled but rather foundational to our nature, to our long first (hunter-gatherer) culture, it may be far more accessible than if it had never been in the human experience.

This book began with Kappeler's look into the evolutionary past; most chapters looked into past history. Ilia Delio turns toward the future, which she describes, following the work of the Jesuit Pierre Teilhard de Chardin, as an "incomplete world" evolving continuously to greater forms of intelligence, love, and understanding. Today, as "our fastest evolver is artificial intelligence. . . . We are heading toward a new techno sapien species and thus need values and principles, including the role of suffering and sacrifice, to both understand and guide our evolution." It is for just such a future that the question of our primary biology and ontology is important. How ready-to-hand will cooperativity and reciprocal regard be to us as we invent our smart machines and proceed as a "techno sapien species"?

Delio distinguishes between sacrifice *ex carentia* (from loss) and *ex abundantia* (from abundance of love for the other) to argue that sacrifice *ex abundantia* is not a societal problem but necessary and vital to developing a future of reciprocal concern and commitment. Here, she echoes Girard's emphasis on ending violence by following the cross's lesson of donative self-sacrifice. At the beginning of this book, Kappeler held that cooperation—sacrifice for the well-being of others and the common good—was critical to our evolution as *Homo sapiens*. Though Delio somewhat startlingly posits a new "techno sapiens," this creature is not so very different from our past and present as cooperative sacrifice is precisely what is critical to its future evolution as well.

Throughout this introduction, it has been important to the understanding of many chapters to look at the long trajectory of Girard's work, including his growing interest in how non-Christian faiths express the "ontology of peace" and the cross's lesson in donative (self-) sacrifice. Had Girard lived longer, we would have learned much from his pursuits in these directions. Like many great minds, it seems he died too soon.

References

Althusius, J. (1603/1964), *The Politics of Johannes Althusius: An Abridged Translation of the Third Edition of Politica methodice digesta, atque exemplis sacris et profanis illustrata*, trans. F. Carney, Boston: Beacon Press.

Antonello, P., and Paul Gifford, ed. (2015), *How We Became Human: Mimetic Theory and the Science of Evolutionary Origins*, East Lansing: Michigan State University Press.

Augustine (426/2014), *The City of God*, Volume 1, ed. M. Dodds. Available online: https://www.google.com/search?q=augustine+city+of+god+pdf&oq=AUGUSTINE+CI&aqs=chrome.2.69i59j69i57j0l4.3775j0j7&sourceid=chrome&ie=UTF-8 (accessed September 15, 2018).

Barash, D. (September 19, 2013), "Is There a War Instinct?" *Aeon*, http://aeon.co/magazine/society/human-beings-do-not-have-an-instinct-for-war/ (accessed October 21, 2018).

Bellah, R. (2011), *Religion in Human Evolution*, Cambridge: Belknap/Harvard University Press.

Bergson, H. (1935), *The Two Sources of Morality and Religion*, trans. R. A. Audra, C. Brereton, and W. H. Carter, London: Macmillan & Co.

Bourdieu, P. (1984), *Distinction: A Social Critique of the Judgement of Taste*, trans. R. Nice, London: Routledge.

Bourdieu, P. (1990), *The Logic of Practice*, trans. R. Nice, Cambridge: Polity.

Bowles, S. (2008), "Being Human: Conflict: Altruism's Midwife," *Nature* 456 (7220): 326–27.

Bowles S., and H. Gintis (2013), *A Cooperative Species: Human Reciprocity and Its Evolution*, Princeton: Princeton University Press.

Canetti, E. (1984), *Crowds and Power*, trans. C. Stewart, New York: Farrar Straus Giroux.

Cawelti, J. (1971/1984), *The Six-Gun Mystique*, Bowling Green: Bowling Green State University Popular Press.

Chantre, B. (2019), "The Ordeal of the Town. Rites and Symbols at Çatalhöyük," in I. Hodder (ed.), *Violence and the Sacred in the Ancient Near East: Girardian Conversations at Çatalhöyük*, 165–187, New York/London: Cambridge University Press.

Christakis, N., and J. Fowler (2009), *Connected: The Surprising Power of our Social Networks and How They Shape Our Lives*, New York: Little, Brown & Company.

Churchland, P. (2012), *Braintrust: What Neuroscience Tells Us about Morality*, Princeton: Princeton University Press.

Clare, L., O. Dietrich, J. Gresky, J. Notroff, J. Peters, and N. Pöllath (2019), "Ritual Practices and Conflict Mitigation at Early Neolithic Körtik Tepe and Göbekli Tepe, Upper Mesopotamia: A Mimetic Theoretical Approach," in I. Hodder (ed.), *Violence and the Sacred in the Ancient Near East: Girardian Conversations at Çatalhöyük*, 96–128, New York/London: Cambridge University Press.

Cowdell, S., C. Fleming, and J. Hodge, eds. (2014), *Violence, Desire, and the Sacred, Volume 1: Girard's Mimetic Theory Across the Disciplines*, London: Bloomsbury.

Cowdell, S., C. Fleming, and J. Hodge, eds. (2015), *Violence, Desire, and the Sacred, Volume 2: René Girard and Sacrifice in Life, Love and Literature*, London: Bloomsbury.

Cowdell, S., C. Fleming, and J. Hodge, eds. (2016), *Violence, Desire, and the Sacred, Volume 3: Mimesis, Movies, and Media*, London: Bloomsbury.

Dawson, D. (2013), *Flesh Becomes Word: A Lexicography of the Scapegoat or, the History of an Idea*, East Lansing: Michigan State University Press.

Delio, I. (2015), *Making All Things New: Catholicity, Cosmology, Consciousness*, Maryknoll: Orbis Books.

Depoortere, F. (2008), *Christ in Postmodern Philosophy: Gianni Vattimo, René Girard and Slavoj Žižek*, London: T&T Clark.

Donald, M. (2001), *A Mind So Rare: The Evolution of Human Consciousness*, New York: Norton.

Dumouchel, P. (2015), *The Barren Sacrifice: An Essay on Political Violence*, trans. M. Baker, East Lansing: Michigan State University Press.

Eliade, M. (1998), *The Sacred and the Profane: The Nature of Religion*, trans. W. R. Trask, San Diego: Harcourt.

Ferguson, R. B. (2013), "The Prehistory of War and Peace in Europe and the Near East," in D. P. Fry (ed.), *War, Peace, and Human Nature: The Convergence of Evolutionary and Cultural Views*, 191–240, Oxford: Oxford University Press.

Fruehwald, E. S. (2009), "Reciprocal Altruism as the Basis for Contract," *University of LouisvilleLaw Review* 47 (3), Hofstra University Legal Studies Research Paper no. 08-09. Available online at SSRN: http://ssrn.com/abstract = 1270117 (accessed November 5, 2018).

Fry, D. (2007), *Beyond War: The Human Potential for Peace*, Oxford: Oxford University Press.

Gallagher, S. (2005), *How the Body Shapes the Mind*, Oxford: Oxford University Press.

Gallese, V. (2005), "'Being like Me': Self-Other Identity, Mirror Neurons, and Empathy," in S. Hurley and N. Chater (eds.), *Perspectives on Imitation*, 101–18, Cambridge: MIT Press.

Garrels, S. (2011), *Mimesis and Science: Empirical Research on Imitation and the Mimetic Theory of Culture and Religion*, East Lansing: Michigan State University Press.

Gilligan, C., and N. Snider (2018), *Why Does Patriarchy Persist?* Cambridge/Medford: Polity Press.

Girard, R. (1977), *Violence and the Sacred*, trans. P. Gregory, Baltimore: Johns Hopkins University Press.

Girard, R. (1986), *The Scapegoat*, trans. Y. Freccero, Baltimore: Johns Hopkins University Press.

Girard, R. (1987), *Things Hidden since the Foundation of the World: Research Undertaken in Collaboration with J.-M. Oughourlian and G. Lefort*, trans. S. Bann and M. Metteer, Stanford: Stanford University Press.

Girard, R. (1996), *The Girard Reader*, ed. J. G. Williams, New York: Crossroad.

Girard, R. (2001), *I See Satan Fall Like Lightning*, trans. J. G. Williams, Maryknoll: Orbis Books.

Girard, R. (2004), "Violence and Religion: Cause or Effect?" *The Hedgehog Review* 6 (1): 8–20.

Girard, R. (2010), *Battling to the End: Conversations with Benoit Chantre*, trans. M. Baker, East Lansing: Michigan State University Press.

Girard, R. (2011), *Sacrifice*, trans. M. Pattillo and D. Dawson, East Lansing: Michigan State University Press.

Girard, R. (2014), *The One by Whom Scandal Comes*, trans. M. B. DeBevoise, *Studies in Violence, Mimesis, and Culture*, East Lansing: Michigan State University Press.

Girard, R., and R. Doran (2008), "Apocalyptic Thinking after 9/11: An Interview with René Girard," *SubStance* 37 (1): 20–32.

Girard, R., and N. Gardels (2005), "Ratzinger Is Right: Interview with Nathan Gardels," *New Perspectives Quarterly* 22 (3): 43–48.

Girard, R., and D. W. Gill (2005), "A Conversation with René Girard," *The Ellul Forum* 35: 19–20.

Girard, R., and G. Meotti (2008), "René Girard's Accusation: Intellectuals Are the Castrators of Meaning," *Modern Age* 50 (2). Available online: http://www.firstprinciplesjournal.com/articles.aspx?article=1086&theme=home&page=4&loc=b&type=cttf (accessed September 18, 2018).

Girard, R., and R. Schwager (2016), *René Girard and Raymund Schwager: Correspondence 1974–1991*, trans. C. Fleming and S. Treflé Hidden, New York: Bloomsbury Academic.

Girard, R., H. Tincq, and T. C. Hilde (2002), "What Is Happening Today Is Mimetic Rivalry on a Global Scale," *South Central Review* 19 (2–3): 22–27.

Goodhart, S. (2014), *The Prophetic Law: Essays in Judaism, Girardianism, Literary Studies, and the Ethical*, East Lansing: Michigan State University Press.

Goodhart, S., J. Jørgensen, T. Ryba, and J. Williams, eds. (2009), *For René Girard: Essays in Friendship and in Truth*, East Lansing: Michigan State University Press.

Gopnik, A. (2009), *The Philosophical Baby: What Children's Minds Tell Us about Truth, Love, and the Meaning of Life*, New York: Farrar, Straus and Giroux.

Halbertal, M. (2012), *On Sacrifice*, Princeton: Princeton University Press.

Hamerton-Kelly, R., and R. Scroggs, eds. (1976), *Jews, Greeks, and Christians*, Leiden: Brill.

Heim, M. (2006), *Saved from Sacrifice: A Theology of the Cross*, Grand Rapids: Eerdmans.

Hobbes, T. (1651), *Leviathan: The Matter, Form and Power of a Commonwealth Ecclesiastical and Civil*. Available online: http://studymore.org.uk/xhob13.htm (accessed September 15, 2018).

Hobson, P., and J. Hobson (2012), "Joint Attention or Joint Engagement?" in A. Seemann (ed.), *Joint Attention*, 115–36, Cambridge: MIT Press.

Hodder, I. (2019), *Violence and the Sacred in the Ancient Near East: Girardian Conversations at Çatalhöyük*, New York/London: Cambridge University Press.

Hrdy, S. (2009), *Mothers and Others: Evolutionary Origins of Mutual Understanding*, Cambridge: Harvard University Press.

Huizinga, J. (1950/1938), *Homo Ludens: A Study of the Play Element in Culture*, Boston: Beacon Press.

Kant, I. (1784/2009), *Idea for a Universal History with a Cosmopolitan Aim: A Critical Guide*, ed. A. Oksenberg Rorty and J. Schmidt, trans. A. W. Wood, Cambridge: Cambridge University Press.

Kirwan, M., and S. T. Hidden, eds. (2016), *Mimesis and Atonement: René Girard and the Doctrine of Salvation*, London: Bloomsbury.

Kracauer, S. (1966/1957), *From Caligari to Hitler*, Princeton: Princeton University Press.

Kracauer, S. (1960), *Theory of Film: The Redemption of Physical Reality*, New York: Oxford University Press.

McDonald, B. (2003), "Violence & the Lamb Slain: An Interview with René Girard," *Touchstone*, December. Available online: https://www.touchstonemag.com/archives/article.php?id=16-10-040-i (accessed September 15, 2018).

Meek, E. (2011), *Loving to Know: Covenant Epistemology*, Eugene: Wipf and Stock, Cascade Books.

Meszaros, M., and J. Zachhuber, eds. (2013), *Sacrifice and Modern Thought*, Oxford: Oxford University Press.

Narvaez, D. (2014), *Neurobiology and the Development of Human Morality: Evolution, Culture, and Wisdom*, New York: W. W. Norton & Company.

Palaver, W. (2013), *René Girard's Mimetic Theory*, trans. G. Borrud, East Lansing: Michigan State University Press.

Palaver, W. (2015), "Parochial Altruism and Christian Universalism: On the Deep Difficulties of Creating Solidarity Without Outside Enemies," in P. Dumouchel and R. Gotoh (eds.), *Social Bonds as Freedom: Revisiting the Dichotomy of the Universal and the Particular*, 153–73, New York: Berghan.

Palaver, W. (2018), "The Abrahamic Revolution," in W. Palaver and R. Schenk (eds.), *Mimetic Theory and World Religions*, 259–76, East Lansing: Michigan State University Press.

Palaver, W., and R. Schenk, eds. (2018), *Mimetic Theory and World Religions*, East Lansing: Michigan State University Press.

Pfaff, D. (2014), *The Altruistic Brain: How We Are Naturally Good*, New York: Oxford University Press.

Reddy, V. (2008), *How Infants Know Minds*, Cambridge: Harvard University Press.

Roca, C., and C. Helbing (2012), "Emergence of Social Cohesion in a Model Society of Greedy, Mobile Individuals," *Proceedings of the National Academy of Sciences*, http://www.pnas.org/content/108/28/11370.full (accessed October 17, 2018).

Sanders, E. P. (1983), *Paul, the Law, and the Jewish People*, Philadelphia: Fortress Press.

Schaik, C. van and K. Michel (2016), *The Good Book of Human Nature: An Evolutionary Reading of the Bible*, New York: Basic Books.

Schmid-Hempel, P. (May 15, 2015), personal communication.

Seyfarth R., and D. Cheney (2012), "The Evolutionary Origins of Friendship," *Annual Review of Psychology* 63: 153–77.

Silk, J., and B. House (2011), "Evolutionary Foundations of Human Prosocial Sentiments," *Proceedings of the National Academy of Sciences* 108 (suppl. 2): 10910–17.

Sklar, R. (1975), *Movie-made America: A Cultural History of American Movies*, New York: Vintage Books.

Stendahl, K. (1976), *Paul among Jews and Gentiles*, London: SCM Press.

Taylor, C. (2004), "Notes on the Sources of Violence: Perennial and Modern," in J. L. Heft (ed.), *Beyond Violence: Religious Sources for Social Transformation in Judaism, Christianity and Islam*, 15–42, New York: Fordham University Press.

Trivers, R. (1971), "The Evolution of Reciprocal Altruism," *Quarterly Review of Biology* 46 (1): 35–57.

Vattimo, G., and R. Girard (2010), *Christianity, Truth, and Weakening Faith: A Dialogue*, trans. W. McCuaig, New York: Columbia University Press.

Waal, F. de (2005), *Our Inner Ape*, New York: Random House/Penguin.

Waal, F. de (September 2014), "One for All," *Scientific American* 311: 68–71.

Wendel, S., and D. Miller, eds. (2016), *Torah Ethics and Early Christian Identity*, Grand Rapids: Eerdmans.

Whitehouse, H., and J. A. Lanman (2014), "The Ties that Bind Us," *Current Anthropology* 55 (6): 674–95.

Wilson, E. O. (2013), *The Social Conquest of Earth*, New York: Norton/Liveright.

Wright, N. T. (2012), "Israel's Scriptures in Paul's Narrative Theology," *Theology* 115 (5): 323–29.

Wright, N. T. (2013), "Paul and the Patriarch: The Role of Abraham in Romans 4," *JSNT* 35: 207–41.

Part One

Our Understanding of Sacrifice, Expanded: Origins, Development, Types, and Valence

1

A Comparative and Evolutionary Perspective on Sacrifice and Cooperation

Peter M. Kappeler

Evolutionary biologist Peter Kappeler reviews the degrees and types of competition and sacrifice—"cooperation" in the world of biology—among humans and their immediate ancestors to note the uniqueness of human "hyper-cooperativity" within kin-groups and larger networks. Kappeler does not argue that humans start out competitive and learn to be cooperative for pragmatic advantage but that human society evolved for substantial cooperation/sacrifice. As the Giradian archaic holds to a competitive, aggressive humanity, Kappeler's work raises the question of whether the long, cooperative period occurred prior to the archaic. Is Girard's archaic the baseline of the human condition or is there an earlier epoch which also informs human nature? Girard held that the crucifixion narrative, told from the victim's perspective, is the Bible's key to ending violence. More optimistically, the biologist might answer that the pacific meaning of the crucifixion narrative can be understood by humanity because we have an a priori, underlying cooperative nature (even if now laboring under later competitive conditions) that is already capable of sympathy for the victim-other. Several chapters throughout this volume directly and indirectly address the question of humanity's foundational nature and thus the role of competition, sacrifice, and cooperation in human societies.

—editor's note

Introduction

Sacrifice has three important meanings in human social behavior. First, in many historical cultures, sacrifice took on a rather passive meaning from the perspective of the person sacrificed, referring to gruesome ceremonies during which one or several victims were killed, often involving torture. This form of human sacrifice was widespread across time and cultures, occurring, for example, in ancient Greece and Rome (Hughes 1991), Aztecs (Harner 1977) as well as among the Maya (Tiesler and Cucina 2007). In some societies, human sacrifice was combined with cannibalism, for example in Polynesia (Obeyesekere 2005). Anthropologists have proposed that these ritual killings act either to placate a supernatural being or as a demonstration of social control (Beatty 1992), through which the social elites display their divinely sanctioned powers to terrorize their subjects into subordination. A recent comparative analysis shows that, for a large sample of Austronesian societies, human sacrifice indeed facilitated the formation of strictly inherited class systems and prevented the development of more egalitarian societies (Watts et al. 2016). The deliberate, ritualized killing of an individual in a religious ceremony in order to formally please a supernatural being, the model Rene Girard posited as "archaic sacrifice," represents a slightly different, though certainly related phenomenon because religious and social powers were often held by the same individual(s). In any event, this type of sacrifice is a cultural phenomenon that has no parallels in the animal kingdom and thus evades comparative analyses.

Second, sacrifice in the sense of voluntarily giving up one's life for the benefit of others, often favoring the members of one's ethnic, racial, religious, or language group, has also been reported for some human societies. This type of behavior can involve public symbolic acts, such as hunger strikes, self-immolation, or nonviolent martyrdom in resistance to external interference or internal oppression, and more recently also suicide terrorism, all of which serve as political statements (Fierke 2013). Epitomized by Japanese *Kamikaze* pilots, self-sacrifice has also been glorified as the ultimate service to one's nation, father- or motherland in heroic altruistic suicide (Gary 1987), but it can also be explained by more proximate factors, such as combat-unit cohesion (willingness to die for one's "brothers") or the soldier's rank (willingness of a soldier of lower rank to "take the bullet" for one of higher rank) as in the case of US military history (Blake 1978).

Self-sacrificial behaviors have also been observed in some animal societies, notably among ants, bees, wasps, and termites. Most cases of self-sacrifice among these animals have a defensive function and typically occur in response to an acute external threat to the colony rather than to the individual. Individuals performing these fatal defensive behaviors die as a result of either sting autotomy (the self-amputation of the stinger and the poison sac following an external threat, typically by a larger vertebrate) or autothysis (secreting of a harmful substance through rupturing of the body) (Shorter and Rueppell 2012). While typically not lethal for the stung individual, the defender dies within hours or days after sting autotomy, whereas in the case of autothysis, both the attacker and defender die instantaneously. Self-sacrificial behavior has also been observed as a form of preemptive defense against parasites and pathogens, where infected ants remove themselves from the nest, thereby reducing the risk of pathogen transmission to nest mates (Rueppell, Hayworth, and Ross 2010; Heinze and Walter 2010). Because the members of these insect colonies are closely related to each other, there are certain parallels between their self-sacrifice and some forms of self-sacrifice in humans in that the beneficiaries of these acts are members of the same social unit, invoking kinship as a potential unifying principle that may help to explain at least some of these instances of convergent evolution of an extremely altruistic act.

Third, a less dramatic meaning of sacrifice refers to behaviors that are associated with a disadvantage or cost for the actor and a benefit for the recipient. Rather than giving up her life, the actor is (only) giving up some personal interest or advantage. This type of behavior, defined in biology as "cooperation," has constituted one of the major puzzles in evolutionary biology because the notion of helping others is at first glance incompatible with a selfish, fitness-maximizing imperative implied by Darwin's theory of natural selection (Darwin 1859). This puzzle contains an additional human-specific piece because *Homo sapiens* have even been classified as "hyper-cooperative" whereas the other great apes are not (Silk et al. 2005; Burkart et al. 2014). In contrast to chimpanzees and other living hominids, humans regularly help strangers while cooperative behavior in nonhuman primates is mainly limited to kin and reciprocating partners and is virtually never extended to unfamiliar individuals (Silk and House 2011). But even this stranger-cooperation is not usually extended where there is substantial cost to oneself. Because parochialism has historically played the dominant role in explaining the evolution of cooperative behaviors (Silk 2009), I will focus on the role of kin selection as one of the evolutionary forces that has shaped human cooperation with relatives in a comparative manner. Altruistic behavior toward strangers is typically explained by mutualism (Clutton-Brock 2002) or reciprocity (Trivers 1971) and, while important for human behavior, is beyond the scope of this chapter.

Cooperation and kin selection in Hominins

Humans are an unusually cooperative species. We care for the sick and disabled, give blood, donate to charity, hunt together, and we punish violators of social norms—altruistic behaviors motivated by empathy, a concern for the welfare of others, and a sense of fairness. Unlike most animals, people not only willingly incur costs to help relatives and other members of their group but sometimes also help strangers, even in anonymous one-shot interactions. Thus, the motivation, magnitude, and scope of individual behaviors that incur personal costs and confer benefits exceeding costs to members of one's group set us apart from all other species.

Here, I focus on cooperation among kin also because it is currently better documented and understood than cooperation with familiar nonkin or strangers. Because of shared interests in the causes, function, and consequences of these behaviors, the study of cooperation unites the social and biological sciences (Hamilton 1996; Hammerstein 2003; Gintis et al. 2005). However, although evolutionary theory provides an elegant framework for studying cooperation in both disciplines, many recent conceptual advances in evolutionary biology have been communicated poorly or even wrongly to the social sciences (West, El Mouden, and Gardner 2011). It is therefore useful to first define some key terms and concepts.

Social behavior can be defined as all acts, signals, and interactions that affect the fitness of the actor and that of at least one conspecific recipient. Four categories of social behavior can be distinguished by their associated fitness consequences (West, El Mouden, and Gardner 2011). First, selfish behavior is beneficial to the actor and costly to the recipient, whereas spiteful behavior, second, is costly for both. Cooperation is the most general term for any behavior that confers a benefit to another individual. Third, mutualistic behaviors confer benefits to both actors and recipients, whereas altruism, fourth, represents a special case of cooperative behaviors that is characterized by the action not only providing a benefit to recipients but costing the actor. Thus, the consequences of behavior are evaluated by their effects on individual fitness.

Fitness has a direct and an indirect component: Direct fitness is gained through the impact of an individual's behavior on the production of its own offspring. Indirect fitness is obtained through aiding kin so that they have a greater probability of transmitting shared copies of alleles that are identical by common descent to the next generation. The sum of direct and indirect fitness is also called inclusive fitness (Hamilton 1963) and can be estimated by assessing the effect of one individual's actions on everybody's offspring production, weighted by the relatedness between the actor and every other individual. When interacting with relatives, individuals should therefore exhibit a restraint of selfishness and may also show altruistic behavior (Gardner and West 2014).

Kin selection has provided one of the most elegant explanations for the evolution of altruism. Despite some criticism (Nowack, Tarnita, and Wilson 2010), the vast majority of evolutionary biologists maintain that patterns of relatedness among group members are an important prerequisite for many patterns of cooperative behaviors (Abbot et al. 2011; Gardner and West 2014). Information on a species' social organization, that is, its size, age, and sex composition as well as the resulting kinship structure, is therefore a key prerequisite for studying kin-based cooperation.

Two processes are responsible for shaping patterns of relatedness within groups: reproductive skew and dispersal. Reproductive skew describes the extent to which reproduction is shared among the same-sexed members of a group (Nonacs and Hager 2011). If reproduction is monopolized by a single individual, reproductive skew is at its maximum; if all individuals of one sex have equal probabilities of reproducing, reproductive skew is minimal. It is important to consider male and female reproduction separately in this context because patterns of reproductive skew can differ substantially between the sexes. For example, if every female of a group has an offspring, female reproductive skew is zero, but if all infants are sired by one and the same male, male reproductive skew is maximal. Because offspring receive half of their genes from their mother and the other half from their father, patterns of relatedness among a cohort of infants differ, depending on whether they share the same father, as in the example above, or whether they were sired by different, often unrelated males (Ostner et al. 2008). It is therefore necessary to take the mating system into consideration when determining patterns of within-group relatedness to acknowledge relatedness through the maternal and paternal line (Widdig 2013).

In most group-living birds and mammals, patterns of natal dispersal have additional important effects on the genetic structure of a group. After offspring reach sexual maturity, members of at least one sex have to disperse into neighboring groups to avoid costly inbreeding (Pusey 1987). In the majority of mammalian species, young adult males leave their natal group (Greenwood 1980), leaving behind closely related females that can often be assigned to different matrilines based on their genealogical relations.

There are, however, several exceptions from this predominant mammalian pattern, including man's closest living relatives (Watts 2012). Orangutans, for instance, are the only solitary species among the great apes. Adult females and their dependent offspring are widely spaced out and rarely meet and interact. Genetic analyses revealed, however, that females remain in their natal area and do socialize from time to time with closely related female neighbors (van Noordwijk et al. 2012). Dominant adult males defend large territories that encompass those of several females, and these males also mate with all females in that area (Spillmann et al. 2016). In gorillas, groups form around one or sometimes two adult males, and several females and their offspring. When male physical condition, and hence their ability to protect females from infanticide by strange males (Watts 1989), declines with old age or poor health, females leave the group and associate with a male in another group (Robbins et al. 2009). As a result of these female dispersals, coresident females are often unrelated to each other though relatives sometimes end up living in the same group. Coresident female relatives have higher rates of affiliation and lower rates of aggression than nonrelatives (Watts 1994). But there is relatively little grooming among gorillas, and other altruistic behaviors commonly seen in other primates, such as alarm calling, allo-nursing, food sharing, or agonistic coalition formation (Langergraber 2012), are absent.

In chimpanzees, and to the extent this is known in much less-intensively studied bonobos, males remain in their natal group and cooperatively defend a joint territory against neighboring communities (Langergraber et al. 2017). Females leave their natal groups upon sexual maturity and disperse into one of the neighboring communities, where they interact relatively little with other females, to whom they are not related or only distantly so (Langergraber et al. 2009). Males, in contrast, actively patrol and defend the borders of their territory together; they hunt smaller mammals cooperatively, share the meat, and they groom each other regularly. It is also noteworthy that bonobos and chimpanzees live in so-called fission-fusion societies, where members of a community form several small, temporary subunits that change in size and composition over the course of a day, so that all members of a community are rarely found together (Aureli et al. 2008), a feature also found human hunter-gatherer societies. The mating systems of chimpanzees and bonobos are characterized by high levels of male and female promiscuity (Muller et al. 2007).

Thus, humans' closest living relatives differ widely in social organization, mating system, and patterns of cooperative behavior, making it impossible to identify a set of shared features that could be used to predict human social organization and kin and sex biases in cooperation.

Kin selection and human social organization

To evaluate the importance of kin selection on human cooperative behavior, the kinship structure of human societies needs to be known. Given the extreme culture-driven diversity and dynamics of human societies throughout history (Hill, Barton, and Hurtado 2009), defining a common human social organization appears impossible. However, we can obtain some insight from hunter-gatherer societies because they represent the social organization that has shaped the social behavior of *Homo sapiens* for more than 95 percent of its evolutionary history (Hill et al. 2011; Bae, Douka, and Petraglia 2017). Because their intragroup interactions include cooperative food acquisition, food sharing, allomaternal child care, and collaborative transportation and construction (Gurven 2005; Marlowe 2005) and because they exhibit prosocial behavior such as inequality aversion in economic games (Henrich et al. 2005), questions about their kin structure and its behavioral consequences are central to this inquiry.

Hunter-gatherer societies are defined by their traditional reliance on wild plants and animals for most of their food. This lifestyle, which includes nomadic movements among temporary settlements, was typical of our ancestors until about 12,000 years ago, when the first human populations became sedentary and engaged in agriculture (Diamond 2012). Though modern hunter-gatherer societies have been exposed to various extents to Western civilizations, comparative studies on different continents revealed robust similarities in social organization, which may constitute the core of the species' ancestral social organization.

The social organization of hunter-gatherer societies is characterized by three levels of functional units. The fundamental unit of hunter-gatherer societies is the "band." This residential or local group consists on average of about thirty members with variation from about six to more than eighty individuals (Hill et al. 2011; Apicella et al. 2012). Bands are not necessarily stable, however. A band typically splits up into several daily foraging parties (the second level of organization), which may subsequently fission and fuse over the course of a day, while some members remain in camp before all subunits reunite in their camp again for the night. A band may also temporarily fuse with a neighboring band and fission off again weeks or months later. In addition, individuals may move back and forth between bands at any time, creating a very fluid fission-fusion dynamic over longer time periods. The stable social elements within bands are conjugal families. Adult men and women form stable breeding bonds, most of which are exclusive, resulting in a unique mating system, consisting of multiple monogamous pairs within each multi-male, multi-female group (Chapais 2013). Finally, several adjacent bands form an ethno-linguistic group or "tribe" (Marlowe 2005). Although all members of a tribe may never assemble in one place, the tribe represents the level of social organization that impacts social relationships through the mating system (see below). Cooperative acts occur across all levels of these multilevel societies, facilitating, for example, sharing of food between men and women as well as kin (Dyble et al. 2016).

What are the consequences of this social organization for patterns of kinship? Across thirty-two hunter-gatherer societies from Africa, Asia, America, and Australia, there was no difference in the mean number of adult sons or daughters though in some societies, parents were more likely to co-reside with adult offspring of one sex (Hill et al. 2011). As a result, adult brothers and sisters typically live in the same band. Thus, there is strong evidence for bisexual philopatry, but also for bisexual dispersal because spouses must come from outside bands to avoid inbreeding. Because there is a greater average tendency for close male kin to reside together, women are more likely to marry into a neighboring band within the tribe (Chapais 2010). As a result of these dispersal and mating patterns, only 7 percent of the adult population in a band are close kin (Hill et al. 2011). When primary and more distant kin are considered, only about 40 percent of adult band members belong to kin of either spouse.

These co-residence patterns in hunter-gatherer societies make it unlikely that the extensive cooperation observed can be attributed to inclusive fitness benefits (Hill et al. 2011). However, this very social organization encourages prosocial tribal behavior that helps explain the evolution of human hyper-cooperation beyond kin relations. Accordingly, the evolution of pair-bonding within groups, after our human ancestors separated from chimpanzees about 6 million years ago, created new challenges for mate acquisition for males with polygynous tendencies, but also new opportunities for the evolution of prosocial tendencies (Chapais 2013). To find unrelated mates, men and women have to either leave their natal band or persuade members of external bands to join them. In contrast to the situation in great apes, this novel solution involves independent decisions by members of both sexes. This increase in female social power compared with other hominin-like ancestors, where females have comparatively little say in mate choice, was presumably a consequence of an increased need for biparental investment because human children are characterized by relatively slower development (Marlowe 2000). Sex inequality reappeared later in human history after men were able to accumulate resources following the transition to agriculture (Dyble et al. 2015).

Sex equality in residential decision-making has two important consequences. First, within-camp relatedness is reduced if men and women have equal influence in selecting camp members (Dyble et al. 2015). This is an unavoidable consequence of both sexes expressing their preference for assorting preferentially with their kin, which reduces average relatedness at the band level (Marlowe 2004). Second, several unrelated males of a band have affiliative relations with the same female because she is one man's daughter, another man's sister, wife, daughter-in-law, etc. With spouses being exchanged across bands, the resulting ties extend across the social borders that define and separate groups in all other primate species (Chapais 2010).

As a result, social networks of affiliative relations spanning several bands allow for cross-group visiting and frequent interactions with kin and nonkin, promoting prosocial tendencies and rapid cumulative cultural evolution (Migliano et al. 2017). The fact that women in contemporary hunter-gatherer societies who are more integrated in these social networks produce more living offspring (Page et al. 2017) indicates that these prosocial tendencies were also beneficial in early *Homo sapiens* and presumably also in some of our ancestral Homo species.

Conclusion

Recent meta-analyses indicated that the best predictor of variation in proactive pro-sociality across primate species is the intensity of allomaternal care (Burkart et al. 2014), which has also been attributed a crucial role in human social evolution (Burkart, van Schaik, and Griesser 2017). However, all types of cooperative behavior in nonhuman primates are mainly limited to kin and reciprocating partners and are virtually never extended to unfamiliar individuals (Silk 2009). In stark contrast, cooperation in all human societies extends beyond close kin and networks of reciprocating partners and is motivated by empathy and concern for the welfare of others (Silk and House 2011).

The kinship structure of the fundamental unit of human social organization throughout most of *Homo sapiens*' evolutionary history suggests that inclusive fitness benefits were not the key drivers of altruistic tendencies in our species. This is not to say that nepotism does not play an important role in everyday life, however; after all, blood is thicker than water (Madsen et al. 2007; Fox et al. 2009; Jaeggi and Gurven 2013). Yet the genetic, psychological, and social consequences of the unique human social organization have produced a social environment characterized by co-residence of close kin and nonrelatives with affiliative social ties within and across social units. While band stability appears to promote cooperation (Smith et al. 2016), other mechanisms, such as reciprocity, demand-sharing, reputation, and other social norms as well as supernatural punishment (Henrich and Henrich 2006; Boyd and Richerson 2009; Fehr and Fischbacher 2004; Lewis et al. 2014; Grimalda, Pondorfer, and Tracer 2016), favored and reinforced multifaceted cooperation under these unique social conditions. Thus, humans are willing to sacrifice themselves despite and because of their biological legacy, and the lethal forms of sacrifice and self-sacrifice mentioned at the outset appear to be extreme outcomes of human cultural evolution.

Acknowledgments

It is a pleasure to thank Marcia Pally for the invitation to the workshop on sacrifice and to contribute this chapter to the resulting volume. I acknowledge and appreciate the support of the Wissenschaftskolleg zu Berlin that permitted me to develop the ideas presented here.

References

Abbot, P., et al. (2011), "Inclusive Fitness Theory and Eusociality," *Nature* 471: E1.

Apicella, C. L., F. W. Marlowe, J. H. Fowler, and N. A. Christakis (2012), "Social Networks and Cooperation in Hunter-Gatherers," *Nature* 481: 497–501.

Aureli, F., C. M. Schaffner, C. Borsch, S. K. Bearder, J. Call, C. A. Chapman, R. Connor, A. Di Fiore, R. I. M. Dunbar, S. P. Henzi, K. Holekamp, A. H. Korstjens, R. Layton, P. Lee, J. Lehmann, J. H. Manson, G. Ramos-Fernandez, K. B. Strier, and C. P. van Schaik (2008), "Fission-Fusion Dynamics: New Research Frameworks," *Current Anthropology* 49: 627–54.

Bae, C. J., K. Douka, and M. D. Petraglia (2017), "On the Origin of Modern Humans: Asian Perspectives," *Science* 358: 6368.

Beatty, A. (1992), *Society and Exchange in Nias*, New York: Clarendon Press.

Blake, J. A. (1978), "Death by Hand Grenade: Altruistic Suicide in Combat," *Suicide and Life-Threatening Behavior* 8: 46–59.

Boyd, R., and P. J. Richerson (2009), "Culture and the Evolution of Human Cooperation," *Philosophical Transactions of the Royal Society of London B: Biological Sciences* 364: 3281–88.

Burkart, J. M., O. Allon, F. Amici, C. Fichtel, C. Finkenwirth, A. Heschl, J. Huber, K. Isler, Z. K. Kosonen, E. Martins, E. J. Meulman, R. Richiger, K. Rueth, B. Spillmann, S. Wiesendanger, and C. P. van Schaik (2014), "The Evolutionary Origin of Human Hyper-Cooperation," *Nature Communications* 5: 4747.

Burkart, J. M., C. P. van Schaik, and M. Griesser (2017), "Looking for Unity in Diversity: Human Cooperative Childcare in Comparative Perspective," *Proceedings of the Royal Society of London B: Biological Sciences* 284: 20171184.

Chapais, B. (2010), "The Deep Structure of Human Society: Primate Origins and Evolution," in P. M. Kappeler and J. B. Silk (eds.), *Mind the Gap: Tracing the Origins of Human Universals*, 19–51, Heidelberg: Springer.

Chapais, B. (2013), "Monogamy, Strongly Bonded Groups, and the Evolution of Human Social Structure," *Evolutionary Anthropology* 22: 52–65.

Clutton-Brock, T. H. (2002), "Breeding Together: Kin Selection and Mutualism in Cooperative Vertebrates," *Science* 296: 69–72.

Darwin, C. (1859), *On the Origin of Species by Means of Natural Selection, or the Preservation of Favoured Races in the Struggle for Life*, London: Royal Linnean Society.

Diamond, J. (2012), *The World until Yesterday*, New York: Viking Press.

Dyble, M., G. D. Salali, N. Chaudhary, A. Page, D. Smith, J. Thompson, L. Vinicius, R. Mace, and A. B. Migliano (2015), "Sex Equality Can Explain the Unique Social Structure of Hunter-Gatherer Bands," *Science* 348: 796–98.

Dyble, M., J. Thompson, D. Smith, G. D. Salali, N. Chaudhary, A. E. Page, L. Vinicuis, R. Mace, and A. B. Migliano (2016), "Networks of Food Sharing Reveal the Functional Significance of Multilevel Sociality in Two Hunter-Gatherer Groups," *Current Biology* 26: 2017–21.

Fehr, E., and U. Fischbacher (2004), "Social Norms and Human Cooperation," *Trends in Cognitive Sciences* 8: 185–90.

Fierke, K. M. (2013), *Political Self-Sacrifice: Agency, Body and Emotion in International Relations*, Cambridge: Cambridge University Press.

Fox, M., R. Sear, J. Beise, G. Ragsdale, E. Voland, and L. A. Knapp (2009), "Grandma Plays Favourites: X-Chromosome Relatedness and Sex-Specific Childhood Mortality," *Proceedings of the Royal Society of London B: Biological Sciences* 277: 567–73.

Gardner, A., and S. A. West (2014), "Inclusive Fitness: 50 Years on," *Philosophical Transactions of the Royal Society B: Biological Sciences* 369, 2013.0356.

Gary, R. J. (1987), "In the Name of the Fatherland: An Analysis of Kin Term Usage in Patriotic Speech and Literature," *International Political Science Review* 8: 165–74.

Gintis, H., S. Bowles, R. Boyd, and E. Fehr (2005), *Moral Sentiments and Material Interests: The Foundations of Cooperation in Economic Life*, Cambridge: MIT Press.

Greenwood, P. J. (1980), "Mating Systems, Philopatry and Dispersal in Birds and Mammals," *Animal Behaviour* 28: 1140–62.

Grimalda, G., A. Pondorfer, and D. P. Tracer (2016), "Social Image Concerns Promote Cooperation more than Altruistic Punishment," *Nature Communication* 7: 12288.

Gurven, M. (2005), "To Give and to Give not: The Behavioral Ecology of Human Food Transfers," *Behavioral and Brain Sciences* 27: 543–59.

Hamilton, W. D. (1963), "The Evolution of Altruistic Behavior," *The American Naturalist* 97: 354–56.

Hamilton, W. D. (1996), *Narrow Roads of Gene Land: I. Evolution of Social Behaviour*, Oxford: W.H. Freeman.

Hammerstein, P. (2003), *Genetic and Cultural Evolution of Cooperation*, Cambridge: MIT Press.

Harner, M. (1977), "The Ecological Basis for Aztec Sacrifice," *American Ethnologist* 4: 117–35.

Heinze, J., and B. Walter (2010), "Moribund Ants Leave Their Nests to Die in Social Isolation," *Current Biology* 20: 249–52.

Henrich, J., and N. Henrich (2006), "Culture, Evolution and the Puzzle of Human Cooperation," *Cognitive Systems Research* 7: 220–45.

Henrich, J., R. Boyd, S. Bowles, C. Camerer, E. Fehr, H. Gintis, R. McElreath, M. Alvard, A. Barr, J. Ensminger, N. S. Henrich, K. Hill, F. Gil-White, M. Gurven, F. W. Marlowe, J. Q. Patton, and D. Tracer (2005), "'Economic Man' in Cross-Cultural Perspective: Behavioral Experiments in 15 Small-Scale Societies," *Behavioral and Brain Sciences* 28: 795–815.

Hill, K. R., M. Barton, and A. M. Hurtado (2009), "The Emergence of Human Uniqueness: Characters Underlying Behavioral Modernity," *Evolutionary Anthropology* 18: 187–200.

Hill, K. R., R. S. Walker, M. Bozicević, J. Eder, T. Headland, B. Hewlett, A. M. Hurtado, F. Marlowe, P. Wiessner, and B. Wood (2011), "Co-Residence Patterns in Hunter-Gatherer Societies Show Unique Human Social Structure," *Science* 331: 1286–89.

Hughes, D. D. (1991), *Human Sacrifice in Ancient Greece*, London: Routledge.

Jaeggi, A. V., and M. Gurven, (2013), "Reciprocity Explains Food Sharing in Humans and Other Primates Independent of Kin Selection and Tolerated Scrounging: A Phylogenetic Meta-Analysis," *Proceedings of the Royal Society of London B: Biological Sciences* 280: 2013.1615.

Langergraber, K. E. (2012), "Cooperation Among Kin," in J. C. Mitani, J. Call, P. M. Kappeler, R. Palombit, and J. B. Silk (eds.), *The Evolution of Primate Societies*, 491–513, Chicago: University of Chicago Press.

Langergraber, K. E., J. C. Mitani, and L. Vigilant (2009), "Kinship and Social Bonds in Female Chimpanzees (*Pan troglodytes*)," *American Journal of Primatology* 71: 840–51.

Langergraber, K. E., D. P. Watts, L. Vigilant, and J. C. Mitani (2017), "Group Augmentation, Collective Action, and Territorial Boundary Patrols by Male Chimpanzees," *Proceedings of the National Academy of Sciences of the United States of America* 114: 7337–42.

Lewis, H. M., L. Vinicius, J. Strods, R. Mace, and A. B. Migliano (2014), "High Mobility Explains Demand Sharing and Enforced Cooperation in Egalitarian Hunter-Gatherers," *Nature Communications* 5: 5789.

Madsen, E. A., R. J. Tunney, G. Fieldman, H. C. Plotkin, R. I. M. Dunbar, J.-M. Richardson, and D. McFarland (2007), "Kinship and Altruism: A Cross-Cultural Experimental Study," *British Journal of Psychology* 98: 339–59.

Marlowe, F. W. (2000), "Paternal Investment and the Human Mating System," *Behavioural Processes* 51: 45–61.

Marlowe, F. W. (2004), "Marital Residence among Foragers," *Current Anthropology* 45: 277–84.

Marlowe, F. W. (2005), "Hunter-Gatherers and Human Evolution," *Evolutionary Anthropology* 14: 54–67.

Migliano, A. B., A. E. Page, J. Gómez-Gardeñes, G. D. Salali, S. Viguier, M. Dyble, J. Thompson, N. Chaudhary, D. Smith, J. Strods, R. Mace, M. G. Thomas, V. Latora, and L. Vinicius (2017), "Characterization of Hunter-Gatherer Networks and Implications for Cumulative Culture," *Nature Human Behaviour* 1: 0043.

Muller, M. N., S. M. Kahlenberg, M. Emery Thompson, and R. W. Wrangham (2007), "Male Coercion and the Costs of Promiscuous Mating for Female Chimpanzees," *Proceedings of the Royal Society of London B: Biological Sciences* 274: 1009–14.

Nonacs, P., and R. Hager (2011), "The Past, Present and Future of Reproductive Skew Theory and Experiments," *Biological Reviews* 86: 271–98.

van Noordwijk, M. A., N. Arora, E. P. Willems, L. P. Dunkel, R. N. Amda, N. Mardianah, C. Ackermann, M. Krützen, and C. P. van Schaik (2012), "Female Philopatry and Its Social Benefits among Bornean Orangutans," *Behavioral Ecology and Sociobiology* 66: 823–34.

Nowack, M. A., C. E. Tarnita, and E. O. Wilson (2010), "The Evolution of Eusociality," *Nature* 466: 1057–62.

Obeyesekere, G. (2005), *Cannibal Talk: The Man-Eating Myth and Human Sacrifice in the South Seas*, Berkeley: University of California Press.

Ostner, J., C. L. Nunn, and O. Schülke (2008), "Female Reproductive Synchrony Predicts Skewed Paternity across Primates," *Behavioral Ecology* 19: 1150–58.

Page, A. E., N. Chaudhary, S. Viguier, M. Dyble, J. Thompson, D. Smith, G. D. Salali, R. Mace, and A. B. Migliano (2017), "Hunter-Gatherer Social Networks and Reproductive Success," *Scientific Reports* 7: 1153.

Pusey, A. E. (1987), "Sex-Biased Dispersal and Inbreeding Avoidance in Birds and Mammals," *Trends in Ecology and Evolution* 2: 295–99.

Robbins, A. M., T. S. Stoinski, K. A. Fawcett, and M. M. Robbins (2009), "Socioecological Influences on the Dispersal of Female Mountain Gorillas — Evidence of a Second Folivore Paradox," *Behavioral Ecology and Sociobiology* 63: 477–89.

Rueppell, O., M. K. Hayworth, and N. P. Ross (2010), "Altruistic Self-Removal of Health-Compromised Honey Bee Workers from their Hive," *Journal of Evolutionary Biology* 23: 1538–46.

Shorter, J., and O. Rueppell (2012), "A Review on Self-Destructive Defense Behaviors in Social Insects," *Insectes Sociaux* 59: 1–10.

Silk, J. B. (2009), "Nepotistic Cooperation in Non-Human Primate Groups," *Philosophical Transactions of the Royal Society of London B: Biological Sciences* 364: 3243–54.

Silk, J. B., and B. R. House (2011), "Evolutionary Foundations of Human Prosocial Sentiments," *Proceedings of the National Academy of Sciences of the United States of America* 108: 10910.

Silk, J. B., S. F. Brosnan, J. Vonk, J. Henrich, D. J. Povinelli, A. S. Richardson, S. P. Lambeth, J. Mascaro, and S. J. Schapiro (2005), "Chimpanzees Are Indifferent to the Welfare of Unrelated Group Members," *Nature* 437: 1357–59.

Smith, D., M. Dyble, J. Thompson, K. Major, A. E. Page, N. Chaudhary, G. D. Salali, L. Vinicius, A. B. Migliano, and R. Mace (2016), "Camp Stability Predicts Patterns of Hunter–Gatherer Cooperation," *Royal Society Open Science* 3: 160131.

Spillmann, B., E. P. Willems, M. A. van Noordwijk, T. M. Setia, and C. P. van Schaik (2016), "Confrontational Assessment in the Roving Male Promiscuity Mating System of the Bornean Orangutan," *Behavioral Ecology and Sociobiology* 71: 20.

Tiesler, V., and A. Cucina (2007), *New Perspectives on Human Sacrifice and Ritual Body Treatments in Ancient Maya Societies*, Heidelberg: Springer.

Trivers, R. L. (1971), "The Evolution of Reciprocal Altruism," *Quartely Review of Biology* 46: 35–47.

Watts, D. P. (1989), "Infanticide in Mountain Gorillas: New Cases and a Reconsideration of the Evidence," *Ethology* 81: 1–18.

Watts, D. P. (1994), "Social Relationships of Immigrant and Resident Female Mountain Gorillas. II: Relatedness, Residence, and Relationships between Females," *American Journal of Primatology* 32: 13–30.

Watts, D. P. (2012), "The Apes: Taxonomy, Biogeography, Life History, and Behavioral Ecology," in J. C. Mitani, J. Call, P. M. Kappeler, R. Palombit, and J. B. Silk (eds.), *The Evolution of Primate Societies*, 113–42, Chicago: University of Chicago Press.

Watts, J., O. Sheehan, Q. D. Atkinson, J. Bulbulia, and R. D. Gray (2016), "Ritual Human Sacrifice Promoted and Sustained the Evolution of Stratified Societies," *Nature* 532: 228–31.

West, S. A., C. El Mouden, and A. Gardner (2011), "Sixteen Common Misconceptions about the Evolution of Cooperation in Humans," *Evolution and Human Behavior* 32: 231–62.

Widdig, A. (2013), "The Impact of Male Reproductive Skew on Kin Structure and Sociality in Multi-Male Groups," *Evolutionary Anthropology* 22: 239–50.

2

Sacrifice Between West and East
René Girard, Simone Weil, and Mahatma Gandhi on Violence and Nonviolence

Wolfgang Palaver

In this chapter, Wolfgang Palaver looks at developments in Rene Girard's later work, in particular, at Girard's assessment that he had earlier unfairly "scapegoated" sacrifice in an effort to rid humanity of violence. In recognition of the need to address—not erase—the violence that is with us, Girard developed his thinking in at least two ways. The first is his growing interest in how an "ontology of peace," which Girard held undergirds all faith traditions, is expressed in non-Christian faiths. Second is his insight that Jesus's death on the cross tells us not only about the evils of sacrifice-as-murder but also about the productive possibilities of sacrifice-of-self, giving for the sake of others. To explore what such donative sacrifice consists in, Palaver investigates the theories of oppression, resistance, and sacrifice in the works of Simone Weil and Mahatma Gandhi. Palaver finds echoes among these thinkers in three areas: in the ontology of peace undergirding all faiths; in the idea that the sacrifice of the self for others is part of making a more just, less violent world; and in the importance of overcoming the passions (Bhagavadgîtâ) that are sources of mimesis, greed, and anger.

—editor's note

Introduction

The complex problem of sacrifice becomes even more perplexing if we compare Western with Eastern approaches. At the time of the Easter feast in 2009, one could find good examples of each. The German philosopher and journalist Uwe Justus Wenzel published an editorial in the Swiss newspaper *Neue Zürcher Zeitung* in which he reflected on Jesus's death on the cross, concluding that it was not a "sacrificial death" but the "end of sacrifice," meaning that sacrifice will remain forever a practice of the past (Wenzel 2009). Wenzel's view represents the typical Western view. At about the same time, the Indian Jesuit and theologian Francis Gonsalves SJ published an article in the *Times of India* in which he emphasized the universality of sacrifice in all religions and cultures. His view was typical of an Eastern approach to sacrifice (Gonsalves 2009). Whereas the West identifies today most often with the end of sacrifice, the East recognizes a continuity from the ancient Vedic sacrifices to Mahatma Gandhi's understanding of it. Both authors referred at least indirectly to René Girard's mimetic theory. Wenzel referred to the work of the German theologian Georg Baudler who connected to early writings of Girard (Baudler 1997), whereas Gonsalves referred directly to Girard, mentioning him together with Sigmund Freud as a key thinker recognizing the importance of sacrifice.

In the following, I will show how these quite different approaches to sacrifice help us to come to a deeper understanding of Girard's mimetic theory by analyzing how nonviolence and sacrifice are related to each other in the works of Simone Weil and Mahatma Gandhi.

René Girard's struggle to reach a comprehensive understanding of sacrifice

Although it took Girard quite a long time to reach a comprehensive view, his evolving thoughts on sacrifice shared insights with both the Western and the Eastern approach (Palaver 2014). In the beginning, Girard's understanding of sacrifice rested on the typical Western framework. He vehemently emphasized the difference between archaic sacrifice and biblical Christianity and rejected the use of the term "sacrifice" to describe Jesus's laying down of his life on the cross (Girard 1987: 240–43). To distance himself from nineteenth-century religious studies and their identification of archaic myth and the Bible, he avoided using the same term for the archaic sacrifice and for Jesus's suffering on the cross. Girard, however, did not maintain his initial and radical rejection of the term "sacrifice." His long-time collaboration with Raymund Schwager, a Jesuit who taught systematic theology in Innsbruck, led him to conclude that emphasizing the difference between archaic sacrifice and Christian self-giving love does not prevent succumbing to the modernist illusion that, in the words of John Lennon, there is "nothing to kill or die for" (cf. Girard and Schwager 2016; Moosbrugger 2014; Palaver 2013b).

Girard recognized that as long as violence is part of human relations, there is no neutral ground to escape its challenge. In an interview with Rebecca Adams, conducted in 1992, he very openly criticized his earlier position, admitting that at that time, he was scapegoating the word "sacrifice," really "trying to get rid of it" (Girard and Adams 1993: 29). The most extensive treatment of his new approach on sacrifice can be found in his contribution to the Festschrift on the occasion of Schwager's sixtieth birthday in 1995 (Girard 1995, 2014: 33–45). Since the publication of this article, he explained his changed attitude regarding sacrifice on a number of occasions (Girard and Treguer 2014: 4, 114–15; Girard 2007: 28, 1001 and 216–17; Vattimo and Girard 2010: 92–94). Most importantly, his new attitude is reflected in the new French volume of Girard's first four books that came out in 2007. In a long footnote, he distanced himself from his earlier position, and he deleted a passage from *Things Hidden since the Foundation of the World* that became most questionable for him (Girard 2007: 28, 998, 1001; cf. Girard 1987: 243). How can we summarize Girard's final position on sacrifice?

First, Girard emphasized that the difference between "archaic sacrifices" and the "sacrifice of Christ" is so great that hardly any greater difference can be conceived (Girard 2014: 41): "No greater difference can be found: on the one hand, sacrifice as murder; on the other hand, sacrifice as the readiness to die in order not to participate in sacrifice as murder" (Girard 2008: 215). Girard maintained his earlier view that there is a fundamental difference between myth and the Bible. Yet this important distinction does not negate all connection between archaic religions and the Judeo-Christian revelation. According to Girard, there exists a "paradoxical unity of religion in all its forms" if we take into account an ontology of peace that is rooted in creation, which had a forming influence on the archaic religions (Girard 2014: 43). Whoever rejects this unity—modern people are tempted to deny that "archaic people" share in it— easily turns toward scapegoating because, by occupying a seemingly innocent and pure position, moderns think it legitimate to condemn all archaic attempts to make peace because they don't understand these efforts (cf. Taylor 2007: 772; Palaver 2017). Modern massacres—the slaughter of indigenous people in Latin America legitimated by the rejection of human sacrifice which, despite its inherent violence, was nevertheless aiming at peace is a telling example of a moralistic and puritan attitude—a corruptio optimi pessima, a corruption of the best leading to the worst (Palaver 2013a: 234–36).

Girard's emphasis on the paradoxical unity of all that is religious opens his theory toward an interreligious perspective because it no longer relies on an unbridgeable gap between Christianity and all other religions. It is also important to understand with Girard that we cannot easily free ourselves from all violence. Violence—as long as it remains part of human relations—is either shifted on someone else (scapegoating) or overcome by someone ready to endure it (Christian self-giving). Girard maintained the distinction between archaic scapegoating religions and Christian self-giving religion, but also understood that due to an ontology of peace going back to creation there is a commonality among all religions.

Girard's later understanding of sacrifice shows to a certain degree an opening toward the East (cf. Palaver and Schenk 2018). This can be recognized, for instance, in his reading of Hölderlin in his last book *Battling to the End*. In it, he highlights Hölderlin's insight that there is not only a discontinuity between archaic religions—the "East" in Hölderlin's view—and Christianity but also a continuity. It is the Greek god Dionysus who stands for the East, for India. He went "as far as the Indus" and "tamed / The fierceness and rage of the peoples" and is also a "brother" of Christ (Girard 2010: 127–28). Girard's openness to the East became even more explicit in his 2002 lecture at the Bibliothèque nationale de France in Paris on the topic of sacrifice in the ancient Indian Vedas and the different forms of transformations developed out of this sacrificial culture. He recognized certain parallels to the biblical critique of sacrifice in the mystic of the Upanishads and also in Buddhism (Girard 2011: xi–xii, 87–95). Similarly, he also mentioned parallels between the Bible and Jainism in an interview with Pierpaolo Antonello and João Cezar de Castro Rocha (Girard 2008: 211–14). He saw in Gandhi a connection between Jainism and Christianity.

Simone Weil: The Gospel and the *Bhagavadgîtâ* complement each other

With the help of the French mystic and philosopher Simone Weil, we can deepen our understanding of sacrifice in regard to war, violence, and nonviolence. She deeply influenced Girard's mimetic theory and shared with him important observations in regard to human violence (Astell 2017). Weil intensely studied the religious traditions of both the East and the West and thus became an important bridge between the two. Influenced by her teacher Alain, Weil early on became a pacifist and remained one up to the Munich Agreement of 1938. She believed France was not ready to sacrifice for Czechoslovakia and that a settlement with Hitler was preferable to a war (Weil 1988: 264–68). Later she criticized herself severely for her naïveté about Hitler's aggression (Doering 2010: 13–40). Close to her death, she wrote in her London diary that her pacifism before 1939 was a "criminal error" (Weil 1970: 345). As she came to realize, Hitler's conquest of Europe meant that, in certain circumstances, violence and injustice would have to be combated violently.

Nevertheless, she still tried to square this insight with her profound critique of violence. She knew how contagious violence is and how easily it escalates. For this reason, she searched for ways to restrain violence in situations in which it could not be avoided. In a personal note on war in spring 1941, we can find important hints about how this might be accomplished (Weil 1956a: 32–34; cf. Doering 2010: 65–68). She emphasized not "to copy the enemy" in order to avoid the escalation of violence and referred to Lawrence of Arabia's efforts "to kill as little as possible." She also underlined the need to detach from the attraction of violence: "Criterion: fear and the taste for killing. Avoidance of each of these." According to Weil, it is important to understand the power of violence fully and yet despise it. Only people close to saintliness are capable of knowing the empire of violence and despising it at the same time. She again referred to Lawrence as an example for such an attitude and also recognized it in Homer's *Iliad* and in the Gospels (Weil 2003a: 116). In her famous reading of the *Iliad*, she again underlined this insight: "Only he who has measured the dominion of force, and knows how not to respect it, is capable of love and justice" (Weil 2005: 212).

Like Girard, Weil understood that a rejection of violence could necessitate the willingness to sacrifice oneself. Only the endurance of violence may lead to its transformation by allowing also the enemy to change his mind when he realizes his victim's willingness to suffer. Weil recognized that Jesus's death on the cross was just such a transformation (Weil 1956a: 25–26). She prefigured Girard when she emphasized that the true God overcomes violence through voluntary suffering whereas all idols turn suffering into violence: "The false God changes suffering into violence: the true God changes violence into suffering" (Weil 1956b: 507).

Weil's insight that overcoming violence may require self-sacrifice does not mean that she had returned to an archaic understanding of sacrifice. Although she definitely endorsed the Western critique of sacrifice, she vindicated self-sacrifice from the charge of masochism, a suicidal attitude, or a rejection of life. Preferring reformist over revolutionary efforts to liberate colonies, she again pointed to Lawrence of Arabia as one who tried to avoid violence as much as possible and who understood that "those who are fighting for freedom want to live to enjoy it rather than die for it" (Weil 2003b: 71, Lawrence 2017: 142). The love of life is key to determining one's attitude toward adversaries as well as to oneself: "To keep the love of life intact within us (not like Achilles); never to inflict death without accepting it for ourselves. . . . We must also desire that the other person should live, although necessity be opposed thereto" (Weil 1956a: 33). By no means may violence become a goal in itself. There are, however, situations in which one could be forced to accept being killed: "Two ways of killing oneself, suicide (Achilles) or detachment" (Weil 1956a: 40).

Weil's emphasis on detachment went along with her turn toward the East and her reflections on the *Bhagavadgîtâ*. In this ancient Indian text, she discovered the spiritual response to an imposed war. According to Weil, the "Bhagavad-Gita and the Gospels complete each other" (Weil 1956a: 25). Because war—"the supreme form of prestige" in Weil's eyes—is so fascinating, it is necessary to develop an inner resistance against its "hypnotizing" pull (Weil 1956a: 25, 32). Arjuna, the main character in the *Bhagavadgîtâ*, had to put his full trust in the god Krishna to fight the unavoidable battle without passion, greed, or any hope to earn the fruits of his action. According to Weil, only such an attitude of detachment prevents one from getting drawn into something like a religious war with all its murderous consequences. For a negative example, she referred to the popular understanding of Joan of Arc, who in Weil's judgment debased God by "making Him a partisan in a war" (Weil 1956a: 55; cf. Doering 2010: 132–33, 175–77). Against such a "nationalist idolatry" (Weil 2002: 254), Weil viewed the *Bhagavadgîtâ* as a spirituality in which God prevents violence from becoming sacralized: "Difference between the spirit of the Bhagavad-Gita and that of the story of Joan of Arc, a fundamental difference: he [Arjuna] makes war although inspired by God, she makes war because inspired by God" (Weil 1956a: 25). In the first case, it is God who prevents a passion-driven sacralization of war; in the second case, God becomes identical with the escalation of violence.

The deeper understanding of detachment that Weil discovered in the *Bhagavadgîtâ* demonstrated an understanding of sacrifice that aims for life and love but is not an end in itself. She distinguished therefore between detachment and renouncement in order to view the first as a lifestyle that aims for life, and she found significant parallels between this and the New Testament (1 Corinthians 7:31): "Detachment and renouncement: often synonyms in Sanskrit, but not in the *Gītā*: here 'renouncement' (*saṃnyāsa*) is the lower form that consists of becoming a hermit, sitting beneath a tree and moving no further. 'Detachment' (*tyāga*) is making use of this world as if not using it" (quoted in Calasso 2014: 222; Weil 2009: 606–07). Similarly, she also discovered in the first verses of the *Ishopanishad*—this was Gandhi's most important mantra—how enjoyment flows from detachment. Let us read these verses first before quoting Weil's comment:

"All this, whatsoever moves on earth, is to be hidden in the Lord (the Self). When thou hast surrendered all this, then thou mayest enjoy. Do not covet the wealth of any man!" (Müller 1962: 311)—"Enjoy through detachment. In the case of the good things, pure joy is the criterion of detachment" (Weil 1956a: 216).

Weil's openness toward the East led her also to examine Gandhi's nonviolent resistance. She was not fully convinced by Gandhi's theory of nonviolence as a universal approach and insisted that nonviolence has to be effective. She believed that there were situations in which only violence could succeed and thus must be preferred (Weil 1956a: 96–97). Only extraordinary people like Saint Francis of Assisi are able to achieve their goals nonviolently. In following their example, she tried to move toward nonviolence as much as possible: "To strive to become such that one may be able to be nonviolent. . . . To strive to substitute *more and more,* in the world, effective nonviolence for violence" (Weil 1956a: 97).

Despite her disagreement with Gandhi, she shared with him the insight that all resistance against violence requires a readiness for self-sacrifice. In her late book *The Need for Roots*, she reassessed Gandhi's nonviolent action and noted that his way would have been preferable for France because it would have excluded any collaboration with Nazi Germany. Writing this, she did not overlook the fact that sacrifice was an essential part of nonviolent action: "It is clear that, in so doing, far greater numbers would have perished, and in far more frightful circumstances. This would be an imitation of Christ's passion realized on a national scale" (Weil 2002: 156). Weil understood very well that an ethical acceptable pacifism must not exclude self-sacrifice: "Pacifism is only capable of causing harm when a confusion arises between two sorts of aversion: the aversion to kill, and the aversion to be killed" (Weil 2002: 157). Whoever wants to avoid any suffering at all may easily sacrifice others. She therefore reproached French pacifists who collaborated with Nazis because they were cowards: "French pacifists of recent years had an aversion to being killed, but none to killing; otherwise they would not have rushed so hastily, in July 1940, to collaborate with Germany" (Weil 2002: 157).

Mahatma Gandhi: Nonviolence and sacrifice

Whereas Girard turned to the East, Gandhi turned to the West. Coming from a Hindu family, he began to reflect on his own religious roots during his studies in London. It was there that he began to study seriously the *Bhagavadgîtâ*. His readings of the Sermon on the Mount and Western and Christian thinkers, like John Ruskin, Leo Tolstoy, and Henry David Thoreau, opened his eyes to the nonviolent potentials in his own tradition: "My young mind tried to unify the teaching of the *Gita*, *The Light of Asia* and the Sermon on the Mount. That renunciation was the highest form of religion appealed to me greatly" (Gandhi 2001a: 78). Whereas Girard started from the Western critique of sacrifice and only gradually developed a more comprehensive approach including the Eastern view, Gandhi discovered in these Western perspectives the potential for his own tradition.

Similar to Weil, Gandhi rejected cowardice as a basis for confrontation with injustice. He preferred violence to cowardice. "I do believe that where there is only a choice between cowardice and violence I would advise violence" (Gandhi 1965: 132). Yet like Weil and Girard, he understood why violence cannot resolve human conflicts and how violence through mimesis easily escalates by turning adversaries into enemy twins. Mimicking violence equalizes all actors. In his famous 1909 book about Indian self-rule, *Hind Swaraj*, he distanced himself from terrorist attacks against the British occupation, referencing Jesus's saying about "those that wield the sword shall perish by the sword" (Gandhi 1997: 89 [Matthew 26:52]). Gandhi feared that, by violently fighting against the occupiers, India would become like the occupying power. According to Gandhi, evil must not be imitated in any way because evil means lead to evil ends. In this respect, his words remind us also of Jesus: "It has been my invariable experience that good evokes good, evil—evil; and that therefore, if the evil does not receive the corresponding response, it ceases to act, dies of want of nutrition. Evil can only live upon itself. Sages of old, knowing this law, instead of returning evil for evil, deliberately returned good for evil and killed it" (Gandhi 1967: 55).

Despite the West's admiration for Gandhi, it often overlooks how strongly he emphasized that the nonviolent struggle against injustice presupposes a readiness to suffer and to sacrifice oneself. Meaning truth- or soul-force, satyagraha became, for him, nonviolent action that explicitly included the willingness to suffer rather than respond violently:

> Its root meaning is holding on to truth, hence truth-force. I have also called it Love-force or Soul-force. In the application of Satyagraha, I discovered in the earliest stages that pursuit of truth did not admit of violence being inflicted on one's opponent but that he must be weaned from error by patience and sympathy.... And patience means self-suffering. So, the doctrine came to mean vindication of truth, not by infliction of suffering on the opponent but on one's self. (Gandhi 2001b: 6)

Gandhi drew on ancient Indian traditions of sacrifice to underscore suffering as a way of transforming violence. For him, satyagraha was simply a new name for "the ancient law of self-sacrifice" or "the law of suffering" (Gandhi 1965: 133). Among his list of the "seven social sins," he also mentioned "worship without sacrifice" (Gandhi 1968: 365).

It is at the same time important to understand how Gandhi's thought contributed to the reform of Hindu tradition. He clearly saw nonviolence as a criterion to evaluate sacrifice. For instance, he rejected animal sacrifices despite its prevalence in the Vedas: "It does not matter that animal sacrifice is alleged to find a place in the Vedas. It is enough for us that such sacrifice cannot stand the fundamental tests of Truth and Non-violence" (Gandhi 1994: 22). It is fitting that Gandhi's grandson Arun extended the Mahatma's insight about sacrifice even further: "Worship without Sacrifice (not of animals, but wealth)" (Gandhi 2017: 194). By referring to wealth and not animals he left archaic practices behind and hinted at human greed as a seminal cause of human conflicts.

Mohandas Gandhi also felt compelled to reject the traditional understanding of untouchability because it contradicted the truth of Hinduism (Gandhi 1994: 50–52). He interpreted the *Bhagavadgîtâ*'s use of warrior images symbolically, as an ethics of asceticism, thereby rejecting a literal understanding with its killing letters (Gandhi 1994: 32–35). According to Gandhi, the *Bhagavadgîtâ* aimed at the overcoming of passions like greed or anger, which are the main roots of human violence. In this respect, there is an affinity with Girard's thesis that mimetic rivalries cause violence.

As in the case of Weil, we have to ask if Gandhi was aware of the dangers that attend a perverted understanding of sacrifice, sacrifice as an end in itself. The answer to this question is similar to the one we found in the works of Weil. For Gandhi, renunciation is neither an irresponsible flight from the world nor an end in itself (Gandhi 1994: 23). Therefore, he understood Christ's sacrifice on the cross—neither flight nor an end in itself—as a "perfect act" of self-giving (Gandhi 1982: 481). Gandhi saw in Jesus a "man who was completely innocent offered himself as a sacrifice for the good of others, including his enemies, and became the ransom of the world." That Gandhi was not seeking renunciation for its own sake becomes clear in his interpretation of the first verses of the *Ishopanishad*. These verses summarize what is essential in the *Bhagavadgîtâ* and became his most important mantra. The renunciation that it voiced freed life for joy. With these three words "renounce and enjoy," Gandhi once answered the question of a journalist about the secret of his life (Easwaran 2011: 125; cf. Groody 2009: 156). His translation of the mantra from the *Ishopanishad* makes this insight explicit: "All this that we see in this great Universe is pervaded by God. Renounce it and enjoy it. Do not covet anybody's wealth or possession" (Gandhi 1994: 18).

The third and last part of this mantra interestingly parallels the last commandment of the biblical Decalogue, warning against mimetic desire. Gandhi interpreted this mantra as a lifestyle, which we have already linked with the help of Weil to Saint Paul, who recommended that people possess things in this world as if they do not possess them (1 Corinthians 7). It is in these deep spiritual insights that the East and the West definitely meet.

The broader view of sacrifice in Girard's later writings is closer to Gandhi's understanding of how the readiness for suffering and self-giving are related to nonviolence. For the three authors—Girard, Weil, and Gandhi—discussed in this chapter, there is a commonality that should be highlighted. They knew that all human engagement against violence depends on the one true God who is essentially love and nonviolence. This ultimately means that we have to trust God's grace to lead us out of violent deadlocks that so often destroy human life. When Gandhi planned a peace brigade, he frequently mentioned faithful trust in God as the first qualification for membership:

> He or she must have a living faith in non-violence. This is impossible without a living faith in God. A nonviolent man can do nothing save by the power and grace of God. Without it he won't have the courage to die without anger, without fear and without retaliation. Such courage comes from the belief that God sits in the hearts of all, and that there should be no fear in the presence of God. (Gandhi 1942: 155)

When the West is not blind to its Eastern roots from which it is an offspring, it strengthens its resolve that nonviolence may require suffering and sacrifice. Conversely, openness to the West allows the East to transcend its origins in the archaic sacred and embrace more fully God's nonviolence because it is the West that moved further away from this foundational murder.

References

Astell, A. (2017), "Mysticism, Girard, and Simone Weil," in J. Alison and W. Palaver (eds.), *The Palgrave Handbook of Mimetic Theory and Religion*, 249–55, New York: Palgrave Macmillan.
Baudler, G. (1997), *Das Kreuz. Geschichte und Bedeutung*, Düsseldorf: Patmos-Verlag.

Calasso, R. (2014), *Ardor*, trans. Richard Dixon, New York: Farrar, Straus and Giroux.

Doering, E. J. (2010), *Simone Weil and the Specter of Self-Perpetuating Force*, Notre Dame: University of Notre Dame Press.

Easwaran, E. (2011), *Gandhi the Man: How One Man Changed Himself to Change the World*. 4th ed., Tomales: Nilgiri Press.

Gandhi, A. (2017), *The Gift of Anger: And Other Lessons from My Grandfather Mahatma Gandhi*, New York: Gallery Boloks.

Gandhi, M. K. (1942), *Non-Violence in Peace and War. Vol. I*, Ahmedabad: Navajivan Publishing House.

Gandhi, M. K. (1965), *The Collected Works of Mahatma Gandhi. Vol.: 18: July — November 1920*, New Delhi: The Publications Division.

Gandhi, M. K. (1967), *The Collected Works of Mahatma Gandhi. Vol.: 24: May — August 1924*, New Delhi: The Publications Division.

Gandhi, M. K. (1968), *The Collected Works of Mahatma Gandhi. Vol.: 28: August — November 1925*, New Delhi: The Publications Division.

Gandhi, M. K. (1982), *The Collected Works of Mahatma Gandhi. Vol.: 85: July 16, 1946 — October 20, 1946*, New Delhi: The Publications Division.

Gandhi, M. K. (1994), *What Is Hinduism?* New Delhi: National Book Trust.

Gandhi, M. K. (1997), *Hind Swaraj and Other Writings*, Cambridge: Cambridge University Press.

Gandhi, M. K. (2001a), *An Autobiography: Or the Story of My Experiments with Truth*, trans. Mahadev Desai, London: Penguin Books.

Gandhi, M. K. (2001b), *Non-Violent Resistance (Satyagraha)*, Mineola: Dover.

Girard, R. (1987), *Things Hidden since the Foundation of the World: Research Undertaken in Collaboration with J.-M. Oughourlian and G. Lefort*, trans. S. Bann and M. Metteer, Stanford: Stanford University Press.

Girard, R. (1995), "Mimetische Theorie und Theologie," in *Vom Fluch und Segen der Sündenböcke. Raymund Schwager zum 60. Geburtstag*, ed. Józef Niewiadomski and Wolfgang Palaver, 15–29, Thaur: Kulturverlag.

Girard, R. (2007), *De la violence à la divinité, Bibliothèque Grasset*, Paris: Bernard Grasset.

Girard, R. (2008), *Evolution and Conversion: Dialogues on the Origin of Culture. With Pierpaolo Antonello at João Cezar de Castro Rocha*, London: Continuum.

Girard, R. (2010), *Battling to the End: Conversations with Benoît Chantre*, trans. M. Baker, *Studies in Violence, Mimesis, and Culture*, East Lansing: Michigan State University Press.

Girard, R. (2011), *Sacrifice*, trans. M. Pattillo and D. Dawson, *Breakthroughs in Mimetic Theory*, East Lansing: Michigan State University Press.

Girard, R. (2014), *The One by Whom Scandal Comes*, trans. M. B. DeBevoise, *Studies in Violence, Mimesis, and Culture*, East Lansing: Michigan State University Press.

Girard, R. and R. Adams (1993), "Violence, Difference, Sacrifice: A Conversation with René Girard," *Religion & Literature* 25 (2): 11–33.

Girard, R. and R. Schwager (2016), *René Girard and Raymund Schwager: Correspondence 1974–1991*, trans. C. Fleming and S. Treflé Hidden, *Violence, Desire, and the Sacred*, New York: Bloomsbury Academic.

Girard, R. and M. Treguer (2014), *When These Things Begin: Conversations with Michel Treguer*, trans. T. C. Merrill, *Studies in Violence, Mimesis, and Culture*, East Lansing: Michigan State University Press.

Gonsalves, F. (2009), "Sacrifice Sanctifies the Entire World," *The Times of India* 10 (4): 16.

Groody, D. G. (2009), *Globalization, Spirituality, and Justice: Navigating a Path to Peace*. 5th ed., *Theology in Global Perspective Series*, Maryknoll: Orbis Books.

Lawrence, T. E. (2017), *Seven Pillars of Wisdom*, Arcadia Press.

Moosbrugger, M. (2014), *Die Rehabilitierung des Opfers. Zum Dialog zwischen René Girard und Raymund Schwager um die Angemessenheit der Rede vom Opfer im christlichen Kontext, Innsbrucker theologische Studien*, Innsbruck: Tyrolia-Verlag.

Müller, F. M., ed. (1962), *The Upanishads: Part I*, New York: Dover Publications, Inc.

Palaver, W. (2013a), *René Girard's Mimetic Theory*, trans. Gabriel Borrud, *Studies in Violence, Mimesis, and Culture*, East Lansing: Michigan State University Press.

Palaver, W. (2013b), "Sacrificial Cults as 'the Mysterious Centre of Every Religion': A Girardian Assessment of Aby Warburg's Theory of Religion," in J. Zachhuber and J. Meszaros (eds.), *Sacrifice and Modern Thought*, 83–99, Oxford: Oxford University Press.

Palaver, W. (2014), "Abolition or Transformation? The Political Implications of Rene Girard's Theory of Sacrifice," in S. Cowdell, C. Fleming, and J. Hodge (eds.), *Violence, Desire, and the Sacred. Volume 2: René Girard and Sacrifice in Life, Love and Literature*, 17–29, London: Bloomsbury Publishing.

Palaver, W. (2017), "René Girard and Charles Taylor: Complementary Engagements with the Crisis of Modernity," in J. Alison and W. Palaver (eds.), *The Palgrave Handbook of Mimetic Theory and Religion*, 335–42, New York: Palgrave Macmillan.

Palaver, W. and R. Schenk, eds. (2018), *Mimetic Theory and World Religions, Studies in Violence, Mimesis, and Culture*, East Lansing: Michigan State University Press.

Taylor, C. (2007), *A Secular Age*, Cambridge: The Belknap Press.

Vattimo, G. and R. Girard (2010), *Christianity, Truth, and Weakening Faith: A Dialogue*, trans. William McCuaig, New York: Columbia University Press.

Weil, S. (1956a), *The Notebooks of Simone Weil: Volume One*, trans. A. Wills. 2 vols. Vol. 1, London: Routledge & Kegan Paul.

Weil, S. (1956b), *The Notebooks of Simone Weil: Volume Two*, trans. A. Wills. 2 vols. Vol. 2, London: Routledge & Kegan Paul.

Weil, S. (1970), *First and Last Notebooks*, London: Oxford University Press.

Weil, S. (1988), *Formative Writings, 1929–1941*, trans. D. T. McFarland and W. Van Ness, Amherst: University of Massachusetts Press.

Weil, S. (2002), *The Need for Roots: Prelude to a Declaration of Duties towards Mankind*, trans. Arthur Wills, London: Routledge.

Weil, S. (2003a), *Intimations of Christianity Among the Ancient Greeks*, London: Routledge.
Weil, S. (2003b), *Simone Weil on Colonialism: An Ethic of the Other*, trans. J. P. Little, Lanham: Rowman & Littlefield.
Weil, S. (2005), *An Anthology*, London: Penguin Books.
Weil, S. (2009), *Écrits de Marseille Vol. 2 (1941–1942): Grèce–Inde–Occitanie*, in *Œuvres complètes*, ed. A. Devaux and F. de Lussy, Paris: Gallimard.
Wenzel, U. J. (2009), "Das Kreuz und das Ende des Opfers," *Neue Zürcher Zeitung* 11 (4): 1.

3

Patterns of Sacrifice and Power Structure

Hassan Rachik

In his study of Islamic sacrifice in Morocco, Hassan Rachik, like Tsvi Blanchard elsewhere in this volume, raises an empirical challenge to Girard's theory: Can all sacrifice be subsumed under one category or type—under Girard's archaic or, for that matter, any other one sort? Rachik's fieldwork finds traditions of sacrifice that resemble Girard's description, but also traditions that do not. To be sure, the strict Girardian (stricter than Girard himself) might argue that the sacrifice forms described by Rachik originally followed the Girardian pattern but were later crystallized and subsumed into the forms that Rachik encountered. But then, our strict Girardian would have to bring evidence of this. As Rachik writes in his conclusion, "Instead of dismissing one pattern of sacrifice to universalize another, it is more productive to note that sacrifice has been adapted to a wide range of situations. Its nature . . . is malleable, negotiable, and manipulable. A theory of sacrifice should take into account this diversity." This lends support to Girard's growing interest in exploring the forms and meanings of sacrifice in other faith traditions.

—editor's note

Introduction

Hubert and Mauss proposed a comprehensive definition of sacrifice based on the opposition of the sacred and the profane: "Sacrifice is a religious act which, through the consecration of a victim, modifies the condition of the moral person who accomplishes it or that of certain objects with which he is concerned" (Hubert and Mauss 1964: 13). Though the French word *sacrifiant* has no exact English equivalent, the word "sacrifier" is used to mean "the subject to whom the benefits accrue . . . or who undergoes its effects" (Halls, in Hubert and Mauss 1964: ix). Hubert and Mauss understood sacrifice as a structured process; the pattern is that of rites of passage. Entry rites ensure the passage of the sacrificer, the animal, and other elements of the ritual from the profane state to the sacred one. The sacrificer, for instance, must perform preliminary rites that rid his body of the imperfections of his profane nature. The slaughtering of the animal, the ritual's culminating point, takes place in a middle stage followed by Exit rites that ensure the return to the profane world (Hubert and Mauss 1964: 19–49).

Hubert and Mauss proposed their model as universal, a description of all sacrifice. The study of Islamic sacrifice below suggests, however, that sacrifice falls into many types. Some resemble the Hubert and Mauss pattern, which emphasizes the sacralization of the (sacrificed) animal and unavoidably echoes Rene Girard's idea that sacrifice was the first ritual and indeed created the sacred. Yet other forms of sacrifice do not follow this pattern as they privilege the sociopolitical over the sacred or communication with a deity. By looking at several types of sacrifice in the High Atlas Mountains and other areas of Morocco, I hope to illustrate the point.

The application of Hubert and Mauss to Islamic sacrifice

This ternary pattern of sacrifice, based on the idea of animal consecration, was applied to Muslim feast of sacrifice (Doutté 1984: 457–80). On the tenth day of the last month of the year (lunar calendar), Muslims celebrate the sacrificial feast, known in Arabic under the name of 'id al-adha. In Morocco, the Arabic-speaking population and Berbers call it by names which mean "the Great Feast." The Little Feast celebrates the break in fasting during the month of Ramadan. The rites connected with the Great Feast stress the idea of consecration of the sacrificial animal and of the people as well. Women paint their hands and feet with henna, their eyes with antimony, and their lips and teeth with walnut root. These are used not only as cosmetics but also as means of purification and protection from evil influences. Men may also have their eyes colored with antimony. On the morning of the feast, a collective prayer takes place, celebrated in the open air, outside the village or the town. The slaughtering of the animal must take place after these prayers.

The sacrificial animal, which must be free from any defect, is also the subject of sanctifying practices that vary according to local customs. It is daubed with henna between its eyes; walnut is applied to its mouth and antimony on its eyes. Just before the fatal act, a woman puts into the mouth of the animal a mixture made of corn or barley, henna, and salt. The head of the animal must be turned toward the East (*Qibla, Mecca*) and the sacrificer must say "In the name of Allah, Allah the most great." These rites must be applied in both religious and profane contexts (butchery, domestic ceremonies), for the slaughtering of animals, in Islam, is always a ritual. Otherwise, the dead animal is considered illicit (Westermarck 1968 ii: 107–14; Hammoudi 1993).

The Hubert and Mauss pattern clearly fits this Muslim sacrifice. Many Muslim rituals could be interpreted as Entry rites that consecrate and prepare the elements of sacrifice for the culminating moment. Once the animal is dead, its holiness is distributed as broadly as possible: "The barely and salt which remain in the mouth of the animal after it has been killed is removed and sewn up in a small rag of piece of leather to be hung on some child or animal as a charm against the evil eye" (Westermarck 1968 ii: 126). The animal's blood is applied to the lintel of the entrance door (horizontal support along the top) and to other parts of the dwelling. It is also applied to hands and feet to heal or prevent the skin from chapping. Other parts of the animal are assigned therapeutic virtues. Against headaches, part of the dried stomach is burnt and inhaled by the patient. Some of the meat which is salted and cured is left to be eaten in future feasts. In so doing, people transfer the holiness of the animal to subsequent occasions (Westermarck 1968 ii: 126–33).

Civic sacrifice

It is this pattern of sacrifice that in 1984 I wanted to apply to the study of sacrifice rituals in the High Atlas Mountains of Morocco. It happened that the first sacrifice I observed, the *maʿruf* (collective and sacred meal), did not fit the ternary pattern. I was disappointed. On the way to the place of sacrifice, a young man who was leading the sacrificial goat behaved with it as he would have done with any animal, that is, by pushing it violently and giving it kicks from time to time. Moreover, no ritual preparation occurred. Except for the location of the slaughtering, near a holy place (a shrine, a mosque), the sacrifice of the *maʿruf* tends toward butchery (Rachik 1990: 27–38). As it would have been absurd to reject these rituals because they failed the Hubert-Mauss theoretical model, all I could do was to note that the ternary model of sacrifice did not fit the *maʿruf*. I had no explanation to offer.

Fortunately, this was not the end of the story. Later on, within the same tribes, I observed a hybrid sacrifice that referred to the sacred during the immolation stage and to politics in the distribution of the meat phase. This sacrifice was at the center of a local religious feast (Rachik 2016). Its social organization entailed two opposing groups: a tribe and a holy lineage, a subgroup of the same tribe. The animal was purchased by the tribe. Several ritual conditions were required. The sacrificial animal must be a black cow, which was held for a night in a cowshed belonging to a member of the holy lineage. On the sacrifice day, this ordinary cowshed was transformed into a sanctuary (by burning incense, candles) which pilgrims visited. The time of the sacrifice was also determined by tradition to be the first Thursday following August 22 in the Julian calendar. The holy lineage governed this stage of the ritual, which culminated in the animal's immolation. They made and held a ritual flag, and they organized the procession during which the cow was led to the place of sacrifice. The owner of the cowshed also had the privilege of giving the knife to the sacrificer. In this case, the role of the sacrificer was inherited.

Though the ternary model of sacrifice adequately describes this ritual so far, references to the sacred became obscured if not absent after immolation. All actions related to the dead animal (skinning, keeping the carcass, selling by auction the head and skin) were performed not by the holy lineage but by the tribesmen. Two days later, the village assembly organized the sharing of the meat. A few tribesmen made a census of the householders, dividing them into *argaz* (man) and afrukh (young). Men got a large share of the meat (*tasghart*), almost three times the amount given to the young as "scraps" (*umagur* means also bribes, leftovers). The rule explaining this distinction was simply stated: whereas the fathers of the householders who received the large portions were dead, the fathers of those who received the "scraps" were still alive.

This distinction went beyond the ritual: the young householder did not attend the community assembly (*jma't*) and was not involved with deciding collective duties. Though he was a head of a family living in an autonomous dwelling, as long as his father was alive, he was not considered a member of the political community. Hence, the sharing of the sacrificed animal followed and reinforced the political rules, notably the rule determining admission to a position of political authority.

The distribution of the meat from the ritual sacrifice was based not only on authority status but also on another political principle, the local definition of citizenship. The foreigner and the person who was banished by the community assembly did not get any part of the meat. Moreover, even the householders of the holy lineage, including the sacrificer, were obliged by the same political rules and received their portions of meat according to their political status. No privilege was accorded to them during this political stage of the ritual.

By contrast, in ritual contexts where the holy lineage exclusively controlled the ritual process, the sanctity of the sacrifice for all participants (rather than politics) was emphasized. Equal parts were given to all those who attended the sacrifice regardless of their tribes, age, or social status.

In sum, where the holy lineage or other religious entity controlled the sacrifice ritual, the rules regarding the animal's consecration and the (symbolic) distribution of this holiness were followed. But in the event that a political community was in charge of ritual sacrifice, there was a chance that political rules would be applied, and the consecration rites weakened and attenuated. The main characteristic of *political* sacrifice is that the sacrificed animal is considered a collective good, subjected to the same political rules applicable to other public goods (mosque, pastures, irrigation ditches). While it is still seen sacred—to express the sacrality of the *ma'ruf*, it is said that the food stays a year in the belly—the process of sacralization is weakened as it is performed by political actors.

Stealth comparisons

Jean Vernant rejected any general theory of sacrifice on the grounds that it is necessarily arbitrary. The relationships between the three partners in sacrifice (sacrificer, animal, and deity) are not constant and change from one culture to another and even within the same culture. To Vernant, the study of sacrifice must be conducted within the limits of a given society and lead to a comparative typology of sacrifices. Any study of the ancient Greek sacrificial system, for instance, requires taking seriously the meaning that people gave to the sacrifice, its vocabulary, its inconsistencies, and the tensions between different conceptions of sacrifice among different subgroups (observers of the official religion, the vegetarians who equate sacrifice with murder, among others). On Vernant's view, sacrificial systems are necessarily original and complex and not easily compared. What should be compared are not specific sacrifice systems, which must be studied in their particularity, but the patterns of sacrifice (Vernant 1980: 5–35) that emerge across many societies.

Our ambition was to compare such patterns in Morocco and in other societies where political sacrifices have been studied. Let's begin by recalling the sanctifying sacrifice based on the idea of the consecration. The marginalization of the civic/political and the highlighting of the "consecration/religious" in the research literature are explained by the fact that researchers have privileged rituals where the sacrificer is a person, which tend toward sacralization rites, and have neglected sacrifice supported by the community.

The theory of Hubert and Mauss was based on individual or family but not community sacrifice, their theory thus emphasizing sacralization. Charles Malamoud notes that in Brahmanic India, sacrifice is essentially a village affair though the *normative* texts of Brahmanism do not admit a "civic" sacrifice whose participants or beneficiaries are members of a political community (Malamoud 1989: 97–101). As the village/civic dimension is absent in Brahmanic normative texts, it is consequently absent in any theory of sacrifice based exclusively on them. It is no coincidence that critics stressing the empirical inadequacy of the Hubert and Mauss (individual/family) pattern often based their descriptions of sacrifice on the ancient Greek civic sacrifice, a prototype of a community sacrifice embedded in political relations.

Détienne argued that the Maussian model, with its movement back and forth between the profane and the sacred, was inadequate to the Greek case, where neither the priest nor the sacrificed animal leaves the profane world but where, on the contrary, it is the participation in the worldly social group or political community that authorizes the practice of sacrifice (Détienne 1979a: 24–25). He offered a careful analysis of how political power and the practice of sacrifice were linked in ancient Greece, showing, for instance, how sacrifice rituals expressed the political inequality of the inhabitants of the city. The right to sacrifice, like political rights, was a privilege granted exclusively to citizens. The foreigner was excluded from the altars, or he required a citizen-mediator to approach them not because he was profane but because he was not a citizen. The exclusion from sacrifice was first political marginalization. The metic, a foreigner with limited citizen privileges, also needed a mediator. However, unlike foreigners, he could be admitted to the large community of commensals, those permitted to eat together.

In sum, it was the political stratification that governed the practice of civic sacrifice within ancient Greece. Unlike the situation in sanctifying sacrifices, it was political rather than religious status that determined who could sacrifice, slaughter, share a collective meal, and approach the Gods and their altars. In principle, every citizen was qualified to perform the various operations of sacrifice. Slaughtering and cutting the sacrificial animal did not require priestly virtues or specialized technical knowledge. In fact, from the fifth century BCE, the various operations of the sacrifice were ensured by the *mageiros*, a butcher-cook-sacrificer, a public servant who was attached to a sanctuary or engaged temporarily for an agreed salary (Détienne 1979b: 9–21, 207).

Concerning the distribution of the sacrificed animal, Détienne showed how this too was based on the political structure of the city. He distinguished two types of sharing, the aristocratic and the isonomic. In the first, the best pieces of meat were given to those who occupied high positions such as the king and priests. The second, similar to the Homeric model of the "meal in equal parts," emphasized the equality of the citizens. The animal was cut into pieces of equal weight which were distributed by lots. The egalitarian meals from public sacrifices, like other public banquets, expressed the isonomic structure of the city (Détienne 1979c: 222-25).

In his analysis of the Bouphonia of Athens (the sacrifice of plowing oxen), Durand too highlighted the links between sacrifice and politics. This ritual was characterized by the negation of the sacrifice and, consequently, of the sacrificer who caused it. No single person assumed the guilt of killing the sacrificial animal, and each participant absolved the others of it, a practice reflecting the political equality of the sacrificers. The question of the sacrificers' guilt is raised only in this Athenian ritual and nowhere else in the ancient Greek sacrifice repertoire. This meant that this issue in Athens was political rather than religious. As the ox was associated in myth with the founding of the city, its sacrifice could not be attributed to a single citizen. The whole city was erected as a collective sacrificer. Unlike religious sacrifice, where the priest was at the center of the ritual, the civic sacrifice blurred the sacrificer's identification.

We can cite many other examples of citizen equality in ancient Greek sacrifice. In the history of Soptratos, the sacrifice of an ox was followed by a feast where the animal was distributed within the civic group according to egalitarian principles (Durand 1986: 43-65). Durand contrasted "civic sacrifice" with "religious sacrifice" (Durand 1986: 57) while Détienne used the expression "political sacrifice" when the sacrifice refers to the city (Détienne 1979b: 195, 205). In sum, where religious actors or entities have greater societal power, the sacrifice ritual emphasized the sacralization of the animal and (symbolic) extension/distribution of this sacralization to the community. But where political entities have greater power, the sacrifice ritual falls under the community's political rules and the importance of the sacralization of the animal dims.

Let's continue these big jumps in time and space to check these assumptions. Half a century ago, Marc Abélés studied Ethiopian sacrifice rituals under conditions of societal conflict between dignitaries who were engaged in political competition and the priests who, as specialists and distinguished by their knowledge and by their practice of sacrifice, are called to act on natural phenomena. However, the priests were dependent on the political community assembly and were therefore removable from office. At certain feasts, every sacrificer, in order to sacrifice his animal, had to call on a priest who was entitled to reserve pieces of meat for himself. However, this practice was questioned by the villagers who rebelled against the priests and began to perform their own sacrifices (Abélès 1983: 13–14, 147, 173–233). Here we see a power structure similar to the one we observed in the High Atlas and in any ritual involving tribe or village assembly: a political community (village assembly, dignitaries) which controls its religious mediators. After the conflict between political dignitaries and priests was resolved, the community's sacrifice acquired an almost entirely political dimension as it shifted from the priests' monopoly to community activity where members are allowed to make their own sacrifices.

Analyzing Kurbania, a Greek community sacrifice studied contemporaneously to the Ethiopian example above, Georgoudi noted the lack of ritual specialization and the interchangeability of actors. The immolation, cutting, preparation, and distribution of meat were performed by various persons: donors of sacrificial animals, churchwardens, or volunteers for these tasks. He also showed how the sacrifice ritual was affected by the local sociopolitical structure. Patriarchal power, for instance, was manifested in the common meals following animal sacrifices. He concluded that the emphasis on consecration diminished and that the sacrifice was civic in nature (Georgoudi 1979: 271–307).

In sum, rituals that retain an emphasis on the sacralization of the (sacrificed) animal are more likely to be observed in societies where religious groups maintain control of the sacrificial rites. This would be the case in Vedic sacrifice and, according to Hubert and Mauss, Hebrew Bible sacrifice. What they define as the *general* model of sacrifice may in fact be not general but simply more common among social groups with clear religious stratification that favors the specialists' monopoly on sacrifice. By contrast, the political or civic sacrifice takes place when a community dispenses with religious mediators and organizes its rituals without them, submitting the sacrifice rite to the same rules that govern the management of community goods. In such cases, access to the sacred is not exclusively determined by one's role in the religious hierarchy or by one's moral purity. The designation of the sacrificer is a political not religious matter.

Importantly, political sacrifice presupposes social structures allowing the political community to directly govern its relation to the sacred.

Humiliating sacrifice

Let's consider the humiliating sacrifice, called *'âr* in the Maghreb, a privileged instance that illustrates more clearly how the political power structure affects sacrifice. The word *'âr* is associated with shameful behavior. According to Westermarck, *'âr* is used in Morocco "to denote an act which intrinsically implies the transference of a conditional curse for the purpose of compelling somebody to grant a request." If a person says to another, "*Ha l'âr 'lik*," "Here is *l'âr* upon you . . . , it implies that if the latter does not grant a request, some misfortune will befall him on account of the conditional curse contained in the *l'âr*" (Westermarck 1968 i: 518). In short, the *'âr* consists of compelling a person or a group to grant a request. The rites by which it is engaged are varied (Hart 1976: 306, 533–48, 553; Eickelman 1976: 149–53; Rosen 1979: 44–46; Brown 1982: 9–34; Rachik 1993: 167–83). If the word "sacrifice" entails consecration, it would be inappropriate to apply it to a ritual associated with the notion of shame.

In situations of minor importance, verbal expressions are sufficient to place a temporary curse on someone. In other cases, the petitioner who seeks to compel an action through the pressure of a curse will perform rituals that express the humiliation of his beseeching position. These include wearing dirty garments, throwing a piece of an old tent-cloth over his shoulders, smearing his face with soot, bowing with his hands behind his back, or putting a tent-cloth round the neck of the horse (used by the defeated party after a fight). On very solemn occasions, the most powerful means of casting the *'âr* is slaughtering an animal close to the house of the person or the mosque of the group from whom a benefit is requested. For example, in the past, a man who killed a fellow tribesman took refuge with an allied tribe. After a year, he and his hosts went to the family of the deceased and slaughtered an animal as an *âr* upon them, a request to forgive the killer for his wrongdoing. The killer came with his hands tied up and a dagger in his mouth. If he was already forgiven, the family of the deceased removed the dagger and unloosed his ties (Westermarck 1968: 520–26), but a "man of honor" would not ask for a pardon and, if unforgiven, had to face the revenge of the victim's relatives (Jamous 1981: 210–14).

In cases of *âr*, the community's sociopolitical structure also significantly affected the sacrifice rite, and the sacramental aspect was diminished. First, the sacrificer could not submit himself or the animal to preliminary purifications. Rather, instead of eliminating the imperfections of his profane nature from his body, he increased its impurity. (Otherwise, it would have been seen as an affront by the person or the group whom he approached with a request.)

Second, the animal was not object of consecration. One form of 'âr, t'argiba, even stressed its humiliation by cutting its hocks ('argub) so that it fell into the posture of a suppliant. This kind of sacrifice was used on solemn occasions, when a tribe sought help or military alliance and when an appeal was made to the Sultan or other high government official (Westermarck 1968 i: 527–32). The t'argiba was also practiced in Mauritania. There the animal, a camel, was taken to the tent of the person from whom the request was being made. Before slaughter, its hocks were sliced with a dagger so that it kneeled. After the sacrifice, the meat was shared among people of low status, such as slaves and blacksmiths (Bonte 1999: 240–41). To accentuate the humiliation, the petitioner might slaughter the animal without performing the obligatory rites of Islam and without pronouncing the name of God (basmala), which renders the animal unlawful for consumption. This omission reduced the sacrifice to a mere killing, which excluded any possibility of partaking of the meat, which was left to servants and poor people (Westermarck 1968 i: 527).

In short, the sacrifier in the 'âr does not seek consecration but rather is obliged to show his humiliation. He is not chosen by virtue of his religious qualities but according to his social position, a killer, a weak or a defeated tribe, or any person who is wronged and has nobody to defend him. The animal is mutilated or reduced to carrion. In contrast to the sanctifying sacrifice that involves God, spirits, and saints, the goal is not to employ sacrifice to approach sacred beings but to manifest or amplify the social gap that separates the sacrificer/supplicator from the recipient of the sacrifice.

The different forms of sacrifice explored here suggest that "sacrifice" does not have only one "nature" nor is there one type of this ritual. In some cases, the relationship between sacrificer and divine beings is paramount, along with the sacralization of the (sacrificed) animal—a sacralization that can be transferred to the sacrificer(s). In others, divine beings and sacralization are far less important—indeed, divine beings may not be present in the ritual at all. The sacrificed animal in this case is seen as more of a "common good" to be distributed according to the sociopolitical rules of the community, thus reinforcing them. In the case of "humiliating sacrifice," sacrifice seems to have even less to do with divine beings or the sacred and again, reflects the sociopolitical status of the parties involved. Sacrifice cannot keep the same "nature" regardless of its structure of power.

Conclusion

The actors in sacrifice are not "prisoners" of a universal pattern founded on an exclusive idea (consecration, gift, redemption) which they automatically perform. Even in the case of sacrifice, we should recognize the opportunities people and social groups have to adapt their ritual practices to the concrete situations in which they are engaged. Sacrifice cannot be reduced to a system of representations and rites endowed with a stability and an exteriority that immunizes it against any political dynamic. It is not so cut off from everyday affairs. As with any cultural form, it would be reductive to abstract it from the social relations that inhabit it.

Hubert and Mauss's pattern of sacrifice is more closely tied to a sociopolitical structure where the priesthood is dominant. What they define as the general pattern of sacrifice is specific to social groups where the specialists of the sacred monopolize the sacrifice ritual. The separation between the sacred and the profane, the rites of consecration, the Entry rites, and the Exit rites are more likely applied when a body of priests or specialists dominates the sacrificial process. But political sacrifice has rituals and purposes that differ substantially from those of sacralization-sacrifice and have more flexible performance requirements. When, in the High Atlas, the holy lineage organized the sacrifice, the time and the place of the immolation were determined, the ritual stages and the division of ritual labor respected, as the holy lineage is a religious body and maintains the sacred/sacralizing and less flexible nature of the sacrifice. But when, in the same region, tribes or other civic assemblies organize the sacrifice, the emphasis is more political, time requirements are more flexible ("when walnut trees bloom," "when barely turns yellow"), and time is negotiated according to the weather and the availability of the members of the group. When it snows, for example, the celebration of the ritual is postponed. Other aspects of sacrifice, such as the distribution of meat and division of labor, also differ from community to community or in different situations within one community.

Instead of dismissing one pattern of sacrifice to universalize another, it is more productive to note that sacrifice has been adapted to a wide range of situations. Its nature, if it is to possess one, is, as with any ritual, malleable, negotiable, and manipulable. A theory of sacrifice should take into account this diversity. The same community can, according to the stakes and contexts, guide sacrifice in a religious or political direction. Importantly, theoretical patterns should not be confused with actual, concrete sacrifices. Even qualifying a given sacrifice as political does not mean that the political dimension exhausts its meaning. The reference to the sacred is not excluded. Patterns at most help us to understand concrete sacrifices that refuse unambiguous interpretation because they are embedded in diverse and changing social arrangements.

References

Abélès, M. (1983), *Le Lieu du politique*, Paris: Société d'ethnographie.
Bonte, P. (1999), "Symboliques et rituels de la protection. Le sacrifice *t'arguîba* dans la société maure," in P. Bonte, A-M. Brisebarre, and A. Gokalp (eds.), *Sacrifices en Islam, Espaces et temps d'un rituel*, 239–61, Paris: CNRS Editions.
Brown, K. (1982), "The Curse of Westermarck," in T. Stroup (éd.), *E. Westermarck: Essay on His Life and Works*, vol. 34, 9–34, Helsinki: Acta Philosophical Fennica.
Détienne M. (1979a), "Pratiques culinaires et esprit du sacrifice," in M. Détienne and et J-P. Vernant (eds.), *La cuisine du sacrifice en pays grec*, 5–35, Paris: Gallimard.
Détienne, M. (1979b), "Violentes 'eugénies' En pleine Thesmophories: des femmes couvertes de sang," in M. Détienne and et J.-P. Vernant (eds.), *La cuisine du sacrifice en pays grec*, 183–214, Paris: Gallimard.
Détienne, M., and J. Svenbro (1979c), "Les loups au festin de la Cité impossible," in M. Détienne and et J-P. Vernant (eds.), *La cuisine du sacrifice en pays grec*, 215–38, Paris: Gallimard.
Doutté, E., *La société musulmane du Maghrib, Magie et religion dans l'Afrique du Nord*, Paris: Maisonneuve J. et Geuthner, P., 1984.
Durand, J.-L. (1986), *Sacrifice et labour en Grèce ancienne: essai d'anthropologie religieuse*, Paris: La Découverte.
Eickelman, D. (1976), *Moroccan Islam. Tradition and Society in a Pilgrimage Center*, Austin and London: University of Texas Press.
Georgoudi, S. (1979) "L'égorgement sanctifié en Grèce moderne: les 'Kourbania' des saints," in M. Détienne and et J-P. Vernant (eds.), *La cuisine du sacrifice en pays grec*, 271–307, Paris: Gallimard.
Hammoudi, A. (1993), *The Victim and Its Masks, Essay on Sacrifice and Masquerade in Maghreb*, Chicago: University of Chicago Press.
Hart, D. (1976), *The Aith Waryaghar of the Moroccan Rif: An Ethnography and History*, Tucson: The University of Arizona Press.
Hubert, H., and M. Mauss (1964), *Sacrifice: Its Nature and Function*, trans. W. D. Halls, Chicago: Chicago University Press.
Jamous, R. (1981), *Honneur et baraka. Les structures sociales traditionnelles dans le Rif*, Paris: Editions de la Maison des Sciences de l'Homme.
Malamoud, Ch. (1989), Cuire le monde Rite et pensée dans l'Inde ancienne, Paris: La découverte.
Rachik, H. (1990), *Sacré et sacrifice dans le Haut Atlas marocain*, Casablanca: Afrique Orient.

Rachik, H. (2016 [1992]), *Le sultan des autres, rituel et politique dans le Haut Atlas*, Casablanca: Afrique Orient.

Rachik, H. (1993), "Sacrifice et humiliation. Essai sur le ʿâr à partir de l'œuvre de Westermarck," in R. Bourqia et M. El-Harras (eds.), *Westermarck et la société marocaine*, 167–83, Rabat: Publications de la Faculté des Lettres et des Sciences Humaines.

Rosen, L. (1979), "Social Identity and Points of Attachments: Approaches to Social Organization," in C. Geertz, H. Geertz, and L. Rosen (eds.), *Meaning and Order in Moroccan Society*, 19–122, Cambridge: Cambridge University Press.

Vernant, J.-P. (1980), "Théorie générale du sacrifice et mise à mort dans la Grecque," in *Collectif, Le sacrifice dans l'antiquité*, 1–39, Vandoeuvres-Genève: Fondation Hardt.

Westermarck, E. (1968), *Ritual and Belief in Morocco*, New Hyde Park: University Books.

4

Rabbinic Reflections on Intentional Sacrifice and Sanctification

Tsvi Blanchard

Blanchard's study of sacrifice in the Hebrew Bible and rabbinic interpretation raises the following question: Can all sacrifice be subsumed under one category or type—Girardian or another? Blanchard's analysis of the actions and especially the intentions required by Hebrew Bible sacrifice finds that these rituals do not easily fall under the Girardian archaic. They are rather means of creating a sanctified space that helps us near God and others in the community. In turn, this "nearing" is part of the reciprocal, covenantal relationship with God, where both God and the Israelites and the Israelites among themselves commit to each other. A Girardian might argue that Hebrew Bible sacrifices were originally of the archaic sacred but developed into other ritual forms which were closer to the non-idolatrous, self-giving type of sacrifice which Girard holds is the salvation of humanity (see Palaver, this volume). Perhaps this later exploration of Girard's into how non-Christian faiths express the universal "ontology of peace" is the productive path. Blanchard's description of sacrifice as creating a space in which to better experience commitment to God and community illustrate the sort of ritual in which Girard was increasingly interested.

—editor's note

Introduction

The word "sacrifice" in English denotes (a) an act of slaughtering an animal or person and (b) surrendering a good or possession as an offering to God or to some other beings, often thought of as supernatural. A derivative use of "sacrifice" refers to any act of surrendering something on behalf of someone or something else (a cause, for instance). In Christian thought, this notion gains in importance. It is linked to the image or conception of Jesus Christ as *giving*—and *giving up* his life—to expiate human sin and redeem humanity. On Rene Girard's view, the second lesson of the cross is indeed that humanity learns to give for the sake of others as Jesus gave for humanity (see, Palaver, this volume). In much of contemporary Western culture, the Christian conception of Christ's sacrifice is also broadened to actions that ordinary persons can do: we can give of what we have for the sake of others, and "sacrifice" here means *giving up* something important in order to benefit others or a cause (Halbertal 2012).

Unfortunately, this shift in focus to "giving up" draws us away from other possible conceptions of sacrifice. In the Hebrew Bible, the sacrificial system is not part of the economy of giving up (for the sake of others) but rather part of holiness. More specifically, sacrifice is related to sanctification or consecration, that is, the act of making the ordinary sacred or holy. In the classic Christian conception, the focus is not on consecration. Jesus does not need to be consecrated by God but instead is *given* or even surrendered—God gives of himself—as an act of love.

In discussing sacrifice, we should not be limited to either the Christian conception or its more popular, less theological versions of "giving up." In this chapter, I hope to expand our conversation about sacrifice by exploring the classic Judaic (biblical and rabbinic) conception of sacrifice as part of sanctification. I am concerned not simply with outlining and explaining the connection between sacrifice and sanctification but also to show why sanctification and sacrifice are important in our present lives.

To do that, I will explore the desert sanctuary and Temple as "covenantal places" of the divine indwelling with the Jewish people *and* also of individual Jews with one another. This will allow us to think seriously about the contemporary search for the sacred and places of holiness in a secular world and about creating rituals of transformation through which the ordinary items and places of our daily life become sanctified and allow us to near the transcendent and other persons. "To follow the Most-High," Emmanuel Levinas wrote, "is also to know that nothing is greater than to approach one's neighbour" (Levinas 1994a: 142).

In the Judaic conception, the purpose of the sacrificial system is not primarily to pacify a God angered by sin or curry favor with an arbitrary and self-interested deity, as in Girardian archaic. Instead, the sacrificial system is meant to maintain and enhance the covenant between God and the Israelite people and among persons—a foundational concept of Judaism developed throughout Jewish history into present scholarship (Borowitz 1990, 1991; Buber 2010; Heschel 1997). The Israelite covenant depends on sustaining a relationship in which (a)

God cares about the physical and spiritual well-being of the Israelites, (b) the Israelites care about the well-being of each other, and (c) the Israelite people are in the service of God. James Alison helpfully explores these interlocking relationships in the Day of Atonement service (Alison 2004). Again in the words of Levinas, the intertwined covenant between God and Israel *and* among persons is not a "figure of speech" but a description of God "who approaches precisely through this relay to the neighbor—binding men among one another with obligation, each one answering for the lives of all the others." This is "the highest possible theological knowledge one can have" (Levinas 1994b: 171).

The act of making an ordinary object or animal sacred or holy has as its goal the creation of a space within which God may dwell with his people, or as God says in Exod. 25:8, "Let them make a sanctuary for Me that I may dwell among them." (Translations of the Hebrew Bible, the Mishnah, and the Babylonian Talmud are my own adaptation of standard versions.) This is most easily accomplished through sacrifice. The logic of sanctification and sacrifice depends on

(a) the existence of a meaningful sacred place that is fundamentally distinguished from the realm of profane life;
(b) a system of rituals with requirements that govern the sacrificial rites;
(c) a model for action that consecrates—that is, that transfers—material reality from the domain of the secular/profane into the domain of the sacred; and
(d) a concept of subjective *intent* that is decisive for an act of sanctification and also significant for the (covenantal) meaning and validity of acts of sacrifice.

Sanctification

Sanctification or consecration is the transformation of the objects and actions that comprise our everyday world into holy objects and actions. In the Hebrew Bible, without holiness (*kedusha*) there is no sanctification.

Fundamentally, holiness in the Bible is an alternative condition distinguished from and seen as *elevated* above the world of ordinary "profane" (*hol*) life. Sanctified/consecrated objects are either inherently sanctified (a firstborn he-goat), become so through an act of consecration, or a combination of both (the Sabbath). The most frequent is objects requiring consecration. The elevation of non-holy objects is possible because we—humanity—are able to link the object, place, person, or time to the divine. In rabbinic law, the proper verbal declaration or thought is sufficient to sanctify the animal, plant, or object.

In both the Bible and rabbinic literature, consecrated items belong to God's domain. In the Mishnah Shekalim 4:6 we learn that consecrated possessions (whose use is not otherwise specified) go toward the upkeep of the Temple. Where such items are fit for public offerings (such as incense, wine, oil, and flour) "they should be given to the craftsman (working for the Temple) for their wages. . . . These are the words of Rabbi Akiva." The Mishnah in b. Talmud Beitsa 36b regards sanctification of a sacrifice as one of the 613 commandments. Nevertheless, the Talmud does not actually require that one perform this commandment except in particular circumstances, for example, if one has sinned. Sanctification was, however, understood as part of good character.

In sum, the act of sanctification is a verbal declaration that a particular animal, plant, or object is being set aside for religious purposes and is now Temple property. Although this is possible through thought alone (b. Talmud Shevuot 26b, Exodus 35:5, 22, II Chronicles 29:31), shared observable consecration rituals are essential to communal religious life.

The Bible and rabbinic literature are not as clear as we would like on whether sacred objects and persons are ontologically different or are simply *treated* differently because they have been sanctified. Our purposes here, however, require only the latter, hence only a functional approach to the practices of sanctification.

Sacrifice

Sacrifice and holiness are found independently in the Bible before the institution of Temple sacrifices. Cain and Abel bring offerings (Genesis 4:3-4). The Talmud suggests that Adam too brought animal sacrifices (b. Talmud Avodah Zarah 8a). Sacrifices are mentioned in connection with special encounters with the divine and covenant renewal (Genesis 13:8, 15:9-21, Genesis 28:10-22) or out of gratitude (Genesis 14:18). Sanctification and holiness are found in the creation story, where God sanctifies the seventh day (Genesis 2:3). Moses must remove his shoes because he is standing on holy ground (Exodus 3:5). The rabbinic concept of holiness too is in part independent of the sacrificial system (Nachmanides, Leviticus 19:2, Isaiah 9:16, b. Talmud Hagigah 18b, b. Talmud Berakhot 53b, among others).

In the rabbinic reading, then, Leviticus 1:1, 2 makes clear that (a) there is an existing social institution of sacrifice running back to the Bible's very beginning, (b) there is to be a national sacrificial system that continues this tradition and in large part replaces the previous system, (c) this sacrificial system represents the will of God, and (d) human beings may of their own free will transform their ordinary "profane" property into sacred/holy property so it now "belongs" to God's sacred domain.

In sum, sacrifice *may be* independent of sanctification. Sacrifice may also be independent of holiness, for example, for expressing gratefulness. Holiness may be independent of sacrifice (the Sabbath). Are they ever joined? Yes, the Temple connects them.

The Temple, sacrifice, and holiness

Dedicating something to the desert sanctuary and Temple is the paradigmatic act of sanctification, of "making holy." The supporting conceptual structure here lies in the primary purpose of the sanctuary and Temple: the communion of God with the people. If the sanctuary and Temple are where God communes with us, dedicating something to these places makes it of God.

Although the wilderness sanctuary is in general termed *mishkan*, Exodus 25:8 uses *mikdash*, usually used for the Temple. This suggests that its purpose is the same as the Temple's, "And let them make a sanctuary for Me that I may dwell among them." Rabbinic literature follows the Bible in understanding the purpose of both the *mishkan* (sanctuary) and Temple as God's dwelling place. The rabbis' reasoning is that while still in the desert, the Israelites, through their closeness to God, enjoyed divine affection greater than at other times in their history. Therefore, he provided his indwelling to them before the permanent Temple was constructed. The primary purpose of both Temple holiness and desert sanctuary holiness is to allow communion with God. The medieval Spanish philosopher Nachmanides parses Leviticus 19:2 as meaning, "And the meaning of the verse saying, 'since Holy am I the Lord, your God,' is that we merit to cling to him by our being holy."

As the Temple and the desert sanctuary are places of communion with God, where heaven and earth meet, each must be holy, and its holiness must be preserved. What happens there protects and rectifies the covenantal relationship between God and his people. One way is by atoning for sin. In the spiritual economy of the covenant, sacrifice eliminates the consequences of error that would otherwise undermine communion with God. Of course, deep gratitude and happiness are expressed as well.

Sacrifice requires a sacred place in which to happen. Thus, the Israelites must be able to consecrate objects, animals, and plants—everything necessary for constructing a place in which God dwells. Consequently, *Israelite society possesses an institution of sanctification that allows for elevating the spiritual status of material realities from profane to holy so that sacred space may be created and so that sacrifice, maintaining relationship with God, may take place there.* The sacrificial system provides many of the details that define the character of holy activity, specifically of holy activity that not only allows for but also "is" communing with God.

Intention and sacrificial rituals

Let us review the Mishnah's understanding of the sacrificial system in Kodashim, tractate Zevachim, which comments mostly on Leviticus (1:1-17, 2:1-3, 3:1-6, 4:1-12, 4:27-32, 5:1-10, 5:14-16, 6:1-2, 6:7-11, 6:17-23, 7:1-8, 7:16-18). Despite the many disputed areas found in the rabbinic discussion, a fairly stable picture, with significant overlaps with the biblical system, is available. The sources of the sacrifices are oxen, sheep, goats, pigeons, turtledoves, flour, wine, olive oil, and water. There are individual/private sacrifices and communal/public sacrifices.

The relevant categories of persons involved are as follows:

(1) The owner of the item to be sanctified and used in the sacrificial process
(2) The designator, or consecrator, who sets the material aside as holy
(3) Priests who perform the sacrificial service in the Temple
(4) Support workers, for example, those who flay the hides of the animals sacrificed

The general types of animal sacrifice are as follows:

(1) Sin offering (*hatat*) and guilt offering (*asham*), obligatory offerings brought to atone for unintentional sins.
(2) Burnt offering (*olah*), often but not always a free will offering, signifying devotion to God and always totally burnt on the altar.
(3) Peace offering (*shelamim*), a voluntary individual offering usually expressing gratitude or hope but also a communal offering on the Feast of Weeks (*Shavuot*).

(4) Thanksgiving offering (*todah*), brought in gratitude for being saved in a dangerous situation.
(5) Firstborn offering (*bekhor*), sacrifice of the firstborn male of a cow, sheep, or goat, expressing the belief that God "owns" and deserves the best of what we obtain. It does not require consecration since it is considered born sanctified.
(6) Tithe-offering, one in ten of animal newborns, signifying God's ownership of the best of what we obtain. New plant growth was also tithed and given to priests, Levites, or the poor.
(7) Passover (*pesach*), a lamb or kid eaten on Passover night in remembrance of God's saving the Israelite firstborns when all the Egyptian firstborn were slain in the tenth plague.

Plant offerings and two additional bird sacrifices are classified separately:

(1) Bird burnt offering (*olat ha'of*), signifying complete devotion to God and burnt completely on altar.
(2) Bird sin offering (*hatat ha'of*), an obligatory offering in atonement for sin.

Vegetable offerings (*minhah*), water libations (*nesakhim*), and possibly wine and oil libations are not relevant to our discussion here. Domesticated mammal sacrifices, bird sacrifices, and the water, oil, and wine libations are considered especially holy (*kodshei kedoshim*) with special stringencies governing how they are treated. The remaining sacrifices are seen as having a lesser degree of sanctity (*kodashim kalim*).

The typical domesticated mammal sacrificial service (*avodah*) proceeds as follows:

(1) A preliminary placing of the owner's hands on the head of animal and leaning down strongly on it while making a confession when required (*semikha*).
(2) The *avodah*: (a) slaughtering the animal, (b) catching the blood in a sacred vessel, (c) carrying the vessel and the blood to the altar, (d) throwing or sprinkling the blood against the altar (in some cases, applying the blood with one's finger).
(3) Parts of the sacrifice, mostly internal organs (*emurin*), are placed and burnt on the altar.
(4) For certain sacrifices, priests and sometimes others, but not the owner, eat the remaining meat of the sacrifice.

For bird sacrifices, the rules for the *avodah* and eating are in part different from those for goat, sheep, and oxen.

Plant sacrifices (*micha*) have a four-part process (matching the *avodah* of domesticated animal sacrifices):

(1) Scooping (*kometz/kemitsah*) corresponding to the slaughtering of the animal.
(2) Putting the scooped material into a consecrated vessel.
(3) Bringing the filled vessel to the altar.
(4) Burning the scooped material (Zevachim 13b).

Importantly, it is through these well-defined rituals at the sacred place (sanctuary or Temple) that sacrifice is connected to holiness and sanctification.

Rabbinic literature, based on the Bible, understands the holy as protected by prohibitions on the personal use of sacred objects, which leads us to the matter of intent. Most sanctification of animals, grains, or vegetables requires designating them as particular types of sacrifice brought on behalf of a particular person or persons who otherwise may benefit from them by, for example, eating, selling, or working them. When a priest makes a sacrifice, he must do so in the name of, that is, on behalf of, the particular person and for particular designated purpose. That is, the priest and persons bringing the sacrifice must have certain intent.

The discussion in the Mishnah Zevachim I:1 begins: "All sacrifices which have been slaughtered *she lo lishmah* are valid but do not count as fulfilling the owner's obligation with the exception of the Passover sacrifice (*Korban Pesach*) and the sin offering (*chatat*)." The standard reading of "*she lo lishmah*" is "not for the designation intended by the person bringing the sacrifice." If the owner brings the sacrifice as a free will offering but the priest sacrifices it as some other kind, the sacrifice "counts" but not as a free will offering.

The Mishnah here has introduced the concept of intended purpose. This is morally and theologically important because it implies that mere correct performance of the ritual is insufficient to fulfill obligations required of the owner and, in the case of the Passover and sin sacrifice, performance absent intent invalidates the sacrifice. To be designated as a particular type of sacrifice, then, depends on the *intent*, that is, thought, of the owner and the priest.

The rabbinic literature distinguishes between an act or condition that invalidates and hence *interrupts* the sacrificial practice and an act or condition that merely prevents it from fulfilling its *intended* function though the sacrifice may still be an act of sacrifice/sanctification (Mishnah Zevachim I:1). If the priest performs the key sacrificial actions with improper intent, the original purpose is not fulfilled. But the sacrificial service itself is not interrupted or canceled because the animal retains its identity as a sacrifice. It is not invalid (*pasul*). The priest is required to perform all of the remaining ritual actions with the proper intent. This preserves the integrity of the ritual process needed for sanctification.

The exceptions noted in Zevachim I:1 are the Passover sacrifice and the sin offering. In these cases, without proper intent, the performance of the sacrifice is actually interrupted and invalidated. The priest does not continue, and no further ritual actions take place. Although the animal is considered sanctified to a particular degree, it is nevertheless now *pasul* and not fit to be offered. Not everything sacred is fit to be a sacrifice.

Although the particulars of these laws are debated in the Talmud (b. Talmud Zevachim 7b, 8a), the implication of these exceptions is that both the type of sacrifice intended and the specific beneficiary of the sacrifice are essential to the sacred character of the Passover and sin offerings in a way that is not required by other offerings.

"Sacrifice" as task or achievement

Lying behind this difference is, I believe, the distinction between sacrifice as a *task* verb and sacrifice as an *achievement* verb. Task verbs are defined by their morphology, that is, by the specific behaviors that constitute the action. In contrast, achievement verbs are defined by their *telos* or purpose, what is to be achieved.

Where "sacrifice" is understood as a task verb, validity attaches to specific actions even if the purpose or intent of the sacrifice is not fulfilled. The instructions for the morphology of the sacrificial performance list a series of behaviors, each one done with proper intent. But, for example, if the second action in the ritual does not occur with proper intent, the third action must still be correctly performed with its proper intent. Although the overall purpose of the series will not be achieved, a failure of a part does not equal a failure of the whole. The integrity of the ritual process itself is preserved, but the specific purpose of the sacrifice is not achieved.

Where "sacrifice" is an achievement verb, the *telos* is essential. That is, the parts are defined as meaningful *only* as efforts to achieve a specific purpose. Each individual act makes sense only in terms of the series of which they are a part, which creates the purpose. If all parts are not as they should be, the entire project falls through. Some sacrifices are defined as a whole by their intended purpose, and hence the failure of a part to be properly intended equals a failure of the whole.

Wrongful or inappropriate intent (*mahshava*)—in both the completely invalidated sacrifice and the sacrifice that "counts" but does not fulfill its purpose—is understood by some commentators as requiring explicit verbal expression, that is, the priest must actually say the wrong intent out loud in order to invalidate or alter the nature of the sacrifice (Tosafot, b Talmud Zevachim 4b s.v. *machashava*, Rashi, b.Talmud Zevachim 41b, s.v. *k'goin she natan*). Maimonides, however, holds that the priest merely having the wrong thought when bringing the sacrifice is sufficient to invalidate it or alter its nature. According to the Talmud, in cases where either the priest said nothing explicitly or we do not know the priest's intent, it is assumed that the intent was correct (*setama lishma kaei*, b. Talmud Zevachim 2b).

Clearly, the Mishnah is working with a subjective "thought" element here. What the priest is thinking or saying determines the meaning of and sometimes the validity or invalidity of the sacrifice. Mere objective behavioral performance is insufficient. The meaning of the act cannot be separated from the intent of the agent. We find here also the rabbinic assumption that people engaged in a specified role within a defined social practice can be assumed to have the requisite intention unless proven otherwise. *Sacrifice and sanctification cannot be fully understood without introducing some notion of subjectivity.*

Except in Maimonides's view, however, subjectivity does not always require explicit consciousness of specific intent. It suffices that an individual actor is situated in a habitus where the meaning of actions and language derive from accepted social practices that organize how individuals perceive their social world. Thus, the agent performing action X is assumed to have the intent to do X. Only an explicit declaration of the priest's thoughts to do other than X would change the assumption that he is not only doing but also intending X—the proper sacrifice. Human beings sanctify and sacrifice within the social systems that, in general, provide meaning in and to their lives.

In the two cases of wrong intentions, priestly intent was associated with the personhood of the owner. Either the intent was for the wrong person or the wrong type of sacrifice requested by/for the person—or in communal offerings, persons. The next category of wrong intent is about time and space.

From the Mishnah Zevachim, it is clear that each type of sacrifice has a time and place assigned to it, within which the sacrifice must be eaten or burnt. Once again, the rabbis introduce the concept of intent. Performing the sacrificial rites with the intention of eating or burning the sacrifice outside of that temporal or spatial limit invalidates the offering. Here, with my interpolations, is Zevachim II: 3:

> This is the general rule: Anyone who slaughters [the animal] or receives [the blood] or conveys [carries the blood] or throws [sprinkles the blood, with the intent] to eat something, that is, as much as an olive of that which is normally meant to be eaten [or] to burn [on the Altar, as much as an olive of] something which is normally meant to be burnt—[if] outside its [required] place [*huts l'mikomo* . . . here the courtyard boundaries], it [the sacrifice] is invalid [*pasul*] but one does not receive the [severe] punishment of *karet*. [If, however, the intent is to do so—eat or burn it outside the prescribed time limit (*huts lizmano*)], it is *piggul* and one does receive the punishment of *karet*.

Once again, certain key sacrificial actions are central, and improper intent invalidates the sacrifice while other auxiliary actions do not do so. As temporal limits attach only to obligatory actions, wrongful intent regarding time applies only to obligatory parts of the sacrifice (what should be eaten or burnt). One who intends to eat the parts that are *not* objects of obligation does not invalidate the offering (Zevachim III: 3, b. Talmud Menahot 17b). Wrongful intent with respect to place (*huts limkomo*) also invalidates the sacrifice.

We have seen that the rabbinic literature places far more overt emphasis on intent than does the plain meaning of the original biblical text. On the whole, rabbinic texts connect intent with the meaning of the sacrifice with respect to its validity, its type, or its function. Thus, a subjective element is at work as a consciously articulated thought or as a mental disposition that is assumed and can be made explicit. For the rabbis, the meaning of sacrifice and sanctification cannot be fully separated from subjectivity.

The purpose of sacrifice as relationship with God

Sacrifice is a form or means of expressing (covenantal) relationship with God. The holiness in the sacrificial system is linked to the divine relationship with the people and his wish to dwell among them. The physical and spiritual realm in which such "indwelling" occurs—the place where heaven and earth meet—is the domain of the holy. Sacrifice is, in large measure, an action focused on the ordinary objects that belong to us and that we use for our own intents and purposes. Certain intentions may remove these objects from our domain and transfer them to the domain of the sacred, "There to create or maintain the holy, the place where heaven and earth meet and where we may thus experience our closest relationship with God."

By implication, then, the "indwelling" of God and communion with God depend on the concept of human subjectivity. Mere action alone is insufficient. Our search for the transcendent requires that we evoke that subjectivity—it is humanity's part of the covenantal relationship—and find ways to express our intent to commune with God in social practices and institutions that we believe constitute a domain of holiness. Sacrifice rituals either move profane objects/time into a sphere where God dwells and so sanctifies them or create a holy space so that we may experience God most closely there.

Conclusion

In contemporary society, our explicitly sacred domains tend to be in religiously affiliated places and institutions as well as in the religious practices associated with them. It is no surprise, then, that many of us imagine communion with God primarily in a church, synagogue, or mosque. As a result, donating money or commonplace objects (or time, for that matter) to these places is seen as holy (i.e., sanctified). Also, such contributions typically involve "making a sacrifice."

Might we, however, think more expansively concerning sanctification—especially as it is the *human* intent, up to us so to speak, that is essential? We already have sophisticated social practices—that is, rituals—that dedicate our time and possessions to distinct kinds of experiences reflecting our values. For example, our eating practices normally involve animals, plants, tables, chairs, textiles, plates, glassware, silverware, etc. All this is "regulated" by rules that express and support our aesthetic and often ethical value commitments—beauty, order, elegance, good taste, environmental and social responsibility, and the value of family and friends. The experience of a good meal shared with family and friends not only is often deeply satisfying but also yields a sense of "communion" with those we love and care about.

We might think about designing or discovering ritual practices that create sacred times and spaces within which we experience something like holiness and a "being with" God and our ultimate values. I would like to suggest an example that I believe merits attention. If we understand all human beings as in the image of God—or even a "fragment" of a transcendent God—then we can create social practices that *intentionally* dedicate (consecrate) ourselves and our property to communion with God through the way we relate to those in his image, other human beings.

That human beings are in the divine image means that we are not "things." Others are not mere props in our own personal drama, mere instruments for accomplishing our particular purposes and interests. To be sure, much human interaction, even where it is ethical, is primarily transactional, that is, profane (as in Buber's I-It relationship, Buber 2010). But human interactions may be sanctified if we "sacrifice"—that is, dedicate—our time and possessions to human moments that are not primarily transactional, not engaging the other for personal benefit.

If we do so, a good meal with family and friends but also with strangers and the disadvantaged—requiring the sacrifice of time, effort, and money to create such a meal—expresses not only our esthetic and moral values but also our vision of the sacred. That is, by treating others to welcome and hospitality, we also welcome in the divine. It is a moment of human-initiated communion with God, much as sacrifice was. Such sacred meals have been a part of Western religious traditions well into the twentieth century.

We should consider developing social practices that promote, celebrate, and share other such potentially sacred moments, among them serious study, music, dance, natural wonders, and the birth of a child. "Ritualizing" these experiences might create opportunities for peak experiences with others as well as with God.

References

Alison, J. (2004), "Some Thoughts on the Atonement," presented at Bisbane, Australia, http://www.jamesalison.co.uk/pdf/eng11.pdf (accessed February 9, 2019).
Borowitz, E. (1990), *Exploring Jewish Ethics: Papers on Covenant Responsibility*, Detroit: Wayne State University Press.
Borowitz, E. (1991), *Renewing the Covenant: A Theology for the Postmodern Jew*, Philadelphia: Jewish Publication Society.
Buber, M. (2010), *I and Thou*, Eastford: Martino Fine Books (original work published 1923).
Halbertal, M. (2012), *On Sacrifice*, Princeton: Princeton University Press.
Heschel, A. J. (1997), *God in Search of Man*, New York: Farrar Straus & Giroux.
Levinas, E. (1994a), *Beyond the Verse: Talmudic Readings and Lectures*, New York: Bloomsbury.
Levinas, E. (1994b), *In the Time of the Nations*, trans. M. Smith, London: Athlone Press.

5

Kant on Sacrifice and Morality

David Pan

Following the chapters by Rachik and Blanchard, describing forms of sacrifice that are not obvious heirs of the Girardian archaic, David Pan analyzes another understanding of sacrifice that differs from Girard's: that of Immanuel Kant. Kant begins from the premise that sacrifice is not an expression of a societal problem but is necessary for moral conduct and the productive organization of human society. Pan's chapter will be followed by several that elaborate on this suggestion.

While Pan agrees with Kant that certain forms of sacrifice are societally productive, he does not think that Kant correctly identified what makes them moral. Kant focuses on the human capacity to sacrifice oneself for principle, and he claims this capacity as the telos *of human morality. But, Pan notes, Kant does not identify the principle or higher good itself, external to the sacrificer, as morality's* telos. *This Kantian focus on the human capacity rather than on the external goal that misidentifies what is societally important about sacrifice. "Sacrifice," Pan writes, "is not ethical merely by demonstrating the capacity to make sacrifices." The Girardian might reply that the very notion of sacrifice for a higher good follows from the archaic sacrifice ritual, developed to ward off competition aggression— that is, for the higher good of aggression reduction. But more importantly, Girard, taking his lesson from the cross, would almost certainly agree with Pan that the effects of sacrifice in world—notably, its outcomes for the downtrodden—are the standards by which a sacrifice is judged as moral.*

—editor's note

Introduction

Liberal theory has imagined a universal basis for order that could overcome political divisions by appealing to principles shared by all. Hobbes bases sovereignty, for instance, in the mutual universal self-interest of actors in a state of nature. In establishing self-preservation and the protection of individual rights as the basic role of the state, Hobbes set up the initial focus on self-interest as the foundational principle of the liberal state (Schmitt 2008: 33–35). This conception replaced the idea, still adhered to by Bodin, that sovereignty comes from God, and Hobbes's vision of sovereignty had the advantage of establishing, in the idea of the common goal of self-preservation, a basis for sovereignty that could transcend religious differences, with the hope of resolving the confessional wars that devastated Europe in the early modern era. But if this conception establishes a universal basis for political order, it sees fear as the motivating force that brings people together in the state. Even if one were to consider such a focus on fear to have been appropriate to the situation of absolute monarchy, it definitely runs into problems with the rise of popular sovereignty. As Paul Kahn argues, the focus on fear and self-interest obscures the way in which sovereignty has come to be understood in the modern era as popular sovereignty, based ultimately on the establishment of a common vision in a people that could align their efforts and aspirations around a unified purpose (Kahn 2005: 274–76). Such a purpose has an essential personal aspect to the extent that individual well-being requires a sense of such a greater purpose and a conception of the way in which the sacrifice of the individual accords with the way in which the individual imagines this purpose—life not as a self-interested struggle but as a consecration of one's life for a greater good. According to this conception, a vision of sacrifice lies at the core of individual conceptions of the self and its relationship to the world. But the history of liberalism has obscured how the representational character of sacrifice is crucial to the establishment of a political system based on popular sovereignty.

The difficulty over the last century is that the ideal of individual fulfillment and happiness that lies at the basis of a liberal conception of order has been implicitly undermined through socialist critiques of capitalism and consumer society. Yet, to the extent that the critique of capitalism retains the liberal focus on individual fulfillment without linking it to some sacrifice to an overarching notion of sovereignty, socialism has been incapable of establishing an alternative political and metaphysical conception of order. The resulting metaphysical void is being filled, on the one hand, by fundamentalist religion and, on the other, by ethno-nationalist movements.

If the European Union has been struggling with Brexit and the rise of populist movements, these difficulties stem from an inability to resolve problems about sovereignty highlighted by terrorism and the refugee problem. Fundamentalist Islam shares in some way with socialism the critique of capitalism and consumerism, and it has been able to combine it with a notion of sacrifice by denying individual fulfillment as an end in itself. Similarly, ethno-nationalist movements have challenged the supremacy of a liberal political order by invoking notions of popular sovereignty based in ethnic or national identity even when such a stance threatens economic well-being, as in the case of Brexit. With such moves, both religion-based terrorism and resurgent nationalism have created an existential crisis for the European order, not just because of the introduction of violence but because they point to a weakness in the liberal idea of individual fulfillment as an end. Because liberalism rejects political symbolism as a kind of distortion of rational thinking, it has generally denied the centrality of sacrifice for maintaining a stable political order.

The meaning of sacrifice

But as Moshe Halbertal argues, some idea of sacrifice is in fact crucial for establishing morality, as morality requires a consciousness of something that goes beyond the self. "Self-transcendence is at the core of the human capacity for a moral life" (Halbertal 2012: 36). The structure of morality requires one to subordinate one's own interests to some ideal that one regards as higher than the self. Some notion of sacrifice lies at the core of any moral conception because it is the movement of sacrifice that is being enacted whenever we choose to subordinate our own interests to those of others or to some greater good. The difficulty that Halbertal identifies is that the notion of self-transcendence implied in both sacrifice and morality leads to an empty middle in the liberal theory of politics.

Focusing on the moral philosophy of Immanuel Kant, Halbertal first points out that Kant's analysis of morality focuses on the difference between self-love and obedience to the categorical imperative, as if these were the sole two human possibilities. "Thus, Kant had a rather complex and sophisticated concept of self-love, and yet a great and significant space still remains between self-love and the obedience to the categorical imperative. Within that space, which Kant didn't recognize, stands the most meaningful arena of moral conflict" (Halbertal 2012: 42). Halbertal points out that the overcoming of self-interest does not necessarily lead to the categorical imperative, which establishes a set of laws that would be equally valid for all people. Rather, a subordination of self-interest can also serve values that are self-abnegating for the individual but nevertheless particular to a specific group—for example, values that serve a particular religion, class, or nation. Halbertal's critique is that Kant failed to see the danger of these types of self-transcendence that are neither affirmations of self-interest nor affirmations of a universal morality but something in between. Halbertal's goal is to differentiate between such lower forms of self-transcendence and the higher forms that would be universal. He does this by establishing certain forms of self-transcendence as the primary ones and designating as "idolatry" those forms that are too culturally particular, idolatrously venerating one political group and thus dangerous to others.

Halbertal describes how Rousseau argues against Hobbes's idea that state sovereignty is based on self-interest. Rousseau argues that individuals find in the national political community a way of understanding the higher meaning of their own existence. But because individuals invest their own nationalist meanings into identification with the political community, this form of self-transcendence, on Halbertal's account, becomes a danger insofar as it benefits not humanity as a whole but only a particular nation. Halbertal consequently distinguishes Rousseau's approach from the more universalizing perspective of Kant:

> Rousseau's general will is understood to consist in the common good of the other citizens in the body politic. It is neither synonymous with humanity as such, nor comparable to some imagined community of all rational creatures, as in Kant's moral theory. Kant saved the general will from this Rousseauian parochialism by shifting the locus of the sacrificial act from the general will of the political state to the categorical universal imperative, thereby preventing the notion from degenerating into a chauvinistic form of collective self-regard. Kant rescued this theme from its idolatrous implication. (Halbertal 2012: 57)

While Halbertal distinguishes the Rousseauian sacrifice for the in-group from the Kantian sacrifice for all humanity, he indicates that even Kantian sacrifice cannot do without some kind of representational form. He does not suggest that one would make a sacrifice to reason itself or the idea of a categorical imperative. Rather, he indicates that there must still be a named beneficiary of the sacrifice.

> When the state becomes the locus of self-transcendence, however, it turns into a false idol. There should be a realm beyond such a sacrificial stage that sets a higher, limiting standard for the political association. Different traditions will articulate that realm in different ways, from human rights that ought to limit state interests, to the image of God that all humans are supposed to share regardless of their associational affinities. A political body that lacks such a category directs the sacrificial urge to an unworthy cause. An absolute commitment to an unworthy cause is the modern form of the old problem of idolatry. (Halbertal 2012: 57–58)

Recognizing that sacrifices cannot be made to the capacity of reason or morality itself, Halbertal suggests "human rights" and "the image of God that all humans are supposed to share" as two possible causes that would transcend parochial interests.

The difficulty, however, in Halbertal's suggestion is particularism: his choice of causes worthy of sacrifice are by no means universal and might themselves spur strife. The idea of human rights is not naturally universal but has a bias toward the individual that not all traditions share. Similarly, the determination of which God has an overarching, universal status has also been at the heart of religious conflicts among faith groups, which then charge each other with idolatry. It may be that not all agree with the categorical imperative as the universal standard of morality, and Halbertal clearly doesn't, but neither is there agreement on Halbertal's replacement. If, as I will try to show, we ultimately cannot avoid particular goals for which we are prepared to sacrifice, then morality will always have a particular character to it.

As Kahn argues, the problem is that self-sacrifice for some higher good makes sense only when the individual feels that the act of sacrifice for this particular good is linked to the way life has meaning for oneself. But because pure reason is not enough to motivate self-sacrifice, the motivation will be linked to not only justice but also love (Kahn 2005: 141). Yet if sacrifice is generally motivated by love, the specific loves will vary from person to person. This necessary variation is the ineradicable crux of the problem.

Duty or love as the basis of morality

If Halbertal sees sacrifice as linked to morality and Kahn sees it as an act of love, in Kant's descriptions of sacrifice the problem is precisely that any particular instance retains a certain ambiguity in that it might be linked to either duty or love. But since Kant considers only pure acts of duty to be morally valid, he tries to purify duty of any admixture of love that would contaminate the morality of the action by turning it into the result of inclination rather than moral duty. "In a word, the moral law demands compliance from duty, not from predilection, which one cannot and ought not to presuppose at all" (Kant 2002: 197). By insisting that the motive for moral action must be confined to duty to the exclusion any type of inclination, Kant understands inclination as a kind of self-love or self-interest. Consequently, he attempts in his examples of moral actions to carefully distinguish duty to the moral law from any kind of inclination, including love. These examples of morality are for the most part situations of sacrifice, which remains central to his moral philosophy (Axinn 2010: 109–15). But because the point is to distinguish duty from inclination as the motive for moral actions, Kant focuses his discussion not so much on the sacrificial actions themselves (which might have self-interested motivations, such as the desire for glory), but on the sense for morality that leads to such actions.

The moral sense must be limited to a sense of duty and separated from any kind of practical goal. Yet, in the examples of sacrifice that he presents, it is very difficult to separate a pure sense of duty from a desire to support a practical and moral goal, whether that goal is justice for an innocent man (Kant 2002: 44), the saving of others or the defense of one's country (Kant 2002: 197–98). The difficulty of making choices between two or more sacrifices that conflict becomes most acute in Kant's example of sacrifice for one's country. In this case, the problem of the goal of the action is key to its morality, but Kant does not address the problem that Halbertal raises about the difference between sacrifice for one's country and sacrifice for humanity as a whole.

> More decisive is the magnanimous sacrifice of one's life for the preservation of one's country; and yet there remains some scruple as to whether it is indeed so perfectly a duty to dedicate oneself to this aim on one's own and without having been ordered to do so, and the action does not contain the full force of a model and impulse for imitation. (Kant 2002: 198)

Rather than taking up the question of the conflict between a duty to humanity as a whole as opposed to one's country, Kant asks only whether one has a duty to sacrifice oneself willingly for one's country without having been ordered to do so as it would indicate a kind of desire that goes beyond the duty to fulfill the law. Yet, he clearly also criticizes the opposite case, in which one *is* ordered to sacrifice one's life for one's country, when, in *Toward Perpetual Peace*, he berates European monarchs for sending their subjects to sacrifice themselves in war (Kant 2006: 78–79).

In focusing on duty to oneself, Kant has difficulty accounting for sacrifice for one's country either as a voluntary act or as something demanded by the sovereign. In this self-focus, Kant echoes Hobbes's position, where the self-preservation of each individual citizen is the ultimate purpose of the state. Yet Kant could not take into consideration how the issue of duty versus love changes in cases of popular sovereignty, where citizens find their own ultimate meaning in their self-identification with the nation. Under these conditions, sacrifice of one's life can be understood not as duty but as love for nation and for oneself, as one identifies with this political entity. And it has become generally accepted as morally valid on these grounds. When Kant retains the example of the sacrifice for one's country as a duty, he treats it as an example of moral duty in a way that would exclude any kind of love or inclination, leading to an ambiguity in his analysis.

This difficulty arises for Kant because he derives freedom from the existence of moral actions, and such actions can only be judged to be moral by looking at the inner motivation for such actions. In analyzing these inner motivations, Kant seeks to limit them to one's sense of duty to the (universal) moral law itself rather than to love of a *specific* value, such as the nation, that transcends the self. But it is precisely in looking at the moral sense that underlies sacrifice that Kant's attempt to distinguish between duty and love begins to break down (Milbank 2003: 14–15). The factor determining the morality of sacrifice in these cases is the way in which one conceives of one's identity in terms of a greater whole, that is, in defining the general object of morality itself.

This determination cannot be a rational one. It is also not a self-interested one but will revolve around the character of a specific group's ultimate values. Kant's examples cannot maintain the distinction between formal adherence to the categorical imperative and the affirmation of a specific group's goals. But neither can Halbertal properly distinguish between a universal God for everyone and each specific group's conception of a universal God. If the sense of morality is always linked to the overall practical goal of the moral system itself, then morality would not be universal but would vary with the decision about ultimate goals and values. Such ultimate goals are not given by reason itself but must come from elsewhere and are linked to the subject's sense of the meaning of her existence. But one always conceives the meaning of one's life to lie in something greater than oneself, and therefore the overall goal of moral action cannot be the rational self as a purpose in itself, as Kant assumes (Kant 1997: 37). The precise nature of the sacrifice is that its very movement is the affirmation that establishes the link between one's own meaning and a value that goes beyond the self. Consequently, Kant's examples cannot properly distinguish between a disinterested duty to a formal law (whose ultimate rationale lies in rational beings as purposes in themselves) and an interest-bound commitment to particular values that go beyond the self.

The sublime as affirmation or subordination of the individual

In *The Critique of Judgment*, Kant ends up rejecting the treatment of the individual as a purpose insofar as the key movement in the sublime is the subordination of the individual natural body to a greater purpose, whereby the individual sacrifices her material concerns for the sake of a principle. This treatment of the individual's body as a means has the effect of demonstrating the human capacity to choose principle over natural impulse, thus affirming the individual human will as purpose in itself. The sublime is an experience that demonstrates to us that "we regard nature's might (to which we are indeed subjected in these [natural] concerns) as yet not having such dominance over us, as persons, that we should have to bow to it if our highest principles were at stake and we had to choose between upholding or abandoning them" (Kant 1987: 121). Kant expresses in this passage the basic congruence between the experience of the sublime, which affirms the human capacity to subordinate nature to rational principles, and the adherence to the moral law, also rational principle, in the moment of sacrifice. The subject affirms nature's material power but then is able to affirm the subject's power to sacrifice materiality for a higher principle. Kant therefore insists on a moment of sacrifice to a principle as central to the definition of freedom.

But even though Kant describes how the sublime involves a sacrifice of the material self for principle, he goes on to emphasize that there is a nobility connected with the self-sacrifice that then accrues to the individual rather than to the cause for which one is sacrificing. Consequently, Kant emphasizes that in the end "the mind can come to feel its own sublimity, which lies in its own vocation" (Kant 1987: 121). Even though the movement of the sublime experience requires the subject to make a self-sacrifice for the sake of some higher principle, what's important to Kant is the individual's *ability and moral decision* to sacrifice herself for principle rather than the principle or higher good itself. Thus, this individual capacity is the final meaning of the sacrifice as it affirms individual freedom. John R. Betz and Marcia Pally focus on this aspect of Kant's discussion to conclude that for Kant "the sublime presents the subject with an enthralling sense of *its own* superiority *over* nature" (Betz 2005: 384), and that Kant "sees reason as a force over world and the cause of whatever it wills" (Pally 2016: 145). While this emphasis on the subject's power over nature is certainly crucial to Kant's mathematical sublime, the situation becomes more complicated in his subsequent discussion of the dynamic sublime.

For there remains in Kant a conflict between the idea that sacrifice creates an affirmation of something greater than the material individual and the idea that this greater thing is the individual's freedom itself, a conflict that Paolo Diego Bubbio characterizes as one between "sacrifice as *suppression*" and "sacrifice as *kenosis*" (Bubbio 2014: 30). Rather than resolving this conflict, Kant creates an ambiguity in his discussion by describing the dynamic sublime in viewing nature on the one hand and then bringing up the example of the warrior on the other, leading to a description of what I call the heroic sublime.

In his description of the dynamic sublime, Kant tries to maintain the nonrepresentational character or "negativity" of the sacrifice by focusing on examples like the consideration of nature ("mountains," "gorges," "raging streams"). Here, one sees a fearful image of nature in the "raging stream," but one also feels oneself superior to nature to the extent that one imagines oneself as willing to succumb to this material power in order to affirm one's highest principles. As there is no image of a specific principle to which one would sacrifice materiality, the result is only the feeling of the soul's superiority over nature's might. Because there is only the imagination of a sacrifice and no specific cause to which one would make it, the experience is "negative," leading Kant to emphasize the power of the individual as the ultimate meaning of the experience of the sublime. "In this way we [feel] our superiority to nature within ourselves, and hence also to nature outside us insofar as it can influence our feeling of well-being" (Kant 1987: 129). The feeling of the sublime depends on the soul's sense of superiority over nature, and the result of this feeling is a self-aggrandizement of the individual. This is the version of the sublime that Betz and Pally emphasize and that one finds in Hegel's dialectic of lordship and bondage, in Nietzsche, as well as in Georges Bataille's and Ernst Jünger's conceptions of the sovereignty of the individual (Betz 2005: 385–86; Pan 2012: 86–88; Pan 2008: 66–74).

But the other example he uses in his discussion of the dynamic sublime, the warrior, indicates that the sacrificial nature of the sublime can also be connected with purposes that go beyond the individual. "For what is it that is an object of the highest admiration even to the savage? It is a person who is not terrified, not afraid, and hence does not yield to danger but promptly sets to work with vigor and full deliberation. Even in a fully civilized society there remains this superior esteem for the warrior" (Kant 1987: 121). Though Kant emphasizes here the self-respect and care for oneself of the warrior rather than the sacrifice for a particular cause, this form of the sublime is still different from the one created through the view of mountains, gorges, and raging streams. In the warrior, there is not just an affirmation of the insignificance of materiality but a linked affirmation of a particular goal that goes beyond the value of the individual. This version of the sublime does not end with an affirmation of the autonomy of the individual as purpose in itself but with a subordination of the individual's purpose to an overall purpose that is both superindividual and particular in orientation.

Though Kant does not explicitly distinguish the dynamic sublime from the heroic sublime, it is only the latter that provides an experience of morality in which the subject experiences a form of self-transcendence in the moral action. Kant describes it as the form of the sublime that one finds in religious traditions, but he also attempts to confine the meaning of this sort of sublime to a moment of negativity, that is, the refusal to imagine any particular transcendent meanings or values.

> Perhaps the most sublime passage in the Jewish Law is the commandment: Thou shalt not make unto thee any graven image, or any likeness of any thing that is in heaven or on earth, or under the earth, etc. This commandment alone can explain the enthusiasm that the Jewish people in its civilized era felt for its religion when it compared itself with other peoples or can explain the pride that Islam inspires. (Kant 1987: 135)

Such examples of the heroic sublime that Kant identifies in religious enthusiasts, savages, and soldiers who sacrifice themselves for a particular cause are, in fact, despite Kant's downplaying of these examples, the only ones that demonstrate a moral law in which the individual sacrifices personal interests for something higher that goes beyond the self.

But Kant does not focus on how the sacrifices for a specific higher good affirm specific representations. Instead, by emphasizing the prohibition on "graven images," he seeks to deny that the sacrifice takes place for the benefit of a "cause" or "principle." He shifts the beneficiary of the sacrifice from a specific representation to the general idea of the "expansion and might" of the subject. While this allows an interpretation of the sublime as an affirmation of the *general* movement whereby the subject subordinates materiality, there is no corresponding affirmation of any particular group or ideal. If Kant contends that "the imagination thereby acquires an expansion and a might that surpasses the one it sacrifices," he describes a process where the individual on the one hand loses freedom but on the other gains it back as a new expansion of individual sovereignty, even over death. Kant's interpretation of the heroic sublime in this way brings it back toward the dynamic sublime in the experience of cliffs and waterfalls, in which there is no direct link to any kind of transcendent cause.

From universality to sovereignty as the basis of morality

Kant's grounding of ethical life in the ability to sacrifice creates a fundamental contradiction in his analysis. On the one hand, the movement of every sacrifice is for Kant one that subordinates the individual to an outside principle, and this represented principle becomes the measure of the individual's value and the basis of ethical life. On the other hand, Kant attempts to cast his argument as a transcendental one that identifies in the movement of the sublime a universal capacity in the human to subordinate material concerns to ideal ones (Kant 1987: 131). The mind experiences the moral law as an intellectual perception of the sacrifice whereby the subject deprives itself of something material to affirm something ideal. This movement of the sublime transcends every specific moral law by revealing the "dominance that reason exerts over sensibility" (Kant 1987: 132). That is, Kant identifies a general human capacity to establish goals that can supersede material ones and reads specific instances of sacrifice as a demonstration of this general human freedom to set and adhere to goals that go beyond self-interest.

But each example of a morally oriented sacrifice in fact demonstrates not just a human freedom to decide on goals but a particular goal to which individual well-being is being sacrificed. This particular goal, whether it be the welfare of one's family, the strength of the nation, or the affirmation of a particular religious conception, becomes a representation of a form of sovereignty that finds its affirmation in the sacrifice. In laying out a particular framework within which sacrifice makes sense, the hero is implicitly affirming that framework as a basis for action and thus as in some sense sovereign. Even the altruistic and unmotivated sacrifice will fit within a specific narrative, either of Christian love or of universal humanity or of some other basis for the decision. Kant thus describes the sublime on the one hand as a representational process that depends for its legitimation upon a sacrifice of self-interest for a designated goal beyond the self and on the other hand, from a transcendental perspective, as evidence of the general human ability to sacrifice material well-being, thus demonstrating the freedom and autonomy of the individual. If his analysis of the sublime reveals both the representational work of sacrifice and the transcendental perspective toward this work, he then seeks to take the transcendental perspective to be the defining one for ethical life.

But he in fact has no basis for making this final move. The transcendental analysis cannot replace the representational one. Instead, the universality that it uncovers is not that of a universal ethic but the universality of sacrifice itself as always being for a higher goal outside the self, which is what makes it part of ethical life. Sacrifice is not ethical merely by demonstrating the capacity to make sacrifices.

Meanwhile, the universal ethic that Kant imagines, which is grounded in the idea of the rational being as purpose in itself, does not recognize, on a transcendental level, the kind of subordination of individual interests to an outside goal that a morally oriented sacrifice requires. The self-sacrifice that leads to morality rather than self-aggrandizement is inseparable from a concrete goal and representational dynamic that undermines the possibility of a universal ethic. For if the condition of value for the individual is its subordination to a higher purpose, the individual can never be its own purpose in an ethical system. Since the effect of a morally oriented sacrifice is not the exaltation of the individual but of the representation, the elevation of the individual is unimportant. Instead, the main focus should be on the representation that structures the sacrifice.

Contrary to Kant's attempt to establish individuals as their own purposes, morality makes sense only within a particular context of goals and principles that establish the framework within which individual self-sacrifice gains meaning. Morality cannot be a pattern of action in which we recognize human freedom as a nonrepresentational universal; it can be only the affirmation of some basis of sovereignty beyond the individual self. At the same time, every particular sacrifice provides a moment in which individual decisions affect the goals and decision processes of the collective. The moment of decision about ultimate goals is what is at stake in the moment of sacrifice, and such moments are not merely examples of moral action but in fact defining for the system of morality itself (Pan 2012: 104–11). The decisive quality of the sacrifice for ethical life means that rational beings can demonstrate their freedom only to the extent that they can subordinate themselves to a purpose that goes beyond the self. This dependence of individual meaning on an outside value is both the motivation and the result of the sacrifice, in which the individual is consecrated to a greater goal.

References

Axinn, S. (2010), *Sacrifice and Value: A Kantian Interpretation*, Lanham: Lexington.
Betz, John R. (2005), "Beyond the Sublime: The Aesthetics of the Analogy of Being (Part One)," *Modern Theology* 21: 367–411.
Bubbio, Paolo D. (2014), *Sacrifice in the Post-Kantian Tradition: Perspectivism, Intersubjectivity, and Recognition*, Albany: SUNY Press.
Halbertal, M. (2012), *On Sacrifice*, Princeton: Princeton University Press.
Kahn, P. (2005), *Putting Liberalism in Its Place*, Princeton: Princeton University Press.
Kant, I. (1987), *Critique of Judgment*, trans. Werner S. Pluhar, Indianapolis: Hackett.
Kant, I. (1997), *Groundwork of the Metaphysics of Morals*, trans. Mary Gregor, Cambridge: Cambridge University Press.

Kant, I. (2002), *Critique of Practical Reason*, trans. Werner S. Pluhar, Indianapolis: Hackett.

Kant, I. (2006), *Toward Perpetual Peace and Other Writings on Politics, Peace, and History*, trans. David L. Colclasure, New Haven: Yale University Press.

Milbank, J. (2003), *Being Reconciled: Ontology and Pardon*, London: Routledge.

Pally, M. (2016), *Commonwealth and Covenant: Economics, Politics, and Theologies of Relationality*, Grand Rapids: Eerdmans.

Pan, D. (2008), "The Sovereignty of the Individual in Ernst Jünger's *The Worker*," *Telos* 144: 66–74.

Pan, D. (2012), *Sacrifice in the Modern World: On the Particularity and Generality of Nazi Myth*, Evanston: Northwestern University Press.

Schmitt, C. (2008), *The Leviathan in the State Theory of Thomas Hobbes*, Chicago: University of Chicago Press.

6

Sacrifice amid Covenant
From Abuse to Gift

Marcia Pally

This chapter explores the nature of sacrifice by focusing not on sacrificial types (archaic, Christian) but on the relationships among the persons involved. Among covenantal relationships, sacrifice, as reciprocal giving for the flourishing of the other and the common good, is not only a necessary component of a just society but our ontological proclivity.

The chapter begins by exploring Girard's early assessment of the First Testament as a transition text that retains the archaic understanding of humanity and thus as a text still bound to scapegoating sacrifice. Noting the methodological requirement of reading the Tanach *as a problem set (reading through its metaphors, flawed human characters, and* longue durée *moral lessons), the chapter suggests that Girard's early view of the* Tanach *under-recognizes its perspective of the victim, its prohibitions against scapegoating, insistence on moral responsibility, and care for the downtrodden. The chapter then investigates the* tanachic *covenant (reciprocal bonds between humanity and God and among persons) and the meaning of sacrifice in the covenantal context. As the brutality of the crucifixion becomes divine love in the Christian understanding, sacrifice-amidst-covenant is a symbolic, dialogic act in the conversation that sustains relationship and reciprocal giving. The chapter agrees with Girard that the Second Testament is a book of "non-violent imitation" and suggests that the First is one of nonviolent education grounded in a covenantal ontology and the "ontological peace" that Girard held is universal to religion.*

—editor's note

Introduction

Among the key issues in looking at sacrifice is whether on balance it is societally beneficial. Under what conditions is it abusive and when is it a necessary component of a flourishing society? Rene Girard holds that sacrifice's valence and usefulness are contingent upon type and purpose (archaic or Christian, scapegoating or donative). Moshe Halbertal (2012) too distinguishes based on type: sacrifice *to* (a deity) and sacrifice *for* (a cause). The latter is productive when its purpose is, for example, the education of children, but dangerous, when terrorism.

This chapter looks at sacrifice not by type/purpose but by the relationship among the persons involved. I follow Girard and others on the social nature of human life that each person becomes who she uniquely is through relations and interactions with others (Pally 2016). But where Girard saw much of that relationality as competitive and violent, I draw on covenantal theology (and evolutionary biology as reviewed in the Introduction to this volume) to suggest that our foundational ontology, prior to the archaic period of Girard's focus, is cooperative, indeed covenantal. Within covenantal relations, sacrifice becomes a mode of reciprocal regard and giving.

Girard in his earlier works distinguishes not only between sacrificial type but also between sacrifice in the First and Second Testaments. While his understanding of non-Christian faiths evolved, I will make some clarifying remarks as his earlier descriptions have been taken to be Girard's consistent position. The First Testament, for instance, has been seen as a transition text retaining archaic sacrifice as a scapegoating ritual to release societal tensions. Thus, it has been understood to offer but harbingers of a world without the sacrifice of innocents. The Second Testament, by contrast, proffers just such a nonviolent vision. "For Girard," Wolfgang Palaver notes, "the only real and nonviolent means to overcoming mimetic rivalry is found in the New Testament. . . . The New Testament shows us another way" (Palaver 2013: 219). That another way is what Girard called "non-violent imitation" (Girard 1987: 430), and I fully support this reading of the later Testament. But I suggest that the First, while not "non-violent *imitation*" is a book of "non-violent *education*" based not on an archaic, competitive view of life but on a covenantal one: the twined covenantal relations with God and among persons. These relations not only are the focus of the prophets, who are often cited as evidence of covenantal tenets, but also run throughout the First Testament or *Tanach*. They are an expression of the "ontology of peace" that Girard held grounds all religions.

Girard's intertestamental investigation

On Girard's view, Christianity's exceptional offer of love—what finally stops mimetic competition and scapegoating sacrifice—is rooted in the crucifixion. Gospel crucifixion narratives, he holds, contain no echo of archaic sacrifice. Their lesson without remainder is God's love and mercy. As Christianity directs human desires toward the divine love shown on the cross, competition-induced aggression is undone since the object of desire, God's love, may be shared by all. There is nothing to compete over. Girard follows Augustine's insight that "if you only love what cannot be snatched out of its lover's hand, you undoubtedly remain unbeaten and are not tormented in any way by jealousy" (*On Christian Belief*, 88, XLVI.86.243). Even Gospel apocalypticism (Matthew 24:1-25, Lukas 17:22-37) reveals no angry deity to be placated by sacrifice, as in archaic myth. Apocalyptic violence, on Girard's view, is the outcome of human violation of God's kingdom (Palaver 2013: 216).

Though on the surface the power of the crucifixion narrative depends on Jesus's literal sacrifice, Girard rightly distinguishes between archaic sacrifice and the crucifixion because the cross is understood as divine donation of love for humanity. As God's loving gift, it fails Girard's criteria for archaic sacrifice: it is neither scapegoating-as-restitution to an angry god nor mob-bonding. Girard, with many contemporary scholars (David Bentley Hart 1993, among others), disallows restitutionary readings of the Passion, where humanity must "pay" God for its sins. Yet his early work finds restitution maintained in the First Testament, which, he holds, makes sacrifices to a vengeful God and does not replace the scapegoating/sacrifice mechanism with *agape* (Girard 1987: 227, 252).

I suggest that this understanding does not encompass the *Tanach*'s vision, about which I'll make a few introductory notes. First is the *Tanach*'s foundation in God's mercy, grace, and covenant with humankind which transcends human law, endures through humanity's breaches, and grounds relations with not only God but also human. In the *Tanach*, giving to neighbor and stranger is situated amid the ritual laws through which the Israelites express bond with God. Thus, the three commitments are not only bound together but bound by giving and mutual care (Leviticus 19:18, 19:34). As Robert Bellah describes, the key features of *tanachic* religion and culture—the centrality of texts and laws independent of reigning elites or monarch, the importance of their interpretation and *critique*, and a conception of a transcendent God against whose ethics of mercy and grace all human acts may be judged—are post-archaic and point to a new conception of God, society, person, and relations among the three (Bellah 2011: Kindle Locations 4239, 4848-49). Sandor Goodhart, among Girard's first graduate students, succinctly writes, "Judaism is nothing if not the exodus from archaic religion" (2014: 245).

Second, the Girardian/Augustinian observation that Christianity undoes competitive violence by directing human desire toward God's ever-available love applies also to the *Tanach*. "The Jewish covenant," Daniel Breslauer (2006) notes, "assumes that monotheism—the God of the covenant—must be accessible to all humanity, not just to Jews." All are invited to God's inexhaustible love that guides humanity to righteousness. The offer is expansively inclusive: observance of ritual is not required nor is conversion (as it is required in Christianity and Islam): one need not accept YHVH as one's savior. All those following the seven basic Noahite morals (against murder, theft, etc.) are held to be righteous and at one with God.

Third, while Girard's archaic sacrifice features mob-bonding and scapegoating-as-restitution, the First Testament repudiates both. The critical binding of Isaac narrative (*Akedah*), like the crucifixion it prefigures, rejects human sacrifice, whether to constitute the Abrahamic line (group bonding) or as restitution to God. Indeed, its point is that such sacrifice—even or especially if the demand appears to come from God—has no part in the covenant with him (Pally 2016: 192–93). Yoram Hazony adds that Abraham knew God does not require this sacrifice as the text twice plainly states and as God, in the text, in fact does not require (2012: 118). Sacrifice of Abraham's other son Ishmael too is impermissible; God makes of him a great nation. The *Akedah* narrative closes with a sacrifice but not of archaic type. The eventual sacrifice of a ram neither expiates sin (restitution)—Abraham has committed no sin— nor does it bond any group. Pointedly, rather than bonding, Abraham's family disperses.

The *Akedah* rejects archaic scapegoating as does the crucifixion, which yet lends itself to difficulties. Even as it seeks to end scapegoating, the crucifixion narrative creates a potential for it in identifying some party as Christ's killer to be murdered in vengeance (Halbertal 2017). History notes the millennia of innocent Jewish victims of Christian violence, ironically justified by a narrative to end the sacrifice of innocents. This human history does not remark on the theology of God's donative love on the cross but rather on the human capacity to employ this theology to scapegoat.

Beyond these introductory notes, I'd like to look further at Girard's important idea that the Second Testament is the first book written from the victim's perspective and so the first to reject scapegoating in favor of moral responsibility. For instance, Girard notes that in asking the mob set on stoning an adulteress "Who is free from sin?" Jesus replaces the crowd's contagious rage with the requirement that the crowd takes moral responsibility for its stone-throwing act—what Girard called "nonviolent contagion" (Girard 2001: 57). This to my mind is correct and draws on Deuteronomy 17:7, which requires anyone stepping forward as witness to a crime to be the first to execute the sentence, to cast the first stone. The moral responsibility for condemning another is not only on those who execute punishment but, earlier, on those who start the rock rolling by giving evidence. Moral self-responsibility is the basis for the Deuteronimic principle as it was for Jesus's later teachings.

The lesson of moral responsibility is found also in the Adam and Eve narrative. This tale—in addition to its concern with leaving one's childhood garden for the responsibilities of childbearing and work—presents a transcendent God and marks the distinction between such a God and humanity. With this distinction, it establishes an epistemological humility that disallows (human) intellectual absolutism. When Adam and Eve are tempted by the unhumble reach for all, absolute knowledge, it loses them nearly everything. The couple and serpent, whose phallic morphology suggests the importance of Adam's role, hide and finger-point (scapegoating each other) to escape moral responsibility, but to no avail. The narrative import—what Goodhart (2014: 112) calls the "heart" of biblical reading—is that one can neither avoid moral responsibility nor scapegoat (111, 113). This, Goodhart continues, is the consistent theme of the *tanachic* and rabbinic oeuvre (114).

Moving from Girard's concern with moral responsibility, we come to a methodological matter. *Tanachic* narratives are neither ideals to be striven for (as portions of the Second Testament are) nor submerged sacrificial violence in the mold of archaic myth. They are problem-sets for the induction of a theology, cosmology, and ethics. They feature metaphor, formulaic (nonliteral) narrative tropes, and flawed human characters through which readers develop a theology and ethics by working out the long-term consequences of multigenerational tales (Alter 1981/2011; Geller 1996: 31). The import of the Noah tale, for instance, is that when humanity's wrongdoings (in this case, sexual) overflow in society (metaphorically speaking), nature responds with overflowing watery emissions of its own. Through metaphor, it remarks on the foundational links between nature and humanity, natural law and ethics. If humanity abuses the workings of the cosmos, the cosmos will no longer work, to the demise of humanity. In another example, the lesson against envy and betrayal that begins with Cain and Abel doesn't end until some forty chapters later, with Joseph forgiving his betraying, envious brothers. This is not archaic myth, where the trace of scapegoating violence is hidden and then "crystallized" for ritual retelling and reenactment (Girard 1987: 142, 275). It is rather the opposite: the envy and scapegoating are not submerged but patent, and the *tanachic* response is forgiveness. The violence is not crystallized for repetition but replaced with grace.

In sum, *tanachic* law and narrative make self-aggrandizement, claims to intellectual absolutism, escapes from moral responsibility, and competitive rage (Joseph's brothers) explicit to condemn and replace them with moral responsibility and forgiveness (Goodhart 2014: 249). Vanessa Avery (2012) is right to note that as the patriarch Jacob blesses Joseph's sons, Ephraim and Manasseh, and makes them leaders alongside Joseph's now-reconciled brothers, Jacob extends the lesson of forgiveness beyond Joseph to the next generation and the Hebrew people as a universal moral principle. David Mitchell (2007) is also right to note a rabbinic *midrash* that works Ephraim into a messianic icon who, prefiguring the Davidic and Christian messiahs, dies as a symbol of reconciliation that redeems humanity. I take issue with Avery, however, where she reads mimetic violence into the Ephraim/Menasseh story. The point of the tale is the *absence* of competitive aggression between the boys, as Avery herself notes. Mimetic violence is also absent from the rabbinic *midrash*, whose point is that sinfulness is overcome not by violence but by giving of oneself and following the Torah given in covenant.

As much of the *tanachic* education in nonviolence lies not in narrative but in law, I'll continue with a closer look there. Law, on the *tanachic* and rabbinic understanding, is a means of living covenantally with God and persons. It helps us repair greed and aggression not through ritualized violence/payment to an angry deity but through covenantal living. Importantly, law is not in a binary against grace and love but a way to prepare for grace and to receive and give love. Its three central commandments are love of God, love of neighbor, and love of the stranger. When Jesus repeats the mandate to love God and neighbor and tells the story of the good Samaritan-stranger, he is reprising this triptych (Lukas 10:27-35). "The [Hebrew Bible] law," Terence Fretheim notes, "stands in the service of a stable, flourishing, and life-enhancing community (the community language is important). Sinai law sketches a vocation to which Israel is called for the sake of the neighbor and the creation" (Fretheim 2005: Kindle Locations 2974–75, 3205).

We may begin with the difficult case of laws for the enemy, who is protected by *tanachic* "just war" criteria (Psalms 7:4, 35:7-8) and importantly, by the requirement that a suit for peace be brought *prior* to any aggression (Deuteronomy 20:10). Captives must be properly cared for (2 Kings 6:22-23); civilians of besieged cities must be allowed to leave unharmed; enemy nations may not be oppressed even during war (2 Chronicles 28:8-15); and truces and peace agreements must be honored even if the enemy breaches them (Joshua 9). From the enemy we may move to the stranger, for whom aid requirements are so extensive that they are cited as a model for treatment of the Hebrew poor (Exodus 22:21; Leviticus 19:34, 23:35-39). Ezekiel 47:22-23 grants strangers even land rights, critical in an agrarian society.

Israelites are mandated to provide aid to strangers as witness to their slavery in Egypt—a victim perspective that is among the most persistent of *tanachic* tropes running throughout the texts (and which is found in the later crucifixion). Yet in keeping with love of enemy, even the enslaving Egyptians are integrated into the community of nations after three generations post-Exodus (Deuteronomy 23:7-8). Here again, we have the inversion of the archaic "crystallization" and reenactment of aggression. Rather than preserving scapegoating violence for (unconscious) societal repetition, the *Tanach* preserves the perspective of the victim, the Hebrew slave, so that *it*—the victim's perspective—may be repeated in acts of compassion for the stranger and needy.

From the laws pertaining to aiding the stranger, we may move to laws for the domestic needy, which prodded the emperor Julian to say, "It is disgraceful that, when no Jew ever has to beg . . . all men see that our people lack aid from us" (Stern 1980: 549–50, no. 482). A sampling of biblical poor laws includes *shmitah* and Jubilee debt cancellation (Leviticus 25:4-6, Deuteronomy 15:1-2); distribution of food to the poor (Deuteronomy 24:19-22); tithing obligations for all others (Deuteronomy 14:22); prohibitions against the return of runaway servants (Deuteronomy 23:15-16) and against the taking of interest from the poor (Exodus 22:25). Manumission of servants is required after six years of work, when they must be outfitted with livestock, grain, and wine (Exodus 21:2; Deuteronomy 15:12).

Importantly, in *tanachic* law, the moral life is not in the end fulfilled by ritual but by care of the downtrodden. While the Girardian archaic imagines that things are set right through sacrifice to the gods, Amos notes the importance of compassion over ritual: "I [God] hate, I despise your religious festivals; your assemblies are a stench to me. . . . But let justice roll on like a river, righteousness like a never-failing stream" (5:21-24). Hosea 6:6 reiterates, "For I desire mercy not sacrifice" as does Proverbs (21:3): "To do what is right and just is more acceptable to the Lord than [animal] sacrifice."

In sum, if archaic myth ritualizes the scapegoating mechanism, the *tanachic* texts rout it in prioritizing humility, compassion, and care for the needy over ritual. And it does so by highlighting the victim's perspective in the continuing reminder of Israel's plight in Egypt.

Sacrifice in the *Tanachic* covenant

So, what is sacrifice in the covenantal context and among covenantal relations? To answer, we return to our methodological matter and note that the literary forms of the *Tanach* are not the sort of logical presentation the West has inherited from the Greeks. Neither argued syllogistically nor presented in declarative statements, meaning and intent are understood from multigenerational narratives, repeating symbols, intertextual references and importantly, from the cosmological and theology context (Alter 1981; Geller 1996; Geller 2005: 12; Hazony 2012; Whybray 1987). That context is, among other things, covenantal. In a period and region where sacrifice was a predominant expression of feeding, flattering, and/or placating inscrutable, volatile gods, sacrifice in the *Tanach* is a dialogic act, symbolic communication that sustains the reciprocal giving and commitment with a God who *seeks* covenant with humanity and who provides understandable guides for sustaining that relationship between persons and God and among persons. That is, archaic sacrifice and covenantal sacrifice differ because notions of the divine and relations with him differ. To explore this, a few preliminaries about covenant are needed.

To begin, in cosmogonic myth, gods are mythopoetic and unchanging: "A cosmogonic myth is beyond discussion," Henri Frankfort writes. "It describes a sequence of sacred events, which one can either accept or reject. But no cosmogony can become part of a progressive and cumulative increase of knowledge" (Frankfort and Frankfort 1959: 251). Covenant, by contrast, is an evolving relationship between a covenant-seeking God and humanity and among persons (Pally 2016: 183–86, 233–36). The *tanahic* God, Stephen Geller writes, is not so much a concept, an "ism," as a relation: "Monotheism involves not just God but also the personality of the believer. The two unities proceed hand in hand" (Geller 2000: 295–96). Humanity is taken to be covenant-responsive and covenant-responsible. Each party is responsible for giving for the flourishing of the other, yet none are subsumed by the bond.

Contra archaic sacrifice, no one in covenant, as seen in the *Akedah*, is sacrifice-able for the group or God. Rather, covenant—unlike contract, which protects interests—protects all involved and their relationship. This is irrevocable, also unlike contract, where breach voids the obligation. Moreover, reciprocal giving and giving of oneself—sacrifice for the care of others—are necessary to the thriving of a covenantal world. It is the principle or foundational law "whose force is of a universal nature, because it derives from the way the world itself was made, and therefore from the natures of the men and nations in this world"

(Hazony 2012: 22, 249). Covenant is understood as for the "blessing of all the nations," said thrice, once to each patriarch (Genesis 12:3, 26:4, 28:14).

Covenants of reciprocal giving among equals are easily imagined as are covenants with asymmetric terms between unequal parties. The *tanachic* innovation is reciprocity among unequals, a direct bond between God and humanity and among persons of different status. So integral is reciprocity that humanity is understood as God's cocreator in the world's development. Positive law, insofar as it develops love of God, neighbor, and stranger, is humanity's contribution to this co-covenantal effort.

This conception of divine-human relations distinguishes covenant from archaic religio-politics where the king is seen as god, god's son, or sole mediator between the gods and the people. The innovation of the ancient Israelites and *Tanach*, Michael Walzer writes (1985), is a vision of society grounded not in a godlike monarch but in a covenant directly between the people and a transcendent God, whose ethics of forgiveness and grace are the standard by which all human acts, including those of kings, are judged. Even Moses, who brings the tablets of covenant to the people, is no king but a flawed, human teacher and prophet, who errs, loses his temper and whose grave, *contra* the Assyrian and Egyptian kings, is unknown. The book of Judges and the "kingly" books, recounting the reigns from Saul through the destruction of Israel and Judah, are *critiques* of monarchy and political power (Noort 2018: 2).

Robert Bellah notes that certain archaic societies (Mesopotamia in the Code of Hammurabi, for one) developed a proto-covenantality in understanding god(s) not only as responsible for life's unpredictabilities but as the people's caretaker. However even here, justice remained closely dependent on the king's decrees and whims (2011: Kindle Locations 3422, 3426). The idea of a reciprocal commitment between a covenant-seeking God and humanity and among persons—an enduring, ethical commitment abstracted from the human personalities involved—evolved along with the evolution of the Hebraic covenant "as a charter for a new kind of people, a people under God, not under a king, an idea parallel to Athenian democracy though longer lasting . . . a people ruled by divine law, not the arbitrary rule of the state, and of a people composed of *responsible individuals*" (2011: Kindle Locations 4700–01, 4864, emphasis mine).

The responsible individuals of covenant have substantial role in sustaining covenant through reciprocity and giving, both to persons in need and to those in symbolic reciprocity with God, who is committed to them. And here we come to sacrifice-within-covenant and its distinction from the archaic. As the meaning of sacrifice is neither argued for nor declared but must be understood within the covenantal premises of the *Tanach*, covenantal sacrifice, like covenant itself, is dialogic. It is a symbolic gesture of giving to God (who has given and committed to humanity) in sustenance of the reciprocal bond. As Marcel Mauss elaborated in *The Gift* (1990/1923), gift is freely given and *given up* as a symbol of one's own spirit granted in covenantal commitment to the other. In the *Tanach*, gift begins bilaterally. God in trust and commitment gives of his Being to create Adam, breathing into humanity God's "spirit" (*nishmat cha'im*, Genesis 2:7). God gives Noah life and covenant; his children give in return in performing the Noahite moral law. God in covenant gives land and Torah to the Hebrews. In reciprocity, they perform the moral and ritual law that sustain covenant. They develop them in cocreation and bring symbolic gifts from the land in reciprocal giving.

Yet this reciprocity and giving does not remain bilateral, between person and God, but triangulates to human relations: persons give to God *by giving* to persons in need, called *hekhdesh*, made holy. Through this triangulation, covenantal giving to others builds covenant with God, and covenant with God sustains persons in giving to others. As covenant extends from bilateral to larger human associations, reciprocal giving becomes giving or gift-exchange networks that sustain intra- and intersocietal relations (Mauss 1990/1923; Godbout and Caille´ 1988; Hyde 1983). That is, they sustain human living.

The triangulation of covenantal giving with God and among persons is reflected not first in the prophets (often cited to illustrate it) but throughout the Pentateuch, notably in the Ten Commandments: three pertain to person-God and the rest, seamlessly, to persons in community (see Palaver's thoughtful passage on Jewish tradition, 2015: 158–60). Leviticus 6:2-3 holds: "If anyone sins and is unfaithful to the LORD by deceiving a neighbor . . . ." Harm to persons breaks covenant with God. Numbers 5:6 repeats the idea: "Any man or woman who wrongs another in any way *and so is unfaithful to the Lord* is guilty." And it is reprised in the frequent biblical formulation, "behave righteously to others; I am the Lord." Rather than a non-sequitur, this refrain is an expression of the linked covenants with God and among persons: righteousness and giving to one entails righteousness and giving to the other. We find a similar linkage in the biblical poor laws: "Leave them [the field corners] for the poor and for the foreigner residing among you. I am the LORD your God" (Leviticus 23:22).

Finally, the triangulated covenant with God and among persons grounds the biblical episodes, such as the Golden Calf, where Israel breaks covenant with God and violence among persons follows or where the natural world erupts in disaster. The narrative import—what Goodhart calls the "heart" of biblical reading (2014: 112)—is this: as covenant with God is broken, the covenantal fabric of society is rent as well. The triangulated covenant is the nature of the cosmos, and a breach in one part breaches all parts. Girard's idea of Gospel apocalypticism resulting from human sin (Palaver 2013: 216) is consistent with the *tanachic* principle of the triangulated covenant: if humanity sins by failing covenant with God and persons, the social and natural worlds themselves fail.

While sacrifice was a predominant approach to the gods in the cultures surrounding the ancient Hebrews, the meaning given to it in the *Tanach* was unusual because it was understood as expression of a covenantal relationship. This is true as well for the crucifixion, which was ubiquitous at the time of Jesus but which—though it involves the tough case of human sacrifice—was given new meaning as God's donative love and new covenant with humanity (Luke 22:20; 1 Corinthians 11:25; 2 Corinthians 3:6; Hebrews 8:8, 9:15, 12:24). In the context of covenant, sacrifice, as dialogic, is symbolic expression by morally accountable persons of giving and gift, which sustain reciprocal commitment with a God who is not unknowable and inscrutable but seeks covenant with humanity. Symbolically, it reflects humanity's acceptance of reciprocal responsibility: God maintains covenant and gives to us as we maintain covenant and give to God and other persons, so sustaining human living. It is part of humanity's role and voice in this covenantal exchange, as prayer later became.

Celebratory sacrifice at the harvest, Sabbath, and other festivals (Numbers 28) is a symbolic return gesture for this life that God, in covenant, sustains. The ritual "offer" of the first son into the priesthood (Levenson 1993) too is a symbolic gesture for the gift of children and emphasizes the *Akedah* point that covenant never demands the sacrifice of a child. The point of the ritual is that God does not take children, not even for priestly worship (as in some archaic religions and with child oblates and monks), but gives children in covenant with humanity. Sacrifice is also a public expression of repentance, a pledge of oneself to community and God that one atones for wrongdoing and will act with righteousness (Leviticus 4, 16). Persons bring atonement sacrifice "when they *realize* their guilt and the sin they have committed becomes known" to the community (Leviticus 4:27-28). Its aim is not to appease the gods, who then will cease their destructive acts against society. Rather, it seeks moral reflection among accountable persons, who are—with God, as his cocreators—responsible for society. The offerings that atone for sin (*hatat*) and guilt (*asham*) as well as the original scapegoat (*se'ir l'azazel*, Leviticus 16: 8-10) do not placate inscrutable gods nor in themselves expiate sin but rather express moral intent and are symbols of accountability to community and God, who seeks covenant.

Unlike archaic sacrifice, the dialogic act of covenantal sacrifice depends on moral responsibility and reinforces reciprocally responsible relationship.

Indeed, sacrifice absent intent is void (see Blanchard, this volume). Thus, covenantal sacrifice fails Girard's criteria for archaic scapegoating. Rather than paying off a distant, angry divine, it is an expression of responsibility *with* the divine for the sustenance of covenant, for reciprocity, giving, and moral living. Moreover, the *tanachic* writings about sacrifice fail Girard's criteria for sacrificial myth. Those criteria are reference (1) to a primordial threat, (2) to a wrongdoing that brought the threat about, and (3) to an *other* who is the perpetrator of the wrong and who thus may be sacrificed. Yet *tanachic* texts about harvest and celebration sacrifices are grounded not in sin or wrongdoing but in relationship and reciprocal giving that sustain the cosmos and human life. *Tanachic* texts about atonement sacrifices do not refer to a primordial threat and wrongdoing. They point to the ever present, quotidian injustices that we ourselves—not an other—commit in failing covenant with God and persons. They aim at sustaining these relationships. They look not at a mythologized past but at moral responsibility and reflection about the way we live in the present and future.

In sum, the shift from archaic person-in-mimetic-competition to person-in-covenant repositions sacrifice from lynch mob to moral responsibility and reciprocal giving with God and other persons. It unites society not by scapegoating and mob frenzy but by grounding personal and public life in an ethics of giving and reciprocal commitment with community and God, who seeks this very reciprocity and giving.

Sacrifice's meaning and valence has changed from abusive to constructive because the understanding of the divine has gone from cosmogonic to covenantal and the understanding of humanity has gone from agonistic to relational.

Conclusion: Covenant as premise for agapic sacrifice

A covenantal worldview may have something to offer us in the way we understand present society and our obligations to give—give up, sacrifice—for each other and the group, what we now call the common good. Just how useful it is hangs on one's notion of human nature as competitive or covenantal with foundational affinities for reciprocity and giving.

The Christian debate, where Girard weighs in, is bookended on one end by Thomist optimism. In Aquinas's *analogia entis*, humanity continues to "analogously" partake of divine goodness—the goodness present at creation—

even given the foundational differences between humanity and God and even after the Fall. "In all things," Aquinas writes, "God works intimately" (Aquinas, 1265-74, Ia, q. 105, art. 5). Thus, as we retain something of this goodness, we retain the possibility of sacrifice as reciprocal giving and exchange of *agape*. The more pessimistic view might be represented by Karl Barth, who feared that the *analogia entis* allows humanity to determine morality too much on its own—out of its own supposed, *imago*-based goodness—without close guidance from revelation and Scripture (Oakes 2007: 595–616). This undue independence from revelation and Scripture, on Barth's view, led to the sorts of "morality" he witnessed in the trenches of the Frist World War and as 1930s Europe capitulated to fascism. Humanity, Barth concluded, could not be trusted to its "good" nature.

In this debate, Girard is something of an Augustinian broker, appropriately wary of humanity's capacity for aggression yet also aware that upon creation, God held humanity to be "very good" and that this goodness is not entirely lost (Augustine 390/1953: 11.21). With something of this goodness still with us, humanity may yet follow God's offer and model of love on the cross.

Tanachic covenant has something of Girard's cautious optimism. It understands humanity as being in an ongoing education toward nonviolence. We are made in the "image" of a covenantal God (our primary condition is covenantal) *and* as we are in reciprocal covenant with him and other persons. Owing to this covenantality, we may give and sacrifice in reciprocal commitment in both personal relations and public policy—as demonstrated by the *tanachic* poor laws and without which no common good can be built. Girard holds that to overcome aggression, we must learn from God's limitless love. The First Testament agrees. It proposes that we are capable of learning from God's love not because it corrects our "natural" competitive violence but because it builds upon our covenantal nature.

References

Alter, R. (1981/2011), *The Art of Biblical Narrative*, New York: Basic Books.
Augustine (390/1953), "De vera religione," in *Augustine: Earlier Writings*, trans. J. Burleigh, Philadelphia: The Westminster Press.
Avery, V. (2012), "The Jewish Vaccine against Mimetic Desire: A Girardian Exploration or a Sabbath Ritual Contagion," *Journal of Violence, Mimesis, and Culture* 19: 19–39.
Bellah, R. (2011), *Religion in Human Evolution*, Cambridge: Belknap/Harvard University Press.

Breslauer, S. D. (November 2006), "Toward a Theory of Covenant for Contemporary Jews," *Covenant* 1 (1). Available online: http://www.covenant.idc.ac.il/en/vol1/issue1/breslauer.html (accessed September 16, 2018).

Frankfort, H., and H. A. Frankfort (1959), *Before Philosophy*, Hammondsworth/Middlesex: Penguin.

Fretheim, T. (2005), *God and World in the Old Testament: A Relational Theology of Creation*, Nashville: Abignon Press.

Geller, S. (1996), *Sacred Enigmas: Literary Religion in the Hebrew Bible*, London: Routledge.

Geller, S. (2000), "The God of the Covenant," in N. N. Porter (ed.), *One God or Many? Concepts of Divinity in the Ancient World*, Transactions of the Casco Bay Assyriological Institute 1.

Geller, S. (2005), "Manna and Sabbath: A Literary-Theological Reading of Exodus 16," *Interpretation* 59 (1): 5–16.

Girard, R. (1987), *Things Hidden since the Foundation of the World: Research Undertaken in Collaboration with J.-M. Oughourlian and G. Lefort*, trans. S. Bann and M. Metteer, Stanford: Stanford University Press.

Girard, R. (2001), *I See Satan Fall Like Lightning*, trans. J. G. Williams, Maryknoll: Orbis Books.

Godbout, J., and A. Caillé (1988), *The World of the Gift*, trans. D. Winkler, Montreal: McGill-Queen's University Press.

Goodhart, S. (2014), *The Prophetic Law: Essays in Judaism, Girardianism, Literary Studies, and the Ethical*, East Lansing: Michigan State University Press.

Halbertal, M. (2012), *On Sacrifice*, Princeton: Princeton University Press.

Halbertal, M. (2017), personal communication.

Hart, D. B. (1993), "A Gift Exceeding Every Debt: An Eastern Orthodox Appreciation of Anselm's *Cur Deus Homo*," *Pro Ecclesia* 7: 333–49.

Hazony, Y. (2012), *The Philosophy of Hebrew Scripture*, Cambridge: Cambridge University Press.

Hyde, L. (1983), *The Gift: Imagination and the Erotic Life of Property*, New York: Vintage Books.

Levenson, J. (1993), *The Death and Resurrection of the Beloved Son*, New Haven: Yale University Press.

Mauss, M. (1923/1990), *The Gift: The Form and Reason for Exchange in Archaic Society*, trans. W. D. Halls, London: Routledge.

Mitchell, D. (2007), "Messiah Ben Joseph: A Sacrificing Atonement for Israel," *Review of Rabbinic Judaism* 10 (1): 77–94.

Noort, E. (2018), *"God of Gods: YHWH": Belonging to YHWH in Joshua 22: 9-34*. Princeton: Centre for Theological Inquiry.

Oakes, K. (2007), "The Question of Nature and Grace in Karl Barth: Humanity as Creature and as Covenant-partner," *Modern Theology* 23 (4): 595–616.

Palaver, W. (2013), *Rene Girard's Mimetic Theory*, trans. G. Borrud, East Lansing: Michigan State University Press.

Palaver, W. (2015), "Parochial Altruism and Christian Universalism: On the Deep Difficulties of Creating Solidarity Without Outside Enemies," in P. Dumouchel and R. Gotoh (eds.), *Social Bonds as Freedom: Revisiting the Dichotomy of the Universal and the Particular*, 153–73, New York: Berghan.

Pally, M. (2016), *Commonwealth and Covenant: Economics, Politics, and Theologies of Relationality*, Grand Rapids: Eerdmans.

Stern, M. (1980), *Greek and Latin Authors on Jews and Judaism: From Tacitus to Simplicius*, Jerusalem: Academy of Sciences and Humanities.

Walzer, M. (1985), *Exodus and Revolution*, New York: Basic Books.

Whybray, R. (1987), *The Making of the Pentateuch: A Methodological Study*, London and New York: Bloomsbury T&T Clark.

7

Generative Sacrifice

Girard, Feminism, and Christ

Anna Mercedes

Anna Mercedes addresses Girard directly in this chapter, investigating his view that humanity will ever reject Christ and Christ-like love until we learn the lessons of the cross. Christ's rejection, on this reading of Girard, is the human condition for the present. Mercedes notes that sacrifice has unquestionably functioned as a mechanism of oppressive patriarchal and colonial systems, including Christian ones. Thus, sacrifice has rightly been a subject of criticism in both feminist theory and in liberative hermeneutics within Christian theology. Yet, Mercedes continues, a feminist theological framework building on the work of Traci C. West and Sarah Coakley argues that sacrificial self-giving even under unjust circumstances is not evidence of only a fallen world, of only our rejection of Christ. Such a unifocal view of sacrifice risks the erasure or dismissal of the very sacrificial acts and actors we deem to be moral—if not blaming the victims then under-valuing their actions. A more nuanced understanding of sacrifice argues for the recognition of resistance strategies in the sacrificial actions of oppressed persons, which can function as means to social and personal transformation. "While persons in targeted social positions," she writes, "have known the dangers of sacrifice, they have also known its power."

—editor's note

Introduction

Perhaps for a moment, a feminist theologian can find respite stepping into Rene Girard's theory. Theologies of Christian sacrifice, most famously in the form of atonement theologies, have mired the capacities of Christian energy. A Christ whose sacrificial death is salvific too quickly lends valor and justification to self-sacrificial suffering and death in Christ's followers. As Catherine Keller aptly summarizes the problem, "Christianity has been perennially tempted to glorify victimization in glorification of its central victim" (Keller 1990: 105–06). In resilient response to Christianity's victimizing tendencies, those dedicated to a liberative theological project have articulated manifold ways that Christianity has more to offer than imitation of Christ as sacrifice. Vividly, for example, Delores Williams insists that Jesus "conquered sin in life, not in death" (Williams 1993: 166). In a vision far from a valorization of violent sacrifice, Williams writes that "the resurrection of Jesus and the kingdom of God theme in Jesus' *ministerial* vision provide black women with the knowledge that God has, through Jesus, shown humankind how to live peacefully, productively, and abundantly in relationship" (Williams 1993: 167; emphasis in original).

In perhaps surprising resonance, Girard, for all his writing on sacrifice, does not champion it. Instead sacrifice for Girard serves as a kind of crutch for humanity; it fundamentally shapes and promulgates all cultures, but sacrifice is just as fundamentally a problem. Christianity in Girard's appraisal succumbs to this perennial problem, and indeed, "historical Christianity took on a persecutory character as a result of the sacrificial reading of the Passion and the Redemption" (Girard 1987: 225). But despite the pernicious trend of Christian history, Girard determines that the Christian Gospel offered the way past sacrifice. Contrary to popular belief about the death of Christ, Girard claims that "the sacrificial reading of the Passion and the Redemption cannot legitimately be extrapolated from the text of the New Testament" (Girard 1987: 224). Nor does Girard see Christ and his death as the key example of sacrifice. Rather, Christ is the counterexample, the evidence of a world gone wrong. For Girard the Christian Gospels "are unveiling the founding mechanism of all worldly prestige, all forms of sacredness and all forms of cultural meaning" (Girard 1987: 429). Girard claims that something without historical precedent takes place in the gospels, something that "discredits and deconstructs all the gods of violence, since it reveals the true God, who has not the slightest violence in him" (Girard 1987: 429).

This ultimate contrast to violence also shows Christian violence to be totally counter to the Christ of its name, revealing to Girard that Christians have not understood "the relationship of Christ to his own death" (Girard 1987: 225). They have not seen that Christ's death reveals a way other than sacrifice and reveals "the founding death of the scapegoat" (Girard 1987: 225). Where Christians have so often turned to hostilities, Girard finds that they have simply perpetuated the sacrificial mechanism cycling through human cultures, missing the radicality of Christ as the "perfectly innocent and non-violent victim" (Girard 1987: 427). Christianity misses its own point when it succumbs to the victim mechanism; thus "What turns Christianity in on itself, so that it presents a hostile face to all that is not Christian, is inextricably bound up with the sacrificial reading. That reading cannot possibly be *innocent*" (Girard 1987: 225; emphasis in original). In sum, Girard refuses a sacrificial reading of Christ and sees in Christ an invitation past violence and sacrifice.

Thus, at least momentarily, stepping into Girard's theory, a feminist theologian can take a deep breath of relief: here is a theory that does not valorize atoning death. Quite the contrary, for Girard, atoning death is not just a bad idea, instead it is like Satan, "the mimetic model and obstacle *par excellence*" (Girard 1987: 419). As sweeping condemnations of violence go, Girard's is rather emphatic!

Happy that someone, and a European man at that, has said no to violence, the feminist may rest a moment. But not for long. Restlessness stirs feminist theology to further explorations of sacred power in a world of violence. The feminist theologian cannot get too comfortable with Girard's theory, for it leaves a gap where agency could be. To demonstrate this point, I will describe this gap in Girard's thought and will juxtapose this description to Traci West's resistance ethics. I will then posit my own claim that resistance can manifest as something like sacrifice and will do so in conversation with Sarah Coakley's theology on sacrifice.

Girard and the Christian life

Girard describes Christian life as a turn away from sacrifice: "Following Christ means giving up mimetic desire" (Girard 1987: 431). For Girard Christ has nothing to do with what Girard sees as the universal cultural production of the victimage mechanism; Christ "offers not the slightest hold to any form of rivalry or mimetic interference. There is no acquisitive desire in him" (Girard 1987: 430). Despite the absence of mimetic violence, Girard's idea of Christian life does contain a different kind of imitation, for the gospels "recommend imitating the sole model who never runs the danger . . . of being transformed into a fascinating rival" (Girard 1987: 430). Girard imagines an "easy" imitation: "Knock, and it will be opened to you" (Girard 1987: 430).

Yet following this Christ may be tricky after all, for it is central for Girard that Christ is repeatedly expelled. This expulsion must necessarily occur because Christ cannot hold amid the cultural production promulgated by the victimage mechanism. Such cyclic production kicks Christ out as a matter of course. Echoing Psalm 118 and the synoptic gospels, Christ is for Girard the stone that the builders rejected; "Christ is that stone in visible form" (Girard 1987: 429). Yet in Girard's theory, these biblical passages take on a meaning particular to his work. These builders are the builders of culture itself. It is as though for Girard, all human cultures are built with the mortar of the victimage mechanism, and Christ, who would unveil this faulty paste, is expelled. Girard sees evidence of Christ's necessary rejection laced into the prologue of John's Gospel, in the lines in which the Logos comes into the world but is neither known nor accepted (John 1:10-11). Girard juxtaposes John's Logos to "the Logos of human culture":

> The Johannine Logos must be specified in the prologue in an obvious and even striking way—even though no one has yet taken note of it, because they have not understood the role of violence in the Logos of human culture. If I have not been mistaken this far, the revelation of the scapegoat principle must be included in the very definition of the Logos: these few lines must reveal all that has been hidden, even though we may not be capable of assimilating that revelation. (Girard 1987: 270)

The whole alternative to the victimage mechanism is there for readers when they discern "the role of expulsion in the definition of the Johannine Logos" (Girard 1987: 271).

Thus, expulsion and refusal figure large in Girard's understanding of Christ. "The Johannine Logos discloses the truth of violence by having itself expelled" (Girard 1987: 271). The Christic nature refuses to be placed in any role in the logic of violence, despite the way Jesus's disciples press him for mastery or dominance (Girard 1987: 419). Christ always "bows out" (Girard 1987: 428). Or in Girard's claim with which I began this chapter: "The Logos of love puts up no resistance; it always allows itself to be expelled by the Logos of violence" (Girard 1987: 274). In this way imitation of Girard's Christ appears breathtakingly passive: to be perpetually rejected, to have oneself expelled, to bow out.

Somewhat in contrast, Girard does allude to the way the Logos, while "always sacrificed," "increases its pressure on us from day to day" (Girard 1987: 444). He finds that "the Logos is still in the process of revealing itself" (Girard 1987: 274) and "a new kind of humanity is in the process of gestation" (Girard 1987: 446). There is an intimation of new possibilities for action. Overall, however, Girard leaves a gap where Christ's agency, or our own, could be. John Milbank has also criticized this lack in Girard's work: "He is undoubtedly right to lay stress upon

Jesus's refusal of violence, but he allows little place for the concrete 'form' taken by Jesus's non-violent practice" (Milbank 2006: 398).

Thus, while it may at first seem that the abolishment of the scapegoat mechanism and Christ as Logos of love would be readily embraced by feminists and others who have advocated for the victims of violence, these activists and scholars are, precisely because of their advocacy, unlikely to align with any movement which will put up no resistance and "always allow itself to be expelled."

Resistance ethics

In illustration of this point, a sharp contrast can be seen between Girard's theory of expulsion and theological ethicist Traci West's work on black women and resistance ethics. In her *Wounds of the Spirit*, West emphasizes both the gravity of the abuse driven at black women and the capacity and strength of abuse survivors and their creativity for resistance. For West this dual emphasis is a necessity:

> This depiction of the relentless, crushing, and variegated pressures of domination on women would be highly inaccurate without attention to the quality of resistance that also occurs. In addition, such an omission would contradict my theo-ethical assumption of the presence of powerful divine resources available to us for resisting the forms of dehumanization leveled at black women. (West 1999: 151)

Thus, it is clear that West would not construct a Christian ethic that "bows out," or one in which love "puts up no resistance." Where Girard writes of a victim, West writes of "victim-survivors" (West 1999: 5).

For West, resistance comes in many forms and is too often overlooked in analysis of violence. And though West does hope for healing in both society and victim-survivors, she theorizes healing as distinct from resistance. Resistance occurs even when healing is still an open question: "Unlike healing, resistance involves any sign of dissent with the consuming effects of intimate and social violence" (West 1999: 151). Importantly, this also means that resistance can still occur in an enduringly violent culture—it is far from utter expulsion by that culture.

Through her analysis, West clearly demonstrates that the concept of "learned helplessness," a concept too often applied to victims of abuse, misses a wide spectrum of possibilities that victim-survivors can and do employ (West 1999:

154–60). In juxtaposition to West's thought, Girard's Christ, a perfect victim, begins to look like an archetype of learned helplessness—an odd fate for the figure Christian communities mark as resurrected and thus rather far from helpless. In light of Easter, West's depiction of victim-survivors of abuse provides a more accurate description of Christ than Girard's image of Christ as perfect victim. Is not a risen Christ, like women who are victim-survivors, "assertive and persistent" (West 1999: 158)?

West writes that "the erasure of black women's resistance behavior is an endemic feature of their subordinate political status" (West 1999: 160). From this, Christian theologians can realize that we should not tell our theological story with an emphasis on violence alone. We only further the subordination of resurrection's stirring when we pull survival and resistance from the transcripts of our discourse and memory. When we support such erasure, our theorizing participates not in the resistance of violence but, even if in small ways, in its further fueling.

It is thus not benign that Girardian theory leaves a gap where theologies of Christ's life, and ours, could be. The gap leaves Girard's Logos of love subordinated beneath what is for Girard the predictable pattern of mimetic violence in the world. West insists that violence must be acknowledged and seen for what it is *and* that resistance must be acknowledged and seen for what it is. Otherwise, it would seem that Girard's Satan can remain ensconced as the main subject of our discourse and the agent of expulsion, fixating us on violence. There is too much violence to leave a gap where agency could be, and that gap only exists in theory anyhow. West finds that "no matter how severely women are brutalized and demoralized, there is still evidence of their resistance. Once we train ourselves to perceive the means that individual victim-survivors utilize for their survival and liberation, our ability to envision broader possibilities for women-empowering change increases" (West 1999: 180).

In pulling West and Girard into juxtaposition, I do not mean to conflate analysis of concepts of Christ and analysis of the struggles of particular victim-survivors. Rather, just as "training ourselves" to see resistance at work in the lives of victim-survivors broadens our capacities for change, Christians can train themselves to see resistance consistently at work in Christ, consistently embedded in God's work as creator, redeemer, sustainer. We can highlight ways that Christ is precisely a resistance raised rather than a victim expelled.

To use Girard's terms, even were Satan's violence revealed for what it is and Christ paradigmatically anti-sacrificial, hidden as a beacon for the future of humanity (none of which I'm precisely willing to grant, but will entertain for sake of the argument), we are left with questions of agency, resistance, and survivor strength (to speak in terms of feminist analysis), or questions of discipleship and Christian life (to speak in terms of Christian theology).

It is very good to emphasize, with Girard, that Jesus should not be seen as a promoter of violent sacrifice. And it is very good for anyone to laud a future for human cultures beyond perpetual victimizing. But what else? What sort of world shall my daughters inhabit, if the "easy" path I teach them to imitate is that of perpetual expulsion?

It is at this point, after acknowledgment of the way sacrifice has widely been a mechanism of violence, that I can speak to the felicities of none other than something like sacrifice. I make my argument from both feminist and Christian commitments, constructing my claims, as does Girard, around the figure of Christ.

Sacrifice on a slant

As West demonstrates, resistance to abuse is diverse. Accordingly, I affirm that resistance does not always look self-giving or self-sacrificial. Sometimes, however, it does, as for instance when victim-survivors dedicate themselves to care in the face of an uncaring culture.

In such a history of resistance, Christ too is a victim-survivor. Christ shows and is a way not beyond sacrifice but of restorative sacrifice, of sacred gift of self for other, in which the new self is also astoundingly born. Christ flows as this sacrificial energy for the sake of a world in need—not as a corrective to all other cultures (as Girard's Christ would be) but as a vivacity at play in and for the world, a greening power, an ever-present holiness and a sacralizing flow, an anima for the world, and an animation of justice and mercy.

This is sacrifice on a slant. Elsewhere I describe it as chrism, as Christ given away (Mercedes 2014) and as "kenosis," echoing Paul in Philippians 2 (Mercedes 2011).

Girard stresses the role of norms and rituals in the success of the victimage mechanism, writing that "culture does not proceed directly from the reconciliation that follows victimage; rather it is from the double imperative of prohibition and ritual" (Girard 1987: 32). I want to press Girard's theory to articulate something it seems to leave out—the norms and rituals serving a culture built with the stone that the builders rejected. Girard explains:

> To understand human culture it is necessary to concede that only the damming of mimetic forces by means of the prohibition and the diversion of these forces in the direction of ritual are capable of spreading and perpetuating the

reconciliatory effect of the surrogate victim. Religion is nothing other than this immense effort to keep the peace. (Girard 1987: 32)

Girard is clear about the innate contamination he sees in every cultural project except that revealed by the Johannine Logos, but his theory does not offer us a similarly descriptive account the possibilities for a culture of the Logos of love. If the rituals and norms of the victimage mechanism were always for him a processing mechanism for the violence at the core of things—if they are cultural forms that kept this violence, to a significant degree, in check—then cannot the logic of love also invoke human cultural response and account as it continues its revelation? Though for Girard, the Logos of love allows itself to be expelled, it nonetheless must have some tenacity or perseverance, even if this perseverance is inherent or perhaps automatic, for it does not after all disappear. As Girard states, "If it tolerates being concealed yet another time, this is to put off for just a short while the fullness of its revelation" (Girard 1987: 274).

So as this logic of love abides in concealed tension, might we not emerge into rituals and norms that celebrate its actualization? Might these rituals and norms have more transparency than the shrouded nature of the rituals and norms of mimetic violence—since for Girard, with the victimage mechanism "the production of the sacred is necessarily and inversely proportional to the understanding of the mechanisms that produce it" (Girard 1987: 34)? And might these norms and rituals and practices for the logic of love have a function of *resistance*?

Christian theologians follow this path when they argue for Christ's incarnation, life, and ministry as the elements of life and love, rather than arguing that Christ's death reveals life and love. Dolores Williams speaks of Christ's "ministerial vision," and many have seen in the synoptic gospels a richer portrayal of Jesus's loving life than in the passion-heavy Gospel of John where Girard finds his expelled "Johannine Logos."

For Girard, the passion of Christ is evidence of the forceful functionality of the victimage mechanism—not because Jesus was a scapegoat but because amid the logic of violence, no one will recognize love; we will expel and crucify it. It does survive in expulsion, which is good news of a sort. Yet the passion need not be read so passively! The passion of Jesus's life, or more broadly, the passion of God in God's life with creation, from mud to Egypt to the prophets of old and the prophets of today, does more than allow itself to be expelled. It puts up steady resistance, though perhaps not what looks like resistance within a logic of violence. That is, it is a nonviolent resistance, or a generative, constructive, creative, fecund resistance.

And sometimes this resistance takes the form of sacrifice, as our lives and loves are drawn up in a movement toward and for the thriving of others: sacrifice on a slant. This is sacrifice in a kinetics of vitality stretching out and forward to insist on more life for the thriving of others. It is one of our strongest indications of life rather than evidence of our position as cogs in an economy of death. It may slant through love and desire, but to characterize this love narrowly as either agape or eros limits its potential, as happens in Girard's own dichotomizing of self-giving and desiring loves with his "assumption that desire expresses lack—and that we value mimetically what others desire" (Skerrett 2003: 794).

In contrast to such a dichotomy, desire for another's thriving, pleasure, and abundance can be as erotic as it is generous, as self-giving as it is self-serving, and as charitable as it is passionate. What is for the self and what is for the other blur in the currents of generative sacrifice, for self and other themselves blur, which is part of the delight and vivacity of this sacrifice on a slant.

That self-sacrifice is too often met with violence and smashed along its way is not the fault of this love. We cede our terms to the logic of violence when we let it rewrite the narrative of what happens to smashed gifts of self, telling us "she sacrificed too much" or "he did not stand up for himself" or "she was masochistic." Those are the terms a logic of violence will use to justify the harm it has done and shift blame to its victims. Rather, we give on our own terms, following a vivacious and loving logic. These terms may sound countercultural: "To do this for you is my strongest self-expression." "In yielding to your cause, I make my own kind of stand." "My power does not rely on dominance." The terms of survival and resistance are passion, love, the fullness of vitality spinning into the future, generating life. And Jesus's life was passion, love, the fullness of vitality spinning into the future, generating life.

Imitating Christ, christened into Christ, bearing a chrism spilling out for the world, we become actors and agent of the logic of love. We ritualize and normalize that love—call it liturgy, call it hospitality, call it spiritual practice—with our passion and generosity amid a world of ongoing violence.

It isn't quite sacrifice, or it is. But what it lacks is competitive mimicry breeding violence; nor is it catalyzed by violence. It creates a different kind of sanctity. And it is as much a gift for others as the expression and reemergence of the giver's own agency. It is something like sacrifice, sacrifice on a slant, sacrifice *for*—for the thriving of others or for the self-made new, the incarnation of holiness in a pained world.

Feminism and sacrifice

This conception of generative sacrifice bears resemblance to that of Sarah Coakley, whose work with the doctrine of kenosis I have engaged elsewhere (Mercedes 2011). Here I will engage her endorsement of sacrifice in order to demonstrate the contrasts between her theological approach and my own and to distinguish our two related but diverging options for embracing sacrifice within Christian feminism.

As in my own argument, Coakley defends sacrifice, well aware of the dangers it has held for women and cognizant of the arguments of feminism. Working with the Genesis narrative of Isaac, she posits that "only sacrifice, *rightly understood*, can account for a feminist transformation of the self that is radically 'theonomous,' rooted and sustained in God" (Coakley 2011: 19; emphasis in original). Isaac, "the ostensibly powerless one," becomes for Coakley "the type of the one who triumphs over human powerlessness, not by a false, compensatory will-to-power and further patriarchal violence, but through the subtler power of a transformative, divine *interruption*"—as God interrupts flow of paternal violence in the Isaac narrative (Coakley 2011: 18). Coakley sees power in the right kind of submission, and she draws her distinction "between submission to the logic of a *false* patriarchal sacrifice (in which male violence and scapegoating dominate), and the choice of an authentic and discerning 'sacrificial' posture of another sort . . . (in which genuine consent is given to the *divine* call to purge and purify one's own desires in order to align them with God's)" (Coakley 2011: 25).

Thus, there is something powerful within the dynamics of sacrifice that is for both Coakley and myself intensely theological and intensely feminist (making us both a bit unusual in our arguments). For both of us, sacrifice is a wider phenomenon than an inherently violent one, as in Girard. In both our conceptions, the sacrificing person encounters, on the other side of sacrifice, herself made new. And in both of our conceptions, God's own self shines rather brightly on the other side of sacrifice.

Nonetheless, in these two arguably Christian feminist conceptions of sacrifice, there are several differences that make a difference. The two parties involved in sacrifice in Coakley's conception are God and the person, in an initial dyad that merges salvifically. In a traditional up-and-down transcendence, Coakley's sacrificial dynamics run on the vertical. In contrast, the parties involved in sacrifice as I am exploring it are less individualized, less dyadic, and somewhat more creaturely, with the sacrificial dynamics running on the horizontal. In Coakley's conception, a self moves toward theonomous transformation. In my conception, the agents of sacrifice give of themselves toward and for the world, spilling chrism forward. God may coalesce with the agent of sacrifice or come to flesh in the christening of the other, or pour out in a holy luminescence between them, a chrism dripping through the interstices of the world (Mercedes 2014).

Without denying the empowerment attainable in Coakley's vision of sacrifice, I am chasing a different stream of power, drawn by sacrifice on a slant. God runs sideways out into the world in the streams of our own self-giving loves. This is the path of God's becoming, and our own. This is incarnation. God flows out toward us in God's own self-giving, mingled into our own, because God is in love with the creatures of this world; God desires our becoming. God pours out for the life of the world, says that it is good, and declares that God will be our God.

I want the wide sweep of this sacrificial energy to filter through, support, and infuse myriad sites throughout space and time. I want that kind of greening power for the world. Thus, it is not so much a self's transformation I am tracking but instead a transformation for my beloveds, and yours, and a desire for them to flourish. And somewhere in the trajectory of this slant toward others, I ride over the next instance of my own self-sacrifice, chasing after a world made new with the spirit of Christ. That I keep coming into myself again, emerging into new self with each expression of self-giving love, I do receive as a theonomous gift—as long as myself shall last, and thereafter, tucked in the currents of God's vivacity for a world whose corners and crevices and creative possibilities are without end in the momentum of God's tenacious unfolding.

Beyond Girard and West, Coakley and myself, in a drastically diverse world, amid big cultural systems that exceed any one theoretical model, there are manifold examples of generous, passionate gestures, as much self-sacrificing as they are self-birthing, constructing who the sacrificer is in the world as she or he "selflessly" extends full reach toward another's thriving. These sacrifices are not the province of any one system, culture, theory, or religion. They are rather obviously part of the fabric of life. Life-giving sacrifice awes, inspires, and catalyzes generativity in large and small ways, some mostly unobserved, every day.

As a Christian theologian, I argue that sacrifice on slant toward the thriving of others is a vital energy of Christianity, a ceaseless gift of Christ for the world, like a tap that does not turn off. This kenotic, kinetic flow offers a way to understand Christian vocation in a messy and manifold world. Christic kenosis empties the self while birthing the self-made new and as such conveys a vivid agency. Christic kenosis resists violence with the refreshing force of its generosity. And Christic kenosis flows as part of the ongoing incarnation of holiness in our world, running on a slant as body of Christ, given away.

References

Coakley, S. (2011), "In Defense of Sacrifice: Gender, Selfhood, and the Binding of Isaac," in L. M. Alcoff and J. D. Caputo (eds.), *Feminism, Sexuality, and the Return of Religion*, 17–38, Bloomington: Indiana University Press.

Girard, R. (1987), *Things Hidden since the Foundation of the World*, trans. S. Bann and M. Metteer, Stanford: Stanford University Press.

Keller, C. (1990), "Scoop up the Water and the Moon Is in Your Hands: On Feminist Theology and Dynamic Self-Emptying," in J. B. Cobb Jr. and C. Ives (eds.), *The Emptying God*, 102–15, Maryknoll: Orbis.

Mercedes, A. (2011), *Power For: Feminism and Christ's Self-Giving*, London: Continuum T&T Clark.

Mercedes, A. (2014), "Christ as Chrism, Christ Given Away," *Dialog: A Journal of Theology* 53 (3): 233–39.

Milbank, J. (2006), *Theology and Social Theory: Beyond Secular Reason*, 2nd ed., Malden: Blackwell.

Skerrett, K. Roberts (2003), "Desire and Anathema: Mimetic Rivalry in Plenitude and Lack," *Journal of the American Academy of Religion* 71 (4): 793–809.

West, T. C. (1999), *Wounds of the Spirit: Black Women, Violence, and Resistance Ethics*, New York: New York University Press.

Williams, D. (1993), *Sisters in the Wilderness: The Challenge of Womanist God-Talk*, Maryknoll: Orbis.

8

Sacrifice and Liberation
A Reading by the Magisterium of the Catholic Church in Latin America

Francisco Canzani

Francisco Canzani, member of the general council of the Focolare Movement in Rome, situates Rene Girard's theory of sacrifice in the reports of the Magisterium of the Catholic Church in Latin America. These reports have both a theological and pragmatic obligation to address the continent's considerable socioeconomic and political problems within the lessons of Christ's sacrifice on the cross. In this sense, the Magisterium Reports, 1955 to 2007, is a case study in whether Girard's proposals work: whether his notions about the mimetic-competitive nature of humanity are explanatory in situ and whether his belief that the solution is found in the cross is helpful in addressing greed. Canzani concludes that the sacrifice of today's poor to the gods of greed and power falls easily within Girard's descriptions of mimetic competition and the sacrifice of some for the benefit of others. He also echoes Girard's later understanding of the crucifixion as a lesson not only in the evils of sacrifice-as-murder but also in the productive possibilities of self-sacrifice, giving for the sake of others, in creating a more just society. Canzani looks at how this productive application of sacrifice appears in the Magisterium reports.
—editor's note

Introduction

The Latin American subcontinent is not well known in the global North, even in the academe. While some of the more famous features of its history are familiar, the "other" Latin America—the indigenous and afro-Latino American subcultures—still remains a bit of a mystery.

In fact, in the famous meeting between René Girard and a prominent group of Latin American liberation theologians (Brazil, June 25–28, 1990), Girard made clear that while the Latin American character impressed him, the cultural background and the professors' approaches and research were unknown to him. Girard was most impressed by the emphasis given to political and social issues (Assmann 1991: 19–20) and noted that his research had many points in common with the work of liberation theologians and scholars researching liberation theology (Assmann 1991: 21).

This is not an uncommon phenomenon. In fact, it's an experience which I, too, have encountered in interactions with international scholars. Allow me, therefore, to offer a brief overview of the history and the sociopolitical context in which my reflection takes place.

Latin America, a continent waiting for better times

From the arrival of the conquerors to what is today known as Hispanic and Portuguese America, the program of the missionaries in the late fifteenth and early sixteenth centuries had two key aspects: first, the evangelization of the newly discovered peoples (Zanatta 2017: 9) and, second, the acceptance, education, and economic development of the indigenous people as full human beings. This was by no means a foregone conclusion in the debates of the era, which were bookended by Fray Ginés de Sepúlveda, who denied the humanity of indigenous peoples, and Fray Bartolomé de las Casas, who recognized it (Fernández Buey 1992: 319–28). The debate concluded with the papal bull *Sublimis Deus* (1537), in which the church accepted the humanity of the pre-Hispanic peoples (Del Popolo 2018: 26).

Ironically, from that moment on, the prohibition against enslaving the indigenous population generated the tragic phenomenon of the African slave trade, which for centuries, the Holy See failed to condemn. During the fifteenth and sixteenth centuries, its policy was attentive to missionary work toward African peoples but more attentive to colonial powers (Barbarani 2016: 28). Descendants of these African slaves formed the third ethnic group in Latin America, together with descendants of the European settlers and indigenous peoples. The various forms of miscegenation that began then continue today. This complex process, creating gradations of "colored" people, and the destruction of the advanced indigenous cultures—albeit disconcerting for Europeans—left a mark on the collective subconscious of the subcontinent. The violence of the conquest is reflected today in the continuing oppression of indigenous peoples, whose fundamental rights—for example, to property and their traditional identity—are constitutionally recognized but not applied or applied only partially (CEPAL 2014: 117–52, 19–84; Del Popolo 2018: 48–55). Many impoverished indigenous communities have no access to ownership of their historic homeland, to decent housing and education, and to accurate information about their rights (CEPAL 2014: 293–318, 258–88; Del Popolo 2018: 25). Descendants of African slaves and the poor on the whole encounter similar obstacles.

On the one hand, the subcontinent in the last decade has experienced marked economic growth. Seventy million people emerged from poverty between 2003 and 2013 (Clark 2016), and in some countries, a stabilization of democratic procedures and institutions can be observed. On the other, Latin America has the highest inequality rates in the world (CEPAL 2018: 45–50). In 2014, the wealthiest 10 percent possessed 71 percent of the region's wealth (Bárcena 2016). This situation was even more grave in 1955, when the CELAM (*Consejo Episcopal Latinoamericano*—Latin American Episcopal Council) was founded and when the First Conference of Bishops of Latin America and the Caribbean took place in Rio de Janeiro.

Brief introductory notes on the theology of liberation

In second half of the twentieth century, one of the most well-known and insightful responses to Latin America's systemic injustices was liberation theology (Gutiérrez 1975: 17).

Christians throughout the subcontinent saw in it not a purely speculative form of theology that pondered God and world through resources in classical philosophy but a theology that began with oppressed peoples. Liberation theologians analyzed the causes and consequences of the systemic, institutionalized injustice in a region with apparently Christian values.

One of the keys to reading liberation theology is its "Marxist" or "Marxian" analysis. The latter term is used to clarify that, while Marxist categories are used to analyze sociopolitical-economic realities, liberation theology does not embrace all Marxist postulates, in particular its materialism.

The basics of liberation theology hermeneutics hold that present sociopolitical and economic realities must be interpreted in light of the Gospel, which seeks the redemption of the human being not only spiritually but also in his or her material and social reality, into his or her dignity and political and economic rights. The challenge, Brazilian theologian Leonardo Boff wrote, is to grant centrality to the poor and oppressed. Only from this "other logic"—beginning from the oppressed—is it possible to break the mimetic circle of violence to which Girard referred, a circle that results from the idolatry of power and money. The neoliberal market, liberation theologians affirm, is "structurally" sacrificial, serving up the poor in an economic ritual it considers the lesser evil in view of the benefits to others (Assmann 1991: 61).

In praxis, liberation theologians took numerous paths. They formulated proposals for living the Christian experience in ecclesial communities (especially in the basic ecclesial communities, BECs). They assisted in the development of social movements (e.g., the *Sem terra*, those without land) that asserted, with mixed results, the rights of the poor and the land rights of indigenous populations in particular. In some cases, they supported forms of armed revolution along with socialist and Marxist groups.

The perspective of the Catholic Church in Rome regarding liberation theologies

Engagement with Marxist principles brought some liberation theologians into conflict with traditional Catholic theology, a conflict which some feared would provoke opposition to the Holy See and condemnation from it. The Holy See's official documents, however, do not condemn liberation theology in totum but rather only the use of Marxist analyses in the construction of theological thought.

Two passages from "Instruction on Certain Aspects of the Theology of Liberation," written by the Congregation for the Doctrine of the Faith, then headed (1984) by Cardinal Joseph Ratzinger (later Pope Benedict XVI), may be helpful in illuminating Rome's position. The "Instruction," it should be said, was not well received by liberation theologians, and in 1985, Boff was condemned to silence by the Congregation and later left the ordained ministry. The introduction to the "Instruction" states:

> Liberation is first and foremost liberation from the radical slavery of sin. Its end and its goal are the freedom of the children of God, which is the gift of grace. As a logical consequence, it calls for freedom from many different kinds of slavery in the cultural, economic, social, and political spheres, all of which derive ultimately from sin, and so often prevent people from living in a manner befitting their dignity. To discern clearly what is fundamental to this issue and

what is a by-product of it, is an indispensable condition for any theological reflection on liberation.

Faced with the urgency of certain problems, some are tempted to emphasize, unilaterally, the liberation from servitude of an earthly and temporal kind. They do so in such a way that they seem to put liberation from sin in second place and so fail to give it the primary importance it is due. Thus, their very presentation of the problems is confused and ambiguous. Others, in an effort to learn more precisely what are the causes of the slavery which they want to end, make use of different concepts without sufficient critical caution. It is difficult, and perhaps impossible, to purify these borrowed concepts of an ideological inspiration which is compatible with Christian faith and the ethical requirements which flow from it. And in the same document, chapter III, number IV,

> The aspiration for "liberation," as the term itself suggests, repeats a theme which is fundamental to the Old and New Testaments. In itself, the expression "theology of liberation" is a thoroughly valid term: it designates a theological reflection centered on the biblical theme of liberation and freedom, and on the urgency of its practical realization. The meeting, then, of the aspiration for liberation and the theologies of liberation is not one of mere chance. The significance of the encounter between the two can be understood only in light of the specific message of Revelation, authentically interpreted by the Magisterium of the Church.

In sum, the "Instruction" recognizes liberation from oppression as deeply rooted in the biblical tradition, noting that the biblical concept of liberation and the theoretical positions of liberation theology are clearly and positively linked. It is necessary, however, to interpret the biblical concept of liberation in light of the traditional teachings of the church, which are incompatible with Marxist ("alien") analyses of Latin American living conditions. The document thus questions the emphasis on liberation from poverty and political oppression while ignoring liberation from sin, the main fruit of Christ's sacrifice.

The church in Latin America

In recent decades, the response of the Latin American Catholic Church to the region's many inequalities has developed on several levels:

(1) The theological and spiritual: the church has privileged the community response to faith and the Christian theological experience lived within

a Christian community, exemplified perhaps most clearly by the Basic Ecclesial Communities of the 1960s to the 1990s, where faith was shared in the context of a parish or a social movement (though each person lived in her own house). In low income areas, the BEC experience helped residents become, together with others, aware of their socioeconomic situation and rights and to organize against injustice and discrimination, sometimes peacefully, sometimes violently. Additionally, the church pioneered the "ecclesiology of communion" (Concilio Vaticano II 1975: 35), formulated theoretically by such theologians as Henri de Lubac, Yves Congar, and Karl Rahner and officially proposed by the Second Vatican Council in *Lumen Gentium* (1964), one of the three "dogmatic constitutions" of the Council.

(2) The social: Christian communities in Latin America have become aware of the church as an "ethical community." It is not only the individual—with his or her praxis and reckoning alone with his or her conscience—who is the agent of political and economic transformation but also organized communities implementing concrete programs that break down the structures of sin. This has been the motivation for involvement in (mainly leftist) social movements and political parties (1960s and after periods of dictatorship in the 1980s and 1990s) and in organizations to aid the poor today.

(3) Cultural mediation: five general conferences, reflecting decades of theological, social, and political work by the Latin American Episcopal Council, were held in Rio di Janeiro (1955), Medellin (1968), Puebla, Mexico (1979), Santo Domingo, Dominican Republic (1992), and in Aparecida, Brazil (2007). Building on these conferences, Latin American bishops have proposed interpretative keys, based on Scripture, to read the reality of a continent that must be transformed. That is, the transition from religious experience to social transformation requires adequate cultural mediation supported by the study of language and in particular the social sciences. The reports issuing from these conferences, called the *Magisterium* of the Catholic Church in Latin America, have guided Latin American communities toward a greater commitment to social and political issues.

Starting from the preferential option for the poor, the *Magisterium* reports have promoted theoretical research, pedagogical projects, and structural transformation of injustice and inequality. Catholic universities have begun study and research programs on specifically Latin American poverty and in the light of Christian faith. Many priests and nuns have moved to marginalized neighborhoods to educate the poor. In every diocese of Latin America today, there are dozens of social programs, often run by the laity, in favor of marginalized populations. The *Magisterium* of Pope Francis is heir to this Latin American effort in praxis and research.

The *Magisterium* of the Catholic Church in Latin America: The concept of sacrifice

The Latin American *Magisterium* was much concerned to address the victims sacrificed to the god of capital, power, and political and social oppression. These reports refer to sacrifice in three semantic ranges. The first is the ongoing concern, framing all the reports, about the sacrifice of the poor to money and power. Because of this foundational issue, many liberation theologians have difficulty incorporating a positive rendering of sacrifice into their thinking about society and justice (Assmann 1991: 37, 38).

The second discussion is theological: the sacrifice of Christ on the cross for the benefit of humankind. The Latin American *Magisterium* follows traditional Christian theology as expressed by the Second Vatican Council. In *Lumen Gentium* (at number 3), the Council writes,

> The Son, therefore, came, sent by the Father. It was in Him, before the foundation of the world, that the Father chose us and predestined us to become adopted sons. . . . By His obedience He brought about redemption. The church, or, in other words, the kingdom of Christ now present in mystery, grows visibly through the power of God in the world . . . in the sacrament of the eucharistic bread, the unity of all believers who form one body in Christ is both expressed and brought about. All men are called to this union with Christ, who is the light of the world, from whom we go forth, through whom we live, and toward whom our whole life strains.

Christ's sacrifice on the cross has redeemed all human beings and restored every lost order in the world. Thanks to it, human beings and world can fulfill the plan of being a single social body, a single human family.

The third discussion of sacrifice should be seen analogically: as Christ sacrificed himself for humankind, Christians sacrifice for the poor, leaving aside selfish interests and giving their lives for those who suffer. This sacrifice is "for" others not sacrifice "to" a deity, a distinction Moshe Halbertal also makes

(Halbertal 2012). The poor become a *locus theologicus*, and in them is rooted the impulse of every Christian to what many theologians call the "gift of self." Later, I will discuss this concept in depth.

The five *Magisterium* reports do not present a systematic theory of sacrifice, and most discussions of it are implicit. Nonetheless, these three levels run through the documents, their aims and intentions.

A fruitful sacrifice?

To build on the first discussion of sacrifice in the Latin American *Magisterium* as it is concerned with the sacrifice of people by socioeconomic structures not only in archaic societies but in this "world of ours," so much of which ironically is concerned about human rights. As Girard wrote, "There is another way of sacrificing people: indifference" (Assmann 1991: 21). In light of this, is there a *fruitful* sacrifice? What would it consist of?

In Christian theology and in Girard's work, Jesus's sacrifice redeems the world. As Wolfgang Palaver succinctly writes, "The only real and nonviolent means to overcoming mimetic rivalry is found in the New Testament. . . . The New Testament shows us another way" (Palaver 2013: 219). Christ's ultimate sacrifice sowed the seeds of freedom from individual and societal evil. Now, it is up to us to cultivate these seeds until the final completion of a world without injustice.

No other sacrifice is needed. The death and resurrection of Christ is the ultimate and fruitful sacrifice. The Puebla conference writes in numbers 194–195 (III Conferencia 1979: 98), "All the suffering of Creation is assumed by the Crucified One, who offered his life as a sacrifice for everyone. . . . This is why . . . his resurrection is the sign and token . . . of the final transformation of the universe." The resurrection of Christ—and by analogy every daily sign of resurrection—says to us that the mimetic circle of violence, as Girard puts it, has been defeated and can still be defeated without new sacrifices.

The church must actualize Christ's ultimate sacrifice and the possibility for redemption in history. As *Lumen Gentium* holds (number 8), the church is called to follow Christ's route in communicating the fruits of salvation to men "in poverty and persecution" because Christ was sent "to give the good news to the poor and to set the oppressed free" (Luke 4, 18) (Concilio Vaticano II 1975: 42). The good news tells that people are redeemed spiritually and also materially on Earth because the kingdom of God not only belongs to Heaven but has already started in world. We see it every time a person is liberated from poverty, discrimination, and oppression by other persons. Because of Christ's sacrifice, Christians have the strength to be committed "To try to save what was lost" (Luke 19:10): the cosmos, a victim of human neglect, and all human beings—both the victims of their own greed and desire for power through the oppression of others and *their* victims, the poor and oppressed.

In every person who suffers, the face of Christ is mysteriously hidden: "In the poor and afflicted, it (the Church) sees the image of its poor and suffering Founder" (*Lumen Gentium* 8). Thus, the way to love the face of God is to love the face of every man or woman but principally, the face of those who most resemble Christ on the cross, the marginalized and suffering. They await redemption by the hands of Christians who will remove them, here and now, from poverty and marginalization (Concilio Vaticano II 1975: 42). That is why the church "does all it can to relieve their need and in them it strives to serve Christ" (*Lumen Gentium* 8).

As God in Christ was in solidarity with every man and woman—a solidarity brought to the extreme, absolute sacrifice—the sacrifice of some for the wealth of others is undone. But this is not accomplished in an instant. It is fulfilled in the course of history. Christianity is a religion of history, and the presence of God manifests itself in our history. God frees us from poverty (whatever name this poverty has) from "below," from within history, not from "on top" with extemporaneous intervention. This is yet another reason why we are called to follow Christ: so that we may realize this redemption from "below." It is we, ourselves, who no longer have to sacrifice others. We can instead free them from poverty and suffering using our sciences, strength, and wisdom. We can do this because we have faith that Christ has freed us, first of all, from our poverty (of whatever kind), and we must do as he did among our fellow men.

The thought and commitment of the Latin American *Magisterium*, described here, follows the conceptual line of the Vatican II Council teachings, affirming that

> in the face of Jesus Christ, crucified and risen . . . the suffering and glorious face, we can see . . . the humiliated face of many men and women of our peoples and . . . their vocation to the freedom of the children of God, to the full realization of their personal dignity and to universal fraternity. (Aparecida report, V Conferencia, number 32)

Indeed, the identification of the innocent crucified one with the innocent victims sacrificed into poverty and marginalization is a theme often repeated by Latin American *Magisterium* documents. Aparecida 420 (V Conferencia 2007) holds that "human suffering is a particular experience of the cross and resurrection of the Lord." Importantly, this identification continues from the crucifixion to resurrection. The "Message to the Peoples of Latin America" (Third General Conference, number 8.2) states, "Christian love goes beyond all categories and all regimes and systems because it contains the insuperable strength of the Paschal mystery, the value of the suffering of the cross and the signs of victory and resurrection."

Thus, Jesus's sacrifice is fruitful because it not only breaks the mimetic circle of violence by being the absolute sacrifice that redeems humanity, freeing us from the sin of sacrificing others but also opens to the signs of resurrection in human history. In Christian faith, the concept of resurrection has not only an eschatological meaning, where resurrection happens in the kingdom of heaven, but an earthly one. In Pope Francis's words,

> The Father desires the salvation of every man and woman, and his saving plan consists in "gathering up all things in Christ, things in heaven and things on earth" (*Ephesians* 1:10). Our mandate is to "go into all the world and proclaim the good news to the whole creation" (*Mark* 16:15). . . . Here, "the creation" refers to every aspect of human life; consequently, "the mission of proclaiming the good news of Jesus Christ has a universal destination. Its mandate of charity encompasses all dimensions of existence, all individuals, all areas of community life, and all peoples. Nothing human can be alien to it" (Pope Paul VI). True Christian hope, which seeks the eschatological kingdom, always generates history. (*Evangelii Gaudium* 181)

The first consequence of the resurrection is that Christ is alive in history in a real but mystical way, which allows the Christian belief that history can be positively transformed. I recently heard of a Syrian Christian couple that had the possibility of leaving their war-beset country for Europe. They had already bought the plane tickets. The decision meant abandoning the school where the husband was director, leaving thirty Muslim children without lessons. The couple decided to remain in Aleppo for the sake of those children. I read this as a sign of resurrection, and we can imagine others from our own lives.

Faith, hope, and love for others are the first and clear signs of resurrection in history. That is why Pope Francis affirms, "An authentic faith—which is never comfortable or completely personal—always involves a deep desire to change the world, to transmit values, to leave this earth somehow better than how we found it. . . . The earth is our common home and all of us are brothers and sisters" (*Evangelii Gaudium* 183). Bringing love to its extreme—following the sacrificed and resurrected Christ—for the sake of the poor and abused is "the fundamental law of human perfection, and therefore of the transformation of the world . . . it is also the dynamism which ought to motivate Christians to realize justice in the world, having truth as a foundation and liberty as their sign" (II Conferencia Medellin 1968: 2).

Violence remains but can be defeated as the fruitful sacrifice and resurrection continues in history with its signs of truth, liberty, love, hope, and care for the other. The alternative is death and its signs: the extermination of innocent people through poverty, marginalization, war, and greed: the human sacrifice.

The mythical and the biblical

In my work on these texts from the Latin American church, I have found many elements that parallel Girard's anti-sacrificial reading of the Gospel. Girard, comparing Christianity with archaic religions, writes, "What mimetic theory shows is that the singularity of Christianity is literally demonstrable, but on a paradoxical basis: the admission of all the resemblances so well observed" (Girard 2011: P.O.C. 443). That is, Girard recognizes the resemblances between the sacrifice of Christ and the archaic, scapegoating sacrifice prodded by mimetic competition. He adds, "It is mimeticism that makes Jesus what he quite evidently becomes at that moment, a scapegoat in the precise sense I have given this expression" (Girard 2011: P.O.C. 458).

Yet while the resemblance between the Gospels and archaic sacrifice "appears inevitable," Girard writes,

> in reality it is not; it is even completely false. We are forced to the opposite conclusion, and for a very simple reason: the [archaic] scapegoat cannot appear as scapegoat, as it does in the Gospels, without losing all credibility. . . . To have a scapegoat is not to know that one has one. As soon as the scapegoat is revealed and named us such, it loses its power. (Girard 2011: P.O.C. 474–75)

This is, "The true difference between the mythical and the biblical. The mythical remains to the end the dupe of scapegoat phenomena. The biblical exposes the lie by revealing the innocence of the victims" (Girard 2011: P.O.C. 496).

Liberation theology and the Latin American *Magisterium* assent to Girard in denouncing the abuse of innocent victims. They accord with Girard also in identifying the victimizers in an economic and political system that favors a mimetic circle in which the rich become increasingly rich and the educated become increasingly cultured. The rich want more in imitation of the richest. The powerful do the same. This understanding of victim and victimizer flows from the commitment of Christians and all persons of good will to leave and dismantle mimetic violence through resurrection—not only from a theological perspective but as a vision for humanity. The resurrection opens the possibility for the Christian community and for every human being to transform the circle of violence into a circle of compassion, sense, dignity, and social and political development.

One last point: Self-sacrifice or gift of self?

The report from the Puebla conference makes a very deep and difficult-to-process appeal (III Conferencia 1979: 119) which requires spiritual and cultural maturity: "We must free ourselves from suffering through suffering, that is taking the Cross upon ourselves to transform it into a source of Paschal life" (Puebla 278).

This appeal relies on a distinction between self-sacrifice and what liberation theologians and classical theology call the "gift of self." We must, Franz Hinkelammert writes, "clearly distinguish between self-sacrifice and gift of self. The gift of self contains a perspective of dissolution and overcoming of sacrificial logic. The self-sacrifice homologues sacrificialism and does not consist in dissolving it" (Assmann 1991: 18). Self-sacrifice alludes to putting ourselves in the position of the scapegoat voluntarily and allowing others to commit violence against us. But for Christians, no sacrifice after Jesus's is needed, including self-sacrifice.

The gift of self implies the sense of living for others. Father Carlos Mugica (1930–74), an Argentinian priest murdered by the military dictatorship, said in a prayer he wrote: "*Quiero morir por ellos: Señor, ayudame a vivir para ellos*" (I want *to die* for them—the poor: Lord help me *to live* for them). The choice is between death, useless suffering, and life, productive suffering. "Life" entails "productive suffering" because misery cannot be transformed from the "outside" of events, with distance or indifference. Only by descending into the abyss of suffering, sharing the life of the rejected—the gift of self—can we hope for a truly redemptive liberation from injustice and death.

A friend of mine, Fr. Vilson Groh, a Brazilian priest who has lived for years among the "favela" (slum) poor, sharing everything with them, embodies this sort of gift of self. In a 2012 lecture in Buenos Aires, he said,

> Jesus's cry of abandonment ("My God, my God, why have you forsaken me")—according to the Aparecida Document the most paradoxical moment of the Paschal mystery—is not a mystical idea. It is not a difficult or lost concept.

We see Jesus Forsaken every day. He is real, concrete; he is the poor, the excluded. His cry is . . . the loss of meaning in life. Jesus forsaken, giving himself for humankind, is the link between the center and the periphery. That cry is a daily challenge to which I open myself to build the joy of the Resurrection.

In a similar vein, the Aparecida Document holds (V Conferencia 2007), "We are asked to devote time to the poor, provide them kind attention, listen to them with interest, stand by them in the most difficult moments, choose to spend hours, weeks, or years with them and strive to transform their situation from within their midst."

I am personally convinced that the "gift of self" in love is destined to break the mimetic circle of violence and contribute substantially to the development of social, cultural, political, and economic dignity.

References

II Conferencia General del Episcopado Latinoamericano (1968), *Documentos finales de Medellín*, Buenos Aires: Ediciones Paulinas.
III Conferencia General del Episcopado Latinoamericano (1979), *Puebla, Conclusiones Finales*, Montevideo: Ediciones Paulinas.
V Conferencia General del Episcopado Latinoamericano y del Caribe, 5ta. Edición (2007), *Documento conclusivo Aparecida*. Bogotá: CELAM, San Pablo, Paulinas.
Assmann, H., ed. (1991), *René Giard com teólogos da libertacao. Um diálogo sobre ídolos e sacrificios*, Petropolis: Vozes.
Barbarani, F. (2016), "La Chiesa, la schiavitù e la tratta di neri," in *Itinerari di Ricerca Storica XXX numero 1 (nueva serie)*: 11–40. Lecce: Università del Salento. Dipartimento di Storia, Società e Studi sull'Uomo.
Bárcena, A. (January 25, 2016), "Executive secretary of the Economic Commission for Latin America and the Caribbean (CEPAL)," in *América Latina y el Caribe, la región más desigual del mundo. ¿Cómo solucionarlo?*. www.cepal.org
Cepal (2018), *Panorama Social de América Latina 2017*, Santiago de Chile: Cepal.
Cepal-Celade (2014), *Los pueblos indígenas en América Latina*, Santiago de Chile: Editorial de la Cepal.
Clark, H. (November 1, 2016), Administrator of the Program of United Nations for Development (PNUD), VIII Foro Ministerial de Desarrollo Social y I Conferencia de Desarrollo Social de América Latina y del Caribe, República Dominicana, www.pnud.org
Concilio Vaticano II (November 1975), *Documentos*. 30th ed., Madrid: Biblioteca de Autores Cristianos de la La Editorial Católica.

Congregation for the Doctrine of the Faith (1984), *Instruction on Certain Aspects on the "Theology of Liberation,"* Vatican City, www.vatican.va

Del Popolo, F. (2018), *Los pueblos indígenas en América Latina (Abya Yala). Desafíos para la igualdad en la diversidad*, Santiago de Chile: Editorial de la Cepal.

Fernández Buey, F. (1992) "La controversia entre Ginés de Sepúlveda y Bartolomé de las Casas," in *Boletín americanista N° 42–43*: 301–40, Barcelona: Revistes Científiques de la Universitat de Barcelona.

Girard, R. (2011), *Sacrifice: Breakthroughs in Mimetic Theory*, trans. M. Pattillo and D. Dawson, East Lansing: Michigan State University Press, Kindle Edition.

Gutiérrez, G. (1975), *Teología de la Liberación. Perspectivas.* 7th ed., Salamanca: Ediciones Sígueme.

Halbertal, M. (2012), *On Sacrifice*, Princeton: Princeton University Press.

Palaver, W. (2013), *Rene Girard's Mimetic Theory*, trans. G. Borrud, East Lansing: Michigan State University Press.

Pope Francis (2013), *Evangelii Gaudium*, Pasay City: Paulines Philippines.

Zanatta, L. (2017), *Storia dell'America Latina Contemporanea*, Urbino: Editori Laterza.

Part Two

Is the "Problem" of Sacrifice a Problem of Conceptualizing Masculinity?

9

Between Victim and Perpetrator
Constructions of Heroic Masculinity and the Religion of Death

Ulrike Brunotte

Underlying Rene Girard's theory of sacrifice is the principle of pars pro toto, part for the whole. In archaic sacrifice, the scapegoated victim represents the larger society and is sacrificed for its sake. In the crucifixion, though the narrative is told from the victim's perspective as a cry against violence, Jesus is nonetheless given—sacrificed—for all humanity, pars pro toto. In a case study of the "heroic male" in Weimar and Nazi Germany, Ulrike Brunotte investigates the transformation of "pars" pro toto into a "toto" willingness to self-immolation. The resulting nationwide death cult is a perverse Nazi elaboration of Girard's archaic, where violence itself is sacralized. The murder of others—the victims scapegoated for societal and geopolitical problems—is both permitted and encouraged to benefit the state. One's own death in the process of such murder is the highest of life's achievements. In her close reading of the Langemar(c)k-myth, the story of school-boy soldiers who ostensibly went willingly to their deaths on the battlefields of the First World War, Brunotte reconstructs the Weimar/Nazi transformation of these young soldiers into self-immolating heroes and "living" brothers of the next generation, to sing and march with the young and so to inspire them to join the eternal "undead" brotherhood of those willing to murder and die in the next war. Brunotte then explores the extension of this sacrificial death cult from Weimar's male youth clubs to all of German society in the Nazi period.

—editor's note

Ambiguity of the hero

In the last two decades, religiously motivated terrorism has returned the ambivalent figure of the hero to the public stage. In 2007, against the background of terrorist attacks and the reappearance of the martyr figure in cultural discourse, Herfried Münkler defined the Western world as "post-heroic societies" (2007: 741) in distinction from "heroic" ones, in which religion and the idea of the sacrifice have been essential:

> Since the idea of sacrifice where one person offers him- or herself up to save the totality is hard to imagine without it referencing religion, heroic societies usually have a religious core. The political religions in the sense of Eric Voegelin, i.e., ideologies which weld together societies as well as communities and furnish them with a symbolism transforming mere death in battle into a heroic sacrifice, can also be attributed to this religious core. (2007: 742)

Today, we observe two trends in the West: first, the return of the hero and martyr figure to the religious and political stages and second, a growing academic and popular fascination with heroism and its ambivalent violence. Despite Münkler's diagnosis that we live in a post-heroic society, the hero and the "aesthetic of heroism" retain their appeal (Merkur Special Volume on Heroes 2009; Immer and van Marwyck 2013; Brunotte 2015). Importantly, constructions of violence and the hero rely on and inform our concepts of masculinity. When violent actors are stylized as religious martyrs, masculinity undergoes a rhetorical sacralization (Kippenberg 2011; Kraß and Frank 2008; Croituro 2003). When violent actors are styled as ethnically marked perpetrators or terrorists, "foreign" masculinity is demonized (Puar 2007). Both the sacralization and demonization, however, draw on the West's own heritage and history.

The Western repertoire of hero figures is seen most often in "crisis-of-masculinity narratives" intertwined with narratives of sacrifice and self-elevation (Glawion et al. 2007). The discursive masculinity crisis is part of a canon of heroic narratives (Haschemi Yekani 2011) and a central model of "hegemonic masculinity" (Connell 1995). In these heroic narratives, masculinity undergoes "superhuman-human elevation" in actions and images (Koschorke 2003: 230) and "narrative structures" (Erhard 2001: 10). They may entail passage through death itself.

While Christian models of martyrdom, self-sacrifice, and redemption remained resilient, evinced in nineteenth-century war narratives and death cults, early modernity—with its classicistic aesthetics and ethics—saw a shift to the antique Greek *pathos-formulae* of heroism (Warburg). George Mosse places the origin of the West's modern masculine ideal in the late eighteenth century. The ideal masculine character and bodily physique, defined through Greek allusions, were integrated into the modernizing state (Mosse 1998). This Enlightenment masculinity was most influentially embodied in the figure of the Trojan priest

Laocoön. The Hellenistic *Laocoön* group, excavated in Rome in 1503 and placed in Vatican museums, shows *Laocoön* in battle at the moment of being fatally bitten by snakes. Johann Joachim Winkelmann's 1775 interpretation of the sculpture, *Reflections on the Imitation of Greek Works in Painting and Sculpture*, was a best seller in European and North America, formulating a new hegemonic ideal of moral conduct and male beauty.

In Winckelmann's interpretation, Laocoön, expressing no pain, shows absolute self-mastery, which became a role model for heroic self-control. In the death struggle, the hero experiences *and* overcomes pain. He performs a stoic body-soul unity in contrast to older male ideals based on the agonized passion of Christ. In medieval illustrations, Christ's weak, vulnerable, and dying body expresses pain and passion. Christ's followers and those who saw him dying reacted with compassion and discipleship. Though Christian theology relies on overcoming death in resurrection, Jesus's *human* body expresses anguish. By contrast, Laocoön's death struggle balances the highly tense muscles of battle with a noble soul to create a modern aesthetic and ethic of masculinity. Pain and its control reveal beauty and "brings the body into view" (Richter 1992: 32).

As Laocoön became a normative ideal of modern masculinity, two parallel images/practices of an elevating death emerged along with the modern nation-state: the Christian ideal of self-sacrifice *to* pain and the classic pagan *control of* pain and affectless death. The latter became a second model for the proper soldierly death, which all men should strive to achieve through training, education, and eventually, death in war. As Hermann Schmale notes, "Through the masses of the copyists and other media, Winckelmann's ideal body-soul model spread to the German 'gymnastics movement' and to the many volunteering for Germany's armies. Finally, this abstract masculine body ideal penetrated the whole national imagination" (Schmale 2003: 171).

In later fascist movements, best represented by the works of Nazi master-sculptor Arno Breker, an obsessive masculinity cult further exaggerated the neoclassic Laocoön ideal to include specific racial requirements and the Nazi body image of the Aryan "New Man" (Diehl 2005). The liberal "image of man" (Mosse 1998) was transformed into a super- or post-human Aryan gestalt (Jünger 1932). As Paula Diehl notes, an "'anti-civilizing reinforcement' of the male image" (Diehl 2005: 68) went hand in hand with transforming a paradigm of sacrifice into a fascist "religion of death" (Jesi 1984: 15).

This chapter, building on ongoing research, focuses on a case study from Germany, the Langemark-myth, to illustrate the transformation of the classically informed, liberal pro patria mori, willingness to die for their country, into the Nazi death cult and fascist ideal of masculinity.

A regime of sacrifice: The singing "Youth of Langemarck"

During and after the First World War, the concept of youth sacrifice permeated the nightmare visions of mass killings, the mutilated bodies of returning soldiers, and the attempt to give a meaning to the lost war (Brunotte 2015; Weinrich 2009; Ulbricht 2017). The invention of the Langemarck narrative provided such meaning by transforming the senseless slaughter in Ypres and Langemarck into a narrative of mythical force. The myth began in the much-cited military bulletin by the Supreme Army Command, November 11, 1914: "West of Langemarck, youthful regiments singing 'Deutschland, Deutschland über alles' [Germany. Germany, above all else] broke forward against the front lines of enemy positions and took them" (Fischer 2007: 35–36; Dithmar 1992: 6). By contrast, the British and Belgian bulletins described the horrors of the battle and the helpless German volunteer soldiers (Unruh 1986).

After the war, conservative nationalists promulgated a counter version of the Flanders slaughter in which the sacrifice of the youth, regardless of outcome, gave meaning to the lost war. Arndt Weinrich argues that with the "growing cult of sacrifice . . . there emerged a social strategy of filling the vacuum of meaning created by the collapse in 1918 'by quenching the trauma'" (Weinrich 2009: 320). In this counter version, the idealistic trope of youths throwing themselves into battle to sacrifice for their country yielded the discursive trope of the *Männerbund* (male band; Brunotte 2004, 2015). The *Männerbund* became not only a key symbol of the Weimar "conservative revolution" but, more broadly, a central concept of Weimar's political culture.

In the male-band-discourse, a warrior-like masculine youth, inspired by the supposed camaraderie of the trenches, became a model for all men in society. The Langemarck myth, fascinating young soldiers from 1914 to 1945, took a central place (Hüppauf 1984, 1993; Ulbricht 2017). Through the images of Langemarck and *Männerbund*, the notion of sacrifice leading to redemption was written into notions of youth and initiation into masculinity. Moreover, as some casualties of the Flanders offensive were members of the German youth (*Wandervogel*) movement, the "'authenticity' of the former *Wandervogel* youth movement was reinterpreted as a willingness to die . . . a hero's death" (Macho 1996: 233). The male band was defined by its willingness to self-sacrifice.

In sum, it was a multilayered notion of sacrifice that brought together discourses of youth, initiation into masculinity, and (self-) sacrifice per se. Sabine Behrenbeck (1996) describes a circularly reasoned sacrificial masculinity where self-sacrifice as such—without pro patria, military success, or other purpose—was valorized and became a major discursive component in Weimar. After the lost war and empire, the enthusiastic performance of youth-willing-to-sacrifice represented a new Germany and gave meaning and hope especially to nationalist circles.

Within the early national socialist movement, which drew heavily on the discursive regime of sacrifice, the myth of Langemarck spilled over further into civilian life. Countless commemorating rituals, songs, poems, and speeches reinvoked the Langemarck youth. In 1938, Baldur von Schirach (Schirach quoted in Kaufmann (ed.) 1938: 23), the head of the Nazi youth movement, easily turned this discourse into an aspiration for the next generation of youth:

> In the prattle of know-it-alls, one eternal element is the legend of the senselessness of the sacrifice of Langemarck. The sense of that sacred act, which meant the flower of youth dying in storming the Langemarck heights, is not evident to those who register the value of a military operation by the sums of success and effort and then, in a schoolmasterly way, grade the General. Look at the millions of youth: That is what gives meaning to Langemarck! That we forget ourselves, that we sacrifice ourselves, that we are loyal, that is the message of the fallen to the living, that is eternity's call to this era.

This new ideology, distinguishing itself from the bourgeois cult of the soldier dying *for country*, was "founded on the heroism of the dead" (Neocleous 2005b: 91). But how was the discourse of sacrifice and victimhood transformed into a cult of the dead, and how did this cult affect the hegemonic model of heroic masculinity?

Youth and the death cult

National socialist ideology made use of a repertoire of sacrifice and heroism models, both Christian and later pagan/Germanic. In many archaic models, the sacrificial victim is elevated and sacralized through his/her death as this death is thought to save society from a wrathful god (Girard 2001: 70). In Rene Girard's view, sacrifice and victim-sacralization are the beginning of ritual and religion. Girard's idea that the sacrifice victim gains, by dint of his/her death, the aura of the sacred (Girard 1997: 37, 247) is applicable here, too. The quality of "sacredness" was granted to the war dead, and the "body of the dead became the sacred body of the dead hero" (Neocleous 2005b: 92–93).

After 1918, in nationalist circles and discourse, the dead of Langemarck were no longer merely mourned as war victims but became the shining symbol of a new, better, youthful Germany. The dead of Langemarck were reimagined and given a dynamic *afterlife* that called to their living successors. In this radical discursive shift, the sacrificial narrative of victimhood was replaced by one of resurrection, and the figure of the dead victims merged with the band of the undead heroes (Brunotte 2015: 61), as represented in Otto Höfler's mythical male band. In his 1934 "Wild Hunt," the demonic "army of ghosts or (un)dead" (Höfler 1934: 220) fights for apocalyptic revenge (Brunotte 2004: 131–36).

The common element in these discursive and ritual constructions was the invocation to the *living* to become one with the sacralized, heroic (un)dead. As early as 1924, during a memorial for the fallen of Langemarck on the Heidelstein (Rhön mountains), the conservative author Rudolf Binding—in the aptly titled speech "German Youth and the War Dead"—claimed, "These events, however, no longer form part of history where someday they—the events and the soldiers—would be paralyzed and buried, but belong to the ever creative, ever rejuvenating, ever vibrant, power of myth" (1924/1966: 60). As if to give an example of myth's power, he described the commemoration itself, mythologizing Langemarck, as partial resurrection of the dead youth and reenactment of the original battle.

In his text, the living German youth and the performatively resurrected Langemarck youth celebrated the commemoration together. They merged within the dramatic performance of a "shared journey" and joined in singing and "fighting games" (1924/1966: 62), suggesting not only the dead youth's spiritual presence but also the possibility of their physical resurrection. "For fascism, the process of commemoration is not just about memory, but *immortalizing* the dead. As one Langemarck veteran was to write in 1935, 'the graves of Langemarck glow with a new heavenly light. *The dead have returned home in us*'" (Matthießen in Dreysse 1934 in Neocleous 2005b: 44).

Hans Schwarz van Berk, Freikorps and later SS member and associate of Joseph Goebbels, completed the transformation of the myth in his 1928 speech "The Rebirth of Heroic Man." Addressing students at the University of Greifswald, Schwarz van Berk stated (1930: 5, 7) that instead of the memory of the

> shadowlike Unknown Soldier, we should mark out the death cult of the youth of Langemarck, because the dead are more real than the living. . . . We need to celebrate a day where we are still together with our dead. For where the dead are

in our very midst and full of life, there begins the fervor of faith, [*die Glut des Glaubens*] which creates myths.

On Schwarz van Berk's view, society must acknowledge myth's rejuvenating power to silence history's catastrophes. The key problem of Weimar and all Western civilization, he claimed, was their inability to give their dead an appropriate place within society. But since "our time has become heroic" (1930: 11), society must establish a political cult around the heroic dead. In the democratic commemoration of the Unknown Soldier, Schwarz van Berk could find only "magical coldness" and the empty, uniform "nameless Man" (1930: 12). In the Langemarck cult, he found the sensory embodiment of the elite fellowship (*Bund*) of the undead. These heroes were not dead but present, "full of life." Out of the most radical existential crisis, a crisis of masculinity *and* survival, they were resurrected and could fight the enemy again. No longer, however, were they the individual fighters of Ypres but an immortal fraternity representing a *future* Germany.

In this myth of heroic undead warriors, a depersonalized post-human masculinity became a cornerstone of the new *Männerbund*. In contrast to the lifeless Unknown Soldier, the dead of Langemarck were granted both "stone-like immortality" (1930: 11) and resurrection. Speaking in the voice of mainstream Nazi ideology, Berk states, "The youth of Langemarck are like a new nobility promised us again! Their features can be sculpted" (1930: 12). Relying on resurrection imagery, he continues, "Youth too has its maturity, and if it has to die before its fulfillment, there only remains to it resurrection in the spirit of those following!" (1930: 12).

Ultimately, the death cult Berk encouraged turned into an aggressive power. The eschatological power of revenge, he claimed, turned "our lives in a transfiguration to an attack, into a threat!" (1930: 27).

The national socialist Ordensburg and the role of education

The Langemarck commemoration cult was given architectural representation, when, shortly before the end of the Weimar Republic, the Flanders war cemetery was redesigned—at the instigation of German students—as a *Totenburg*, a "fortress of the dead" whose "defiant and somber character was intended to awaken the semblance of a 'front still active'" (Pallaske and Völlmecke 1996: 22). After accession to power, the Nazi regime sought to reinforce the sacrificial, heroic spirit of this new generation—especially future state and military elites—

by inculcating these beliefs in special "Adolf Hitler" schools, other schools and universities in Germany, and in other sites in Flanders. "If only the dead are truly heroic, then [they] must be educated for death" (Neocleous 2005b: 91). That was the goal of the elite Ordensburgen Vogelsang academy [Castles of Order] of the national socialist German Workers' Party (Eifel Mountains). Today, it is the only well-preserved Nazi-training camp (Wunsch (Catalogue Vogelsang) 2016), transformed into a museum in 2016.

"The aesthetic and instructional program at Ordensburg educated German youth into an Aryan ideal of the 'New Man' linked death and killing" (Figure 9.1).

Through the Vogelsang architecture, sculptures, training rooms, and museum, one can study the ideology and idealized bodies of the Nazi-education program shaping the heroic *habitus* and the inhabitants' "education to members of the master race. The cult of heroes and the dead, the central theme in Vogelsang's iconographic program and political cult, was not just a point of reference for the national socialist concept of breeding a 'new Man,' but also for the Ordensburg's ritual practices" (Thamer 2016: 262). The Vogelsang exhibition shows that many of its first graduates were sent to eastern Europe to assist the Wehrmacht and SS (Wunsch 2016: 310–15; Schmidt in Wunsch 2016: 316–23). According to Hans Ulrich Thamer, this deployment to the violent eastern front points to "the real orientation of this training in the spirit of a national socialist worldview which, in essence, was dedicated to eradication and destruction" (Thamer 2010: 100).

Figure 9.1 Vogelsang. Gesamtansicht: VIP 010885: Archiv Vogelsang IP; Fotograf: Foto-Atelier Schmeck, Aachen.

Resurrection or immortality of the dead hero: Drawing on Christian and neoclassic tropes

After 1933, the newly established spirit of the undead or resurrected hero at times merged with and at times ran parallel to the discourse of heroic self-sacrifice. As the leading SS member Baldur von Schirach declared in 1933, "The German dead are resurrected. Together with them we march with fluttering flags into eternity" (Schirach in Kaufmann 1938: 24). "In the Nazi era," in Klaus Heinrich's words (2006: 100), "the national cult of sacrifice is increased, is internalized and totalized." Importantly, here we also find the distinction from the pars pro toto of patriotic sacrifice (some for the sake of all) and the pro patria mori tradition: the key notion of rebirth or even the immortality of the dead who demanded successors among the living, action and revenge for the lost war.

This newly found spirit of the immortal perpetrator was a central trope in Nazi-propaganda, which underscored both death and resurrection. Everywhere—in monuments, words, and notably in songs like the "Host Wessel Lied," where Germany's dead comrades were also marching alongside—one *had to* keep alive the "spirit of the front" and the "armies of the dead" (Behrenbeck 1996). The lure of the "death zone" between the fronts, sacralized by writers such as Ernst Jünger as a special liminal sphere between life and death, pervaded civilian life. As Saul Friedländer noted, "This is an attraction for death in itself as something elemental, opaque, intractable to analysis. . . . For death as revelation and communion" (1984: 42). Within the Nazi death cult, this meant the total mobilization of the living *and* the dead for the sake of the future. The catchwords were resurrection and immortality, not suffering, death and rebirth. The most famous fascist slogan was "Long live death." As Mark Neocleous writes, "There is much more at stake when fascism talks about the dead. In this sense, the idea of resurrection is a far more telling category than rebirth. For resurrection, as Mussolini comments, *has to begin with the dead*" (2005a: 32).

To be sure, religious sacrifice cults have always required a pars pro toto. The sacrificial victim always dies so the majority may live. This was central to Girard's notion of the sacrificial victim acquiring the aura of the holy because of the victim's *salvific* value to the group which the victim's sacrifice/death "saves" (Girard 1997). But the national socialist's death cult reversed this structure to become *toto pro toto*: all are under the mandate of the death-sacrifice in order to gain real life:

> Life in its entirety is placed under the dominion of death. Only those ready at any time to sacrifice their lives for the sake of death are living a genuine life; only

the violent martial death provides the transition to the mythical collective of the eternal warriors. (Hüppauf 1984: 89)

In place of pars pro toto, the Girardian principle of substitute sacrifice still operative in pro patria mori, living soldiers and indeed all citizens were understood as attaining authentic life only through the sacrificial fellowship of the front, where all enter the "sacred" sphere of death. In this sphere, no one finds peace, not even the dead, who are recruited for mobilization in the next war. In the Langemarck cult, which soon fused with the Nazi cult of martyrs, the fascination was not in death and destruction as such, but in the ubiquitous and ever renewed, returning dead.

For this, national socialism drew on and exaggerated not only neoclassic *Laocoön*-type images but also the reservoir of religious iconography, recruiting a wide range of Germany's traditions to enhance Nazi appeal. The Christian motif of resurrection was overlaid with the Germanic-coded revenant cult that we've seen in the "Wild Hunt" or the myth of the "undead ghost army" (Höfler 1934). At this point, the discursive invocation of the undead iron warrior and the cult of masculinity merge. The marble hero of classicism, which Winckelmann saw in *Laocoön's* perfect white body, was already unporous, homogeneous, and sharply contoured. In Breker's sculptures and in those at Vogelsang, the male body was further solidified and transformed into Jünger's heroic machine-like gestalt.

The common denominator among the fascist cult of martial warriors and masculinity lies in the paradoxical image of a moving army of the dead. This *Männerbund* of the dead soldiers stands as a sculpted bulwark against the amorphousness of mass death, decaying corpses, and maimed living bodies. The *Untoten* [undead] carved in stone, wood, and cast in steel are mythically and ritually invoked for revenge, again exemplified in the "army of ghosts" or "Wild Hunt." This "*active embrace of death* is about much more than just sacrifice" (Neocleous 2005b: 101; emphasis in original) (Figure 9.2).

The cult of the undead/resurrected hero is well represented in the architecture and instructional program at Vogelsang. In the Ehrenhalle (Hall of Honor), in place of a cross in an altar room modeled on Christian church architecture stood the naked superhuman figure of an "ideal man," a "martyr" of the Nazi movement, bearing the legend the "Deutsche Mensch" (German Man) on its plinth. Willy Meller's larger-than-life wooden sculpture of a dead hero was intended not solely to recall the national socialists killed in the failed Hitler-putsch in Munich from 1923. Instead "as a model for the participants in training, the naked hero symbolized a 'New Man'" (Neuen Menschen) (Thamer 2016: 262). This ideal "New Man" symbolized the immortal dead of the Nazi movement.

Figure 9.2 Statue. VIP003257 Privatsammlung; Fotograf: Karl Frauenkron, Gemünd.

"For fascism, the cult of the fallen soldier and the memory of the dead went far beyond commemoration; rather, it became a philosophy of life. 'Death *is*,' says Heidegger; 'Long Live Death!', cry the fascist activists" (Neocleous 2005b: 100). That the Vogelsang sculpture was designed to evoke the "religion of death" was evident not solely from the sculpture's right arm raised in the Nazi salute but also by the word *Hier* (here) inscribed on the base of the wooden figure. The dead man was not really dead but resurrected and present.

References

Behrenbeck, S. (1996), *Der Kult um die toten Helden. Nationalsozialistische Mythen, Riten und Symbole, 1923 bis 1945*, Vierow b. Greifswald: SH-Verlag.

Binding, R. G. ([1924] 1966), "Deutsche Jugend vor den Toten des Krieges. Rede gehalten bei der Enthüllung des Ehrendenkmals für die Gefallenen von Langemarck auf dem Heidelstein in der Rhön," in Weyer A. (ed.), *Reden an die deutsche Jugend im zwanzigsten Jahrhundert*, 59–65, Wuppertal/Bremen: Jugenddienst-Verlag.

Bohrer, K. H., and K. Scheel, eds. (2009), "Special Issue Heldengedenken. Über das heroische Phantasma," *Merkur* 63: 9/10.

Brunotte, U. (2004), *Zwischen Eros und Krieg. Männerbund und Ritual in der Moderne*, Berlin: Wagenbach.

Brunotte, U. (2015), *Helden des Todes. Studien zur Religion, Ästhetik und Politik moderner Männlichkeit*, Würzburg: Ergon.

Connell, R. W. (1995), *Masculinities*, Cambridge: University California Press.

Croitoru, J. (2003), *Der Märtyrer als Waffe. Die historischen Wurzeln des Selbstmordattentates*, Munich/Vienna: Carl Hanser Verlag.

Diehl, P. (2005), *Macht-Mythos-Utopie. Die Körperbilder der SS-Männer*, Oldenbourg/Berlin: Akademie Verlag in de Gruyter.

Dithmar, R., ed. (1992), *Der Langemarck-Mythos in Dichtung und Unterricht*, Berlin: Hermann Luchterhand Verlag.

Erhard, W. (2001), *Familienmänner. Über den literarischen Ursprung moderner Männlichkeit*, München: Fink.

Fischer, J. (2007), *Disciplining Germany: Youth, Reeducation and Reconstruction after the Second Word War*, Detroit: Wayne State University Press.

Friedländer, S. (1984), *Reflections of Nazism: An Essay on Kitsch and Death* (translated from the French by Thomas Weyr), Bloomington: Indiana University Press.

Girard, R. (1997), *Violence and the Sacred*, Baltimore: Johns Hopkins University Press.

Girard, R. (2001), *I See Satan Fall Like Lightning*, trans. J. G. Williams, Maryknoll: Orbis Books.

Glawion S., E. Haschemi Yekani, and J. Husmann-Kastein (2007), *Erlöser. Figurationen männlicher Hegemonie*, Bielefeld: transcript.

Haschemi Yekani, E. (2011), *The Privilege of Crisis. Narratives of Masculinity in Colonial and Postcolonial Literature, Photography, and Film*, Frankfurt a.M.: Campus Verlag.

Höfler, O. (1934), *Kultische Geheimbünde der Germanen*, Frankfurt/M: Diesterweg.

Hüppauf, B. (1984), "'Der Tod ist verschlungen in den Sieg.' Todesbilder aus dem Ersten Weltkrieg und der Nachkriegszeit," in B. Hüppauf (ed.), *Ansichten vom Krieg. Vergleichende Studien zum Ersten Weltkrieg in Literatur und Gesellschaft*, 31–89, Königstein i. Ts: Forum Academicum.

Hüppauf, B. (1993), "Schlachtenmythen und die Konstruktion des 'Neuen Menschen,'" in G. Hirschfeld G. Krumeich, and I. Renz (eds.), *Keiner fühlt sich hier mehr als Mensch . . . Erlebnis und Wirkung des Ersten Weltkriegs*, 43–84, Essen: Klartext Verlag.

Immer, N., and M. van Marwyck, eds. (2013) *Ästhetischer Heroismus. Konzeptionen und figurative Paradigmen des Helden*, Bielefeld: transcript.

Jesi, F. (1984), *Kultur von rechts*, Frankfurt/M: Stroemfeld.

Jünger, E. (1932/2013), *Der Arbeiter. Herrschaft und Gestalt*, Stuttgart: Klett-Cotta.

Kaufmann, G. (1938), *Langemarck. Das Opfer der Jugend an allen Fronten, hg. in Verbindung mit dem Arbeitsausschuss Langemarck beim Jugendführer des Deutschen Reiches*, Stuttgart: Belser.

Kippenberg, H. (2011), *Violence as Worship: Religious Wars in an Age of Globalisation*, Stanford: Stanford University Press.

Koschorke, A. (2003), "Theologische Maskerade. Figurationen der Heiligen Familie in 'Star Wars,'" in C. Benthien and I. Stephan (eds.), *Männlichkeit als Maskerade*.

Kulturelle Inszenierungen vom Mittelalter bis zur Gegenwart, 316–35, Cologne/Weimar/Vienna: Böhlau Verlag.

Kraß, A., and T. Frank, eds. (2008), *Tinte und Blut. Politik, Erotik und Poetik des Martyriums*, Frankfurt a.M: Fischer.

Macho, T. (1996), "Jugend und Gewalt. Zur Entzauberung einer modernen Wahrnehmung," in M. Wimmer, C. Wulf, and B. Dieckmann (eds.), *Das zivilisierte Tier. Zur historischen Anthropologie der Gewalt*, 221–44, Frankfurt a.M.: Fischer Taschenbuch.

Matthießen, W. (1934). "Einleitung," in W. Dreysse (ed.), *Langemarck 1914. Der Heldische Opfergang der Deutschen Jugend*, 2–14, Minden/Berlin/Leipzig: Köhler.

Mosse, G. L. (1998), *The Image of Man*, New York/Oxford: Oxford University Press.

Münkler, H. (2007), "Heroische und Postheroische Gesellschaften," *Merkur* 61: 742–52.

Neocleous, M. (2005a), "Long Live Death! Fascism, Resurrection, Immortality," *Journal of Political Ideologies* 10 (1): 31–49.

Neocleous, M. (2005b), *The Monstrous and the Dead. Burke, Marx, Fascism*, Cardiff: University of Wales Press.

Pallaske, C., and D. Völlmecke (1996) "'Deutschland muß leben, und wenn wir sterben müssen!' Gedenken und Totenkult nach dem Ersten Weltkrieg: Der Mythos von Langemarck," *Geschichte lernen* 49: 20–25.

Puar, J. (2007), *Terrorist Assemblages. Homonationalism in Queer Times*, Durham: Duke University Press.

Rack, J., and K. Heinrich (2006), "Wir und der Tod. Ursprungskult oder Bündnisdenken – über die Mitbestimmung der Toten," *Lettre international* 72: 100–03.

Richter, S. (1992), *Laocoon's Body and the Aesthetics of Pain: Winckelmann, Lessing, Herder. Moritz, Goethe*, Detroit: Wayne State University Press.

von Schirach, B. (1938), "Hitlerjugend – Träger des Erbes von Langemarck," in G. Kaufmann (ed.), *Langemarck. Das Opfer der Jugend an allen Fronten, hg. in Verbindung mit dem Arbeitsausschuss Langemarck beim Jugendführer des Deutschen Reiches*, 21–24, Stuttgart: Belser.

Schmale, W. (2003), *Geschichte der Männlichkeit in Europa (1450-2000)*, Wien/Köln/Weimar: Böhlau.

Schwarz van Berk, H. (1930), *Die Wiedergeburt des heroischen Menschen, Rede am 11. November 1928*, Berlin: Verlag des Nahen Ostens.

Thamer, H.-U. (2010), "Der 'neue Mensch' als nationalsozialistisches Erziehungsprojekt. Anspruch und Wirklichkeit in den Eliteeinrichtungen des NS-Bildungssystems," in Vogelsang ip gemeinnützige GmbH (ed.), *"Fackelträger der Nation." Elitebildung in den NS-Ordensburgen*, 95–120, Cologne/Weimar/Vienna: Böhlau.

Thamer, H.-U. (2016), "Heilsversprechen und Sendungsbewusstsein – Der 'neue Mensch' in der Ikonografie und im politischen Kult der NS-Ordensburgen," in S. Wunsch (ed.), *Bestimmung Herrenmensch. NS-Ordensburger zwischen Faszination und Verbrechen*, 274–81, Dresden: Sandstein Verlag.

Ulbricht, J. H. (2017), "Vom Weiterleben der Toten und dem Sinn des Opfers. Literarischer Jünglings- und Kriegerkult des 19. und 20. Jahrhunderts," in R. Faber and A. B. Renger (eds.), *Religion und Literatur Konvergenzen und Divergenzen*, 307–40, Würzburg: Königshausen & Neumann.

Unruh, K. (1986), *Langemarck. Legende und Wirklichkeit*, Koblenz: Bernard & Graefe.

Weinrich, A. (2009), "Kult der Jugend – Kult des Opfers: Langemarck-Mythos der Zwischenkriegszeit," *Historical Social Research* 34 (4): 319–30.

Wunsch, S., ed. (2016), *Bestimmung Herrenmensch. NS-Ordensburger zwischen Faszination und Verbrechen*, (Catalogue Vogelsang) Dresden: Sandstein Verlag.

10

The Ambiguity of Sacrifice in a Post-Heroic Nation
A Military Perspective

Rolf von Uslar

As Wolfgang Palaver holds in this volume, Girard in his later works declared that he had unfairly "scapegoated" sacrifice in an effort to rid humanity of violence. To address violence, he concluded that we must learn from the crucifixion not only about the evils of sacrifice-as-murder but also about productive uses of sacrifice-of-self, of giving for the sake of others. In this chapter, Colonel Rolf von Uslar follows the late Girard in looking at sacrifice in the military context. He proposes that understanding how self-sacrifice is necessary to build a less violent world is precisely what is needed to contribute to a moral military. Even in the context of present-day Germany, which, "owing to guilt over its role in the twentieth century world wars, is likely the most post-heroic country on this planet," von Uslar argues not for an abstention from violence as this leaves the world to those willing to perpetrate it. Rather, recognizing that we must address the violence around us, von Uslar argues that certain forms of self-sacrifice are likely to yield humane conduct even across enemy lines. He posits a military sacrifice as katéchon, *"the one who restrains."*

—editor's note

Introduction

Carl von Clausewitz, the famous theorist of war, described war as "a true chameleon that slightly adapts its characteristics" (Clausewitz 1984: 89). Although armed conflict constantly changes its face, according to Clausewitz one thing remains always the same: "What is most needed . . . is courage and self-sacrifice" (Clausewitz 1984: 140). However, this perception was not limited to the military itself; civilians used to share this view. One could argue that Clausewitz's "holy trinity" (Clausewitz 1984: 89)—society ("people"), the military ("commander"), and the government—used to be in perfect harmony with the idea of (self-)sacrifice as a basis for military service. Today, it seems to be a different story; at least from a German viewpoint, the former common perception of sacrifice has been lost. This raises pivotal questions about the use of military power in principle and about the civil-military relationship. In the following I would like to discuss the following theses:

(a) There is a problem in the unwillingness of post-heroic societies like Germany, owing to guilt over its role in the violence of the twentieth century, to develop a modern notion of sacrifice.
(b) There used to be and there still is a need for self-sacrifice in order to successfully accomplish current (and future) military operations.
(c) There is an urgent necessity for a concept of sacrifice in the military itself because it helps to strengthen comradeship, leadership, and humanity in war.
(d) Sacrifice can help to understand military service as "katechonian," which might bridge the civil-military gap in post-heroic societies like Germany.

Sacrifice and the civil-military relationship in Germany

Thesis: There is a problem in the unwillingness of post-heroic societies like Germany, owing to guilt over its role in the violence of the twentieth century, to develop a modern notion of sacrifice.

Similar to other languages (like Hebrew, Spanish, and Arabic), the German term for sacrifice, *Opfer*, has more than one meaning (Halbertal 2012: 2). *Opfer* denotes not only a gift to somebody or the giving up of something for a higher cause but also victim. Since the Second World War, "victim" rather than "sacrifice" has been at the center of German public discourse (Münkler and Fischer 2000; Münkler 2008; Schieder 2016).

Even the military casualties in the International Security Assistance Force (ISAF) mission in Afghanistan were considered "victimized" as many Germans think these war casualties were "accidents" that could have been avoided by better concepts of "safety at work" (Kremp 2005). For many civilians in Germany, it is unthinkable that the profession of soldiering should *today* imply the readiness for self-sacrifice (Wagner 2016). This perception did not come out of the blue. In the first half of the twentieth century, Germany had the second highest number of military casualties, after Russia, of all countries involved in the world wars. In the First World War, two million German soldiers were killed in action (KIA) or died of wounds (DOW) compared with 885,138 in Britain and 116,516 in the United States (Overmans 2004a; Department of Defense 2018). In the Second World War, at least 5.3 Million German soldiers were KIA and DOW (Overmans 2004b) compared to 270,825 in Britain and 405,399 in the United States (Department of Defense 2018). The nearly complete annihilation of the male cohort born in 1922 reflects those figures (Müller 2014). Beyond the pure numbers it was, at least in the Second World War, more than obvious that these sacrifices had been made for a wretched cause. With every day that the German divisions continued to fight bravely against the Allied forces, the death camps were able to continue to systematically kill thousands of innocent civilians. The willingness for (self-) sacrifices of German soldiers had been misused for a tyranny that was responsible for one of the most brutal crimes in the history of mankind.

So, it has been argued that a skeptical attitude toward sacrifice was a moral and intellectual "lesson learned" from the twentieth century, where millions were sacrificed "on the altar of the Fatherland." As a consequence, the willingness to sacrifice and acceptance of casualties have clearly been on a downward trend since Second World War in many so-called post-heroic societies (Luttwak 1995). And Germany, owing to guilt over its role in the twentieth-century world wars, is likely the most post-heroic country on this planet (Münkler 2008; Klonovsky 2011; Kümmel 2009). Much of the United States, by contrast, seems to be "still pre-post-heroic" (Carruthers 2014: 180; Rotte and Schwarz 2010).

As a staff officer moving through several echelons of command, I experienced the tensions between the German societal post-heroic and the military heroic perspectives. As a commanding officer, I told my soldiers that their courage— including their willingness to (self-) sacrifice—is meaningful and necessary. Within the Ministry of Defense (MOD), however, I had to euphemistically rephrase my sentences so as not to unsettle the (civilian) political representatives of post-heroic society. Official statements of the MOD must avoid any appearance of a positive connotation of sacrifice. "Think of the effects on the motivation of the soldiers," I might say. "If their sacrifice is only seen as an unintended, negligible, trivial accident, does it make sense to be a soldier?"

Münkler argues that one cannot wage war without a political explanation for war casualties. If there is "nothing to kill or to die for" (Münkler and Fischer 2000), one cannot use military force at all. However, doing nothing in the world's conflict zones is also a decisive political action one has to account for because there will always be reasons that *others* kill, and the absence of intervention allows this killing to occur. If there is no reason to die, no one will be willing to stop the violence. This consigns the unwilling-to-die to observer status of genocides like those in Rwanda or Bosnia.

In 2009, the German government built a new memorial to German servicewomen and servicemen who lost their lives in accidents and combat, "Ehrenmal der Bundeswehr" [Memorial of Honor of the German Military Forces]. "Honor as a motive for making sacrifices" (Olsthoorn 2005) is widely accepted in the German military (Wagner 2016) but again, not by the majority of the civil society. So, the discussions around the new "Ehrenmal" reflect the significant gap between German civilians and the military in attitudes about *Opfer*—sacrifice or victim (Naumann 2007). Strategies to bridge this gap are not at hand (Werber 2009). Münkler describes the present political task to explain the need for sacrifices in a wealthy society geared toward self-fulfillment and comfort, what Charles Taylor in *A Secular Age* called "the immanent frame" (2007: 551), where one sees one's circumstances immanently, absent an overarching picture of the self amid world, transcendent, and purposes or aims larger than one's personal well-being. Or what Münkler calls the *Spaßgesellschaft*, the fun society (Münkler and Fischer 2000).

The politico-strategic effect of sacrifice within conflict

Thesis: There used to be and there still is a need for (self-) sacrifice in order to successfully accomplish current (and future) military operations.

Many believe that the military is about killing other people. I, on the contrary, follow van Creveld, who holds that serving in the military means more to be prepared and to be willing to risk one's life than to endanger other lives (van Creveld 1991).

One could argue that military technology provides tools that have kinetic effects over large distances without any risk to one's own safety or the safety of one's own forces. Drones, for example, are such weapons (Münkler 2013). However, can one win a war with only drones? We have relearned the lesson that it takes "boots on the ground" to win the better peace, as Clausewitz carefully worded it. So, with the use of military force, soldiers have to risk their lives (as well as the lives of their subordinates)—and must be willing to sacrifice. Being the hierarchical organizations that the armed forces are, sacrifice in a military context always includes self-sacrifice of the individual and the leader's responsibility to sacrifice his servicemen to achieve an objective. Experienced commanders have often described that the latter is far more difficult and stressful than the first (Seeckt 1929). Using the three historical cases below, I would like to further discuss the political and strategic needs for sacrifice in the military.

First, Leonidas and his 300 warriors in the Battle of Thermopylae (480 BCE) exemplify a military operation where soldiers sacrificed themselves for a critical objective. In this case, the brave but unwinnable battle was fought to gain time. This allowed the Greek city-states to successfully regroup and organize their defense against a superior Persian enemy. So, the sacrifice of Leonidas and his 300 warriors likely made the difference in ensuring the survival and freedom of thousands of inhabitants and possibly of Greek culture as a whole (Strauss 2005).

Second, why did the British Army win the fight against the Irish Republican Army (IRA) in Northern Ireland? The two political positions were completely incompatible with each other: the British Government insisted on keeping the *status idem* whereas the IRA wanted a (re)union of Northern Ireland with the Republic of Ireland. In the escalating conflict, the IRA used violence as a guerilla tactic against British institutions, especially the UK armed forces. The British Army thus sustained more casualties than the IRA. Yet paradoxically, that could be why they won the conflict. On one analysis, the local population in Northern Ireland regarded these casualties by the British Army as (self-) sacrifices and therefore as a significant commitment to their cause. In contrast, the IRA did not demonstrate a similar commitment and so underline strongly enough their "claim to power" by a willingness to sustain sacrifices (van Creveld 2008a: 235, b).

Third, in the first years of the ISAF's commitment in Afghanistan, the participating German military held to a strategy focused on avoiding casualties (Noetzel 2010)—the so-called zero losses policy. Consequently, the members of the Afghan National Security Forces (ANSF) did not rely on their German comrades in the same way as they relied on the US or UK forces (King 2014: 278–81). It became obvious that the Afghans' acceptance of foreign soldiers was significantly correlated with the foreigners' willingness to take risks. Afghan attitudes toward the German military changed fundamentally when, in 2008, Germany took over the so-called Quick Reaction Force (QRF), a battalion-sized fighting unit in the north of the country. In this capacity, the German military no longer avoided battles but attacked the Taliban in their strongholds. The QRF suffered casualties, and its reputation in the ISAF community and among the ANSF improved significantly. In turn, this had the effect of substantially improving the partnering strategy between ANSF and ISAF because mutual respect was a prerequisite for such an intense cooperation and a successful strategy. To put it in a nutshell, from a military viewpoint, a "zero losses policy," a strategy without the willingness to make sacrifices, is the way to defeat (Luttwak 1999).

Ethicists of war have argued that fomenting notions of sacrifice (to a cause, for a leader) fuels wars by giving them "both psychological and wrong moral justification" (Halbertal 2012: 89; Hedges 2003). I am not convinced that the "sacrifice fuels war" thesis is empirically correct. Research on the First World War shows that the high numbers of soldier deaths contributed heavily to "war weariness" in Germany and France (Keegan 1978: 322) and likely contributed to persuading Germany to surrender. That is, a negative correlation may in some cases emerge between the number of sacrifices and the willingness to pursue a war. This is *not* to argue for provoking a high soldier death toll as a moral position but rather to understand the complex, even dismaying empirical outcomes of the war situation.

The effect of sacrifice on the forces

Thesis: There is an urgent necessity for a concept of (self-) sacrifice within the military itself because it helps to strengthen comradeship, leadership, and humanity in war.

A second popular misunderstanding of military service is that soldiers are willing to die primarily for a political idea. In fact, they are willing to risk their lives primarily for their comrades (and for their military leaders). Sebastian Junger spent twelve months, in 2007 and 2008, with a US company of 173rd Airborne Brigade in Kunar province, Afghanistan. Kunar used to be the region with the most intense fighting in the whole Afghanistan theater. In his book *War* (Junger 2010), Junger describes the relationships among the servicemen within the unit. The obvious and frequently evinced willingness to risk their lives for each other formed a "band of brothers." The last section of Junger's book has the title "Love." Or to say it in the words of the Bible: "Greater love has no one than this, that one lay down his life for his friends" (John 15:13). A similar phenomenon occurs between troops and their leaders. Research on the Vietnam War clearly highlights the difficulties encountered if leaders do not share risks with their subordinates: "To a great extent then, military cohesion can be seen as a function of the quality of the officer corps, its skill, dedication and its readiness to sacrifice"

(Gabriel and Savage 1978: 36). So, the willingness to sacrifice is indispensable for the cohesion and morale of any armed forces (Shils and Janowitz 1975; von Uslar and Walther 2012).

Research on the correlation between combat motivation and coping styles under duress has shown that the collective and individual willingness to engage in the risks of combat, to self-sacrifice for the sake of one's comrades, is highly correlated with more successful strategies in coping with stress (Ben-Shalom and Benbenisty 2016). This suggests that a risk-averse mind-set might be inadequate preparation for avoiding Post-Traumatic Stress Disorders (PTSD). In order to provide the maximum preparation and protection for those being sent to the most dangerous places in the world, the German armed forces might be well advised to rethink the psychological training given to soldiers since at present, the Bundeswehr's corporate philosophy, the so-called *Innere Führung* (Inner Leadership), understands a soldier's mind-set as being as close as possible to the civilian citizen: *Staatsbürger in Uniform* (citizen in uniform). And the German civilian approach is post-heroic and risk-averse.

Paradoxically, even the relationship to the enemy depends on the soldier's understanding of sacrifice. The Law of Armed Conflict is based on the distinction between soldiers and civilians. Soldiers, unlike civilians, are combatants and therefore legitimate targets for the enemy. It is this "belligerent privilege" (Halbertal 2012: 80) that allows them to use lethal force. So, the *legal* and *moral* right to kill is based on the willingness to *self*-sacrifice. This sets soldiers facing one another as moral equals not because both are willing to kill but because both are willing to die (Walzer 1991). Mader (2002) suggests that this idea reaches back to the self-concept of the medieval chivalry.

A remarkable example of self-sacrifice from the Second World War might help to understand this perception of the enemy as a brother serving contingently on the "other side of the hill." In 1994, the 22nd US Infantry Society—a unit that fought in the Second World War—mounted a memorial in the Huertgen Forest next to the German city of Aachen. The Battle of Huertgen is better known in the United States than in the German military. During the four-month battle, the United States suffered 33,000 casualties, the Germans 28,000. It is the longest, bloodiest single battle the US troops have ever fought (Astor 2000). The Huertgen Forest witnessed not only fierce fighting but also acts of bravery, sacrifice, and humanity. In November 1944, a three-day ceasefire on the Kall Trail enabled medical personnel on both sides to take care of the wounded, recognized by each side as moral actors, odd "brothers" of a sort, deserving of respect—and even aid. This saved the lives of hundreds and is documented both by a painting entitled *A Time for Healing* by Robert M. Nisley and by a memorial sculpture at the Kall Bridge. The 22nd US Infantry Division memorial preserves this moment for history, with the inscription in both English and German:

> In Memory of Lieutenant Friedrich Lengfeld, 2nd CO, Fues BN, 275th Inf Div
> Here in Huertgen Forest on November 12, 1944, Lt. Lengfeld, a German officer, gave his life while trying to save the life of an American soldier lying severely wounded in the Wilde Sau minefield and appealing for medical aid.
> Placed at this Site on October 7, 1994.

The most important sentence, however, can be found at the top of the memorial stone, rephrasing John 15, 13 (Figure 10.1):

> No man hath greater love than he who layeth down his life for his enemy.

However, if this concept of moral equality fails, for instance due to ideological radicalism, such humanity and restrictions on violence too will fail (Uhle-Wettler 2001: 87–111). Because of the Nazi ideology of the Second World War, German Army Headquarters ordered that Red Army soldiers not be seen as moral equals:

> *Wir müssen vom Standpunkt des soldatischen Kameradentums abrücken. Der Kommunist ist vorher kein Kamerad und nachher kein Kamerad. Es handelt sich um einen Vernichtungskampf.* (Uhle-Wettler 2001: 99)
> (We must abandon the standpoint of soldierly comradeship. The communist is not a comrade before [the fight], and not a comrade afterwards. This is a war of annihilation.)

As a consequence, German forces on the eastern front, especially in the *Waffen-SS*, followed this order (Snyder 1990), and more than 2.5 million of Russian soldiers died as Prisoners of War (PoW) in German PoW camps. Unfortunately, the twentieth century is full of such examples.

Here one also sees the difference between the self-sacrifice of a "moral warrior" (Coker 2012; Cook 2004) and a suicide bomber: The moral warrior, that is, the (professionally educated) soldier of a regular armed forces, respects limits of violence because he accepts his opponent as a moral equal whereas for the suicide bomber, all targets and all ways of violence are permissible. Suicide bombers use violence to kill primarily non-soldiers; they deliberately ignore the moral concept of war as a fair duel. The suicide bomber is the archetype of a fighter in a civil war, where enmity is so vicious that fighters don't recognize

Figure 10.1 Lieutenant Friedrich Lengfeld's memorial stone. Creative Commons, Attribution-ShareAlike 4.0 International license.

those on the other side as moral equivalents. Already Wellington knew that one opens up "the gates of hell" when starting a guerilla or civil war.

Coming back to our starting point: Acceptance of the concept of (self-) sacrifice for (own and opposing) military forces is the basis for a profound understanding of the construction of the combatant, and therefore essential to accept rules in armed conflict, essential to a restrict violence, essential to keep humanity in war. So, sacrifice has been and always will be an indispensable element of a warrior's ethos (Cook 2004).

Katéchon—the new post-heroic warrior?

Thesis: Sacrifice can help to understand military service as "katechonian," which might bridge the civil-military gap in post-heroic societies like Germany.

When we put the results together, the situation is as follows:

- German society does not have a positive perception of sacrifice due to historical reasons and based on an understanding that there is "nothing to kill and to die for."
- Sacrifice, however, is indispensable for the use of any military power.
- A concept of sacrifice is essential for the military forces itself.

So, where is the way out of this dilemma—especially in societies lacking powerful narratives and visions?

Maybe here: When the German (left-wing) government decided to contribute its armed forces to the NATO mission KFOR (Kosovo Force), the legitimacy of that step was widely discussed beforehand because there was no official war resolution by the United Nations Security Council. The decisive argument—based on available intelligence on ethnic cleansing, both already done and planned in a larger scale—was "No more Auschwitz!" (Fischer 1999). Thus, the narrative that the pacifistic Green Party accepted for the participation of the German armed forces was the moral mandate to stop the ethnic cleansings.

Paul addresses this aspect (2 Thessalonians 2, 6–7), saying that the power to stop evil is the *katéchon*, "the one who restrains." An extensive discussion of Bonhoeffer (1998) and Schmitt's (1988; Grossheutschi 1996; Laska 1997) thoughts on the *katéchon* is not possible here, but I would like to highlight one aspect: the *katéchon* always implies the willingness to sacrifice. So, the question: Could the *katéchon* be a new post-heroic warrior (Bohn 2011)—an inspiration for soldiers from post-heroic societies such as Germany? Even post-heroic societies have to come to terms with the reality of violence and evil and develop an understanding of the need for sacrifice to stop it—a use of sacrifice regulated as morally as possible (as the just war literature extensively details), as a productive contribution to the world. Bohn (2011, 2013) goes a step further. He understands the *katéchon* as fighting evil with post-patriotic heroism (Frisk 2017), lacking even a political narrative and acceptance in society. This is Kant pretty upside down since his approach to sacrifice for the sake of the community was based on mutual acceptance and respect between society and soldier (Schlink 2016). Irrespective whether Bohn is right, the figure of the *katéchon* offers opportunities for a modern concept of sacrifice.

We can find *kátechonial* inspirations in the German military tradition of the twentieth century. Today's German armed forces honor the memory of General Major Henning von Tresckow (1901–44), who served in both world wars. When he understood Hitler's intentions, he organized a German military resistance against the Nazis. It was the one and only resistance powerful enough to endanger Hitler and his minions. A couple of plots to assassinate Hitler had failed; the last was in July 1944 with the so-called Operation *Walküre* (Valkyrie). Tresckow knew that the chances for a successful *coup d'etat* were low but he pushed forward because for him it was not the result but the visible attempt to stop the evil that made the difference:

> What matters now is no longer the practical purpose of the coup, but to prove to the world and for the records of history that the men of the resistance dared to take the decisive step. Compared to this objective, nothing else is of consequence. (Scheurig 1987: 210)

After the failure of Operation Valkyrie, Tresckow committed suicide in order to protect his family and his coconspirators whom he might have revealed under the expected torture by the SS. His last words to his aide-de-camp, Lieutenant von Schlabrendorff, underlined his perception of self-sacrifice and the *katéchonian* approach:

> The whole world will vilify us now, but I am still totally convinced that we did the right thing. Hitler is the archenemy not only of Germany but of the world. When, in few hours' time, I go before God to account for what I have done and left undone, I know I will be able to justify what I did in the struggle against Hitler. God promised Abraham that He would not destroy Sodom if only ten righteous men could be found in the city, and so I hope for our sake God will not destroy Germany. No one among us can complain about dying, for whoever joined our ranks put on the shirt of Nessus. A man's moral worth is established only at the point where he is ready to give his life in defense of his convictions. (Scheurig 1987: 217)

References

Astor, G. (2000), *The Bloody Forrest: Battle of Huertgen September 1944 — January 1945*, New York: Presidio Press.

Ben-Shalom, U., and Y. Benbenisty (2016), "Coping Styles and Combat Motivation During Operations: An IDF Case Study," *Armed Forces & Society* 42 (4): 655–74.

Bohn, J. (2011), "Pflichterfüllung nach dem Ende der Ideen," in J. Bohn, T. Bohrmann, and G. Küenzlen (eds.), *Die Bundeswehr heute: Berufsethische Perspektiven für eine Armee im Einsatz*, Stuttgart: Kohlhammer.

Bohn, J. (2013), "Soldatentum im Rechtsstaat," in M. Böcker and F. Springer (eds.), *Soldatentum – Auf der Suche nach Identität und Berufung der Bundeswehr heute*, 13–26, Reinbek: Lau Verlag.

Bonhoeffer, D. (1998), *Ethik*, ed. Ilse Tödt, Gütersloh: Gütersloher Verlagshaus.

Carruthers, S. L. (2014), "Casualty Aversion: Media, Society and Public Opinion," in S. Scheipers (ed.), *Heroism & the Changing Character of War: Towards Post-Heroic Warfare?* 221–36, Hampshire: Palgrave Macmillan.

von Clausewitz, C. (1976/1984), *On War*, trans. and ed. Michael Howard and Peter Paret, Princeton: Princeton University Press.

Coker, C. (2012), *The Warrior Ethos: Military Culture and the War on Terror*, Abingdon: Routledge.

Cook, M. L. (2004), *The Moral Warrior. Ethics and Service in the U.S. Military*, Albany: State University of New York Press.

van Creveld, M. (1991), *The Transformation of Warfare*, New York: Free Press.

van Creveld, M. (2008a), *The Culture of War*, New York: Presidio Press.

van Creveld, M. (2008b), *The Changing Face of War: Combat from the Marne to Iraq*, New York: Simon and Schuster.

Department of Defense (2018), *Defense Casualty Analysis System (DCAS)*. https://dcas.dmdc.osd.mil/dcas/pages/casualties.xhtml

Fischer, J. (1999), "Auszüge aus der Rede vor dem Parteitag der Grünen," *Der Spiegel*, May 13, 1999. http://www.spiegel.de/politik/deutschland/wortlaut-auszuege-aus-der-fischer-rede-a-22143.html

Frisk, K. (2017), *Post-Heroic Warfare Revisited: Meaning and Legitimation of Military Losses*. http://journals.sagepub.com/doi/pdf/10.1177/003803851668031

Gabriel, R. A., and P. L. Savage (1978), *Crisis in Command: Mismanagement in the Army*, New York: Hill and Wang.

Grossheutschi, F. (1996), *Carl Schmitt und die Lehre vom Katechon*, Berlin: Duncker & Humboldt.

Halbertal, M. (2012), *On Sacrifice*, Princeton: Princeton University Press.

Hedges, C. (2003), *War Is a Force That Gives Us Meaning*, New York: Anchor Books.

Junger, S. (2010), *War*, New York: Twelve.

Keegan, J. (1978), *Das Antlitz des Krieges. Die Schlachten von Azincourt 1415, Waterloo 1815 und an der Somme 1916*, Frankfurt/New York: Campus.

King, A. (2014), "Cohesion: Heroic and Post-Heroic Combat," in S. Scheipers (ed.), *Heroism & the Changing Character of War: Towards Post-Heroic Warfare?* 221–36, Hampshire: Palgrave Macmillan.

Klonovsky, M. (2011), *Der Held. Ein Nachruf*, München: Diederichs.

Kremp, H. (November 26, 2005), "Tod in Afghanistan: Es war kein Busunglück," *Die Welt*. https://www.welt.de/print-welt/article180694/Tod-in-Afghanistan.html

Kümmel, G. (2009), "'Gestorben wird immer'?! Oder: Postheroismus, 'Casualty Shyness' und die Deutschen," in U. Hartmann (ed.), *Jahrbuch Innere Führung 2009*, 92–108, Eschede: Miles-Verlag.

Laska, B. A. (1997), *"Katechon" und "Anarch". Carl Schmitts und Ernst Jüngers Reflexionen auf Max Stirner*, Nürnberg: LSR-Verlag.

Luttwak, E. (1995), "Towards Post-Heroic Warfare", *Foreign Affairs* 74 (3): 109–22.

Luttwak, E. (1999), *"Post-Heroic" Warfare and Its Implications*. http://www.nids.mod.go.jp/english/event/symposium/pdf/1999/sympo_e1999_5.pdf

Mader, H. M. (2002), "Ritterlichkeit: eine Basis des humanitären Völkerrechts — und ein Weg zu seiner Durchsetzung," *Truppendienst* 41: 122–26.

Müller, R.-D. (2014), "Das Zeitalter der Weltkriege," in A. Pöhlmann, H. Potempa, and T. Vogel (eds.), *Der Erste Weltkrieg 1914–1918. Der deutsche Aufmarsch in ein kriegerisches Jahrhundert*, München: Bucher-Verlag.

Münkler, H. (2008), "Der asymmetrische Krieg. Das Dilemma der postheroischen Gesellschaft," *Der Spiegel* 44: 176–77.

Münkler, H. (2013), "Neue Kampfsysteme und die Ethik des Krieges," *Heinrich-Böll-Stiftung* vom 21. Juni 2013. https://www.boell.de/de/node/277436

Münkler, H., and K. Fischer (2000), "'Nothing to Kill or Die for.' Überlegungen zu einer politischen Theorie des Opfers," *Leviathan* 28 (3): 343–62.

Naumann, K. (2007), *Große Geste, kleine Öffnung. Zur Debatte um das Soldaten-Ehrenmal des Bundesverteidigungsministeriums*. Available online: http://www.zeitgeschichte-online.de/thema/grosse-geste-kleine-oeffnung

Noetzel, T. (2010), "Germany's Small War in Afghanistan. Military Learning amid Politicostrategic Inertia," *Contemporary Security Policy* 3: 486–508.

Olsthoorn, P. (2005), "Honor as a Motive for Making Sacrifices," *Journal of Military Ethics* 4 (3): 183–97.

Overmans, R. (2004a), "Kriegsverluste," in G. Hirschfeld, G. Krumeich, and I. Renz (eds.), *Enzyklopädie Erster Weltkrieg*, 663–66, Paderborn: Schöningh.

Overmans, R. (2004b), *Deutsche militärische Verluste im Zweiten Weltkrieg*, München: Oldenbourg.

Rotte, R., and C. Schwarz (2010), "Das Gespenst des Postheroismus: Die Ablehnung des Einsatzes in Afghanistan wurzelt in der Unaufrichtigkeit der Politik," *Die politische Meinung. Monatsschrift zu Fragen der Zeit* 487: 64–67.

Scheurig, B. (1987), *Henning von Tresckow. Ein Preuße gegen Hitler*, Berlin: Ullstein.

Schieder, R. (2016), "Die Inszenierung einer Tragödie. Praktisch-theologische Überlegungen zu einer Trauerfeier im Kölner Dom am 17. April 2015," *Berliner Theologische Zeitschrift (BTHZ)* 33/1: 88–105.

Schlink, B. (2016), "Das Opfer des Lebens," *Berliner Theologische Zeitschrift (BTHZ)* 33 (1): 55–68.

Schmitt, C. (1988), *Der Nomos der Erde im Völkerrecht des Jus Publicum Europaeum*, Berlin: Duncker & Humboldt.

von Seeckt, H. (1929), *Gedanken eines Soldaten*, Berlin: Verlag für Kulturpolitik.

Shils, E. A., and M. Janowitz (1975), "Cohesion and Disintegration in the Wehrmacht in World War II," in M. Janowitz (ed.), *Military Conflict: Essays in the Institutional Analysis of War and Peace*, 177–98, Beverly Hills: Sage Publications.

Snydor, C. W. (1990), *Soldiers of Destruction: The S.S. Death's Head Division 1933–1945*, Princeton: Princeton University Press.

Strauss, B. (2005), *The Battle of Salamis: The Naval Encounter That Saved Greece — and Western Civilization*, New York: Simon & Schuster.

Taylor, C. (2007), *A Secular Age*, Cambridge: Harvard University Press.

Uhle-Wettler, F. (2001), *Der Krieg: gestern, heute – morgen?* Hamburg: Mittler & Sohn.

von Uslar, R., and M.-A. Walther (2012), "Kampfmoral. Voraussetzung für das Bestehen im Kampf," in U. Hartmann (ed.), *Der Soldatenberuf im Spagat zwischen gesellschaftlicher Integration und sui generis-Ansprüchen. Gedanken zur Weiterentwicklung der Inneren Führung. Jahrbuch Innere Führung 2012*, 73–87, Berlin: Miles-Verlag.

Wagner, G. (October 7, 2016), "Großartige Erregung. Der Krieg als Glücksfall für den Soldaten: In Deutschland entsteht eine neue Kultur des Heldentums," *Frankfurter Allgemeine Zeitung (FAZ)* 234: 13.

Walzer, M. (1991), *Just and Unjust Wars*, New York: Basic Books.

Werber, N. (2009), "Soldaten und Söldner. Krieg, Risiko und Versicherung in der 'postheroischen' Epoche," *Merkur — Deutsche Zeitschrift für das europäische Denken*, 9/10: 793–802.

Part Three

An Expanded Understanding of Sacrifice Applied to the Economic, the Political, and the Future

11

Gift or Sacrifice?
History, Politics, and Religion
John Milbank

John Milbank looks at the contexts in which ritual sacrifice occurs (sacral, tribal, theocratic, political, secular) to reconsider Girard's idea that sacrifice aims at containing competitive aggression. Engaging the work of Marcel Gauchet, Philippe Descola, and Moshe Halbertal, Milbank argues against the idea that the political is of necessity a move away from the archaic religious toward the ostensibly more civilized secular. He holds instead that a gift-giving reciprocity grounded in religion is not only the first form of human living but the prevailing one. Sacrifice, Milbank concludes, is not foundationally murderous and scapegoating but "retains . . . its primordial subordination to gift." Indeed, Milbank holds, the move from tribal to monarchical forms of living "was not a shift to the political and secular but rather a mutation within a religious, gift-exchanging vision and practice. . . . In a sense, this renders not just the social but the economic more primary than the political in an ultimately divine oikonomia of distributive care adapted to the minutiae of circumstances and person. . . . The passage of gift through loss and death that characterizes sacrifice only serves to suggest an unlimited sway of gift and of gift-exchange."

—editor's note

Introduction

For the French philosopher Marcel Gauchet (2005), the entire history of the world is the history of secularization.

This *longue durée* is not, however, undergirded by any evolutionary or dialectical theory about inevitable progress nor by any claim for social or economic determinism. Rather, Gauchet (1997: 21–97) stresses the role of human freedom and fortuitous contingency, which nonetheless operate within a certain fixed set of *a priori* possibilities: nothing *has* to happen, but only certain kinds of thing *can* happen.

These possibilities derive from the universal circumstances of the insertion of human subjectivity within the world. First of all, the human subject is oriented toward the *other* because she is reflexively capable of thinking of herself as if from another person's perspective. Second, human subjects are collectively situated in time and may orientate themselves either to the unalterable givenness of the past, or to the new immediacy of the present, or else again, to the open horizon of the future. Third, human subjects are driven to speculate about the invisible and yet unavoidably implied undifferentiated whole of reality.

Within this *a priori* repertoire, history is played out. The entire Comtian-Durkheimian legacy is refused by Gauchet, who denies any "necessity" for religion and insists instead that it was always and everywhere a contingent invention. There is then for him no reason why primitive people should have resorted to magical instead of to simple naturalistic explanations for natural phenomena. Nor is there any reason why they should not have resorted to merely pragmatic accounts of the need for social cohesion (Gauchet 2005: 50–57).

Given his rejection of any human necessity to be religious at any stage of development, the collective adoption of religion becomes for Gauchet a deliberate if semiconscious choice within the permanent repertoire of human possibilities: a choice for the priority of the past, which ensures absolute security and a consequent absence of self-questioning and uncertainty. Thus "societies without a State" are governed by an unchanging ritual order which is taken as reflecting a now inaccessible primordial foundation. For Gauchet, it is such an arrangement which most of all defines "the religious," since it attributes everything legitimate within the human realm to a non- or trans-human, sacred "other."

These (for Gauchet) alone fully religious early societies were tribal ones, where religious ritual suffused the whole of life and expressed an entire unity of the social with the cosmic order. In doing so, it usurped in advance the place of law and government, because its function was precisely to secure, by sacralization, an untrammeled primitive communism and rule of egalitarian gift-exchanging reciprocity. Hence the reign of the all-religious was secretly motivated by a primacy of the political and its social exigencies. But once the purely political escaped and differentiated itself in the archaic kingships of the Neolithic to the Bronze Age, then one had already the first and still the most decisive "secularization." For ritual now leached away from everyday life to concentrate round the royal court and was itself desacralized to the degree of becoming more dependent upon the king's arbitrary and at root sheerly political will (Gauchet 1997: 33–76, 2005: 45–89).

But once more, Gauchet continues, this arrival of "the state" (though the term is anachronistic before early modern times), with its imperative for totalizing enclosure and often also for conquest and ever-widened domination, is not to be accounted for by any deterministic mechanism or response to prior contradiction. Instead, the persistence of the primitive through and beyond the Neolithic discovery of agriculture would rather seem to suggest that the superstructural is all important. Hence "the state" represents a different fundamental choice: this time for the authority of the present. Here the subjective, willed, and capricious power of the monarch usurps the invariable and impersonal power of the inherited ritual order. Such power is correlated with—and for Gauchet brings into being through a choice at once political and existential—an equivalent displacement of the sacred from a founding past, forever re-presented, to a perpetual presence projected into a remote transcendence. The distance and control of *space* is substituted for the distance and control of *time*. The modern, emancipated age then is understood by Gauchet in terms of the third option for the priority of the future.

But is Gauchet right about the priority of an ahistorical transcendental repertoire? And in consequence about the transhistorical primacy of the political over the religious? And can one see primitive gift-exchange, sacrally grounded, as simply an instrumentalist device to guarantee equality and ward off the arrival of the state? In the human beginning, did there lie a fear of the monopolizing of power by the other? Or was there rather a reciprocal binding to the other that blended an element of mutual guarantee with an equal element of trust that admitted some possibility of vulnerability and wounding if there was also to be cooperation and shared achievement? I will now try to address these questions.

(1) In terms of the question of "primitive agency," Gauchet is somewhat coy about the degree of deliberation that he is here prepared to recognize. If one refers to the specific mode of tribal as being freely chosen and not a developmental inevitability, then why did everyone, at first, choose the same social path? To sustain his courageous voluntarism, Gauchet would have to be prepared to entertain the idea that an alternative choice—for "the state"—was primordially latent or semi-emergent. Such a position would also begin to break up the still evolutionist uniformity of Gauchet's picture of the primitive: perhaps one should rather say that in *some* compact societies a more purely "ritual" rule pertains while in others there is something more like "personal and political" rule?

Likewise, Gauchet's account of rule by the past somewhat suppresses the variety of primitive construals of time: as cycle, lapse, perpetual presence, or expected return.

More fatally, it ignores all the recent evidence, summed up by Descola (2005: 311–406), that animistic and totemistic societies tend not to specifically remember ancestors at all because their repetition of the past is so perfect and identical. The dreamtime of the aborigines, for example, was not the time of the ancestors but of the primordial. On this evidence, one could argue that tribal societies opt for the primacy of the present, not the past, and that what is normative for them is not an inheritance but a shared polity with nonhuman beings, whether in terms of an animistic shared interiority or a segmentally variegated coincidence of the inner and the outer in totemic groupings. On Descola's alternative quadripartite typology, pivoted around the culture-nature complex rather than time, what he calls "analogical" societies mix the inner spiritual and the outer physical in much more fluid and complex ways than in the totemic mixture. And they do so precisely through systems of spatial correspondence and patterned linear descent, without which any sense of identity and authority would tend to collapse. Thus, it is in "state" formations that an increasing but articulated *spatial* distance was accompanied by an increasing but articulated *temporal* distance—clean contrary to Gauchet's universal narrative. For on the Descola view, it would be the state formation, not the tribal-religious, that favors the priority of the past, though as one aspect of its general construal of the relation of humans to the cosmos.

(2) Gauchet's account of primitive reciprocity assumes, after the structuralists, that this was primarily a secular matter of reinforcing shared symbolic norms. But if we return to Marcel Mauss (1990) and acknowledge that the gift was at once thing and symbol, thereby embracing the real material economy as well as the ritual one, then we can see how the symbolic order could not be readily confined to a collective self-awareness of culture over against nature, or to nature culturally regarded, but was also seen more holistically as the extra-human "gift" of nature herself. It is for this reason that Mauss saw the primitive gift as a somewhat subjective reality which demanded "of itself" to be returned, according to the *hau* or "the spirit of the gift"—while equally the Maussian giver is somewhat objectified such that he exists only within webs of physically realized mutuality where each is "materially" bound to each and each to all. All this assumes a vitalized cosmos for which mind and matter are not alien to each other in a manner that owes much more to Lucien Lévy-Bruhl and his ideas of primitive "participation" than is usually allowed.

Here I am both agreeing with and dissenting from Descola. He allows that the modes of gift, exchange, and predation are linked to a non-duality of nature and culture but oddly fails to see that the paradox of gift-exchange, or of a gift that in some way expects a return, belongs to such a non-duality. By contrast, the strict division of measurable contract over against an intended pure gratuity is surely part and parcel of the modern, naturalistic paradigm. Yet in effect, Descola's own account of gift as involving trust in the forthcoming generosity of others amounts to systematic, through asymmetrical, reciprocity after all even though he strangely denies this (2005: 311–21).

The Maussian paradigm, as Descola does allow, assumes that gift-exchange systems include also supernatural forces such that the original obligation to return gift is to repay a debt to the divine realm and its human representatives, often themselves identified with gods and spirits. Mauss firmly noted this while not fully developing its import: "It is they [the spirits of the dead and the gods] who are the true owners of the things and possessions of this world" (Mauss 1990: 16–17). However, that this debt can never fully be repaid is not, as yet in primitive society, an inevitably sinister circumstance since for the logic of gift-exchange, this condition also pertains among humans and has in either case a positive valence as guaranteeing the perpetuity of giving and exchanging in relationship (Godbout 2007: 162–73; Caillé 2007: 93–130, 131).

To argue instead—with Gauchet and many others, including (perhaps surprisingly) some members of MAUSS (*Mouvement Anti-Utilariste des Sciences Sociales*) like Alain Caillé (2007: 123–81)—that gift-exchange was initially a defensive mechanism to ward off the threat of hierarchy and violence begs the question as to where such a threat might "originally" have come from? Since "violence" as intentional and subject to judgment is an entirely cultural reality (we do not judge the wolf for snaring her prey), the notion of an original contagion of violence must be considered a Hobbesian or Girardian fantasy. By the same token, Camille Tarot (2008: 631–41) is surely wrong to consider sacrifice older than gift, with sacrifice taken as a mutation of a Girardian scapegoating mechanism. It would rather seem that the preagricultural tribal gifts to divine forces were generally unbloody, or else sought to honor and placate the hunted animal or else again were rituals of animistic or totemistic belonging, as Robertson Smith long ago surmised (Hénaff 2002: 209–68). Evidence of tribal sacral violence against humans looks more like sheer judicial excluding or else indeed like scapegoating but not like sacrifice—even if we can by no means be sure of the exactitude of these symbolic boundaries which are fixed in terms of our western terminology. But overwhelmingly, human sacrifice seems to be something commanded by later sacral kings in archaic empires or in extreme instances to involve the reverse sacrifice of the kings themselves. Both measures assume an extension of the logic of debt-paying now turned darker and more unilateral—if not, one wants to say, outright diabolical.

(3) One cannot plausibly interpret the switch to archaic kingship (as a secularizing liberation of the political) to be a societal organization more "natural" than tribal/gift-exchange—unless one dogmatically doubts the reality of any sacral cosmic order or else fails to see the perennial human cultural necessity to ascribe to one. Here Gauchet (2005: 50–57) fails to allow that religion's manner of describing and explaining cosmic forces is not to be regarded as a proto natural science which is secondary to its main, political function, since this is an integral aspect of its other function (admitted by Gauchet) of interpreting existential perplexity. What is more, any notion that the secular political is more "natural" to humans amounts to a vicious paradox of the naturalness of the cultural as arbitrary which fails to attend to Descola, Bruno Latour, and Marshall Sahlin's genealogical demonstration that a dualism of the culturally constructed over the naturally given is *itself* an arbitrary construct of the modern, naturalist paradigm.

In any case, the shift to sacral kingship is not, as Gauchet avers, already a qualification of sacral cosmos. It is rather the beginning of a more personal and free apprehension of this sacrality as rooted in something unattainable and ineffable that is one mode of an "analogical" ordering: The focus of such a sense for a long historical moment in the person of the king allowed this more personal aspect still to be blended with a more diffused and impersonal social embodiment of the cosmic. It is certainly true that kingship could assume terrifying aspects and could tend, as in Hawaii and other Pacific islands, to a cult of pure force. Yet this could also be tempered, as Bellah (2011: 210–64) stresses, by a new sense of care, justice, and mercy that originates with the kingly function itself. For while tribal gift-exchange could secure a balanced relationality in terms of collectively acknowledged goods (of all kinds, both material and symbolic), it was less adept at attending to situated individual needs and to providing specialized attention. For this one required the more elevated social perspective, just as only kingship (in the first "social democratic" instance of the "state" balancing the "market") could counteract the always threatened monopoly achieved by the hoarder of gifts who later became their main provider. It was Near Eastern kings who first offered a compensating "justice" to widows and orphans just as it was the kingly function that was more able to consider a just apportioning and distribution in terms of needs and abilities and functions. Primitive gift-exchange either secured a literal base equality or rapidly encouraged inequities. The same tendencies ensured that it was unable to resolve early tendencies to endemic warfare and indeed often exacerbated them when gift-giving assumed a predominantly agonistic character. Equally, gift-exchanging communities tended to be closed round a particular understanding of the sacred thing that was bound to return, whether spirit or totem, and so they could negotiate with each other through modes of predation whose well-intentioned assimilation as stressed by Descola must nevertheless be adjudged retrospectively as deplorable violence.

This is not to say that gift-exchange did not later remain, as in the archaic imperial period, the primary "social fact" (in Maussian terms). It did but it was now blended with elements of top-down unilaterality and distributive fairness (according to shifting historical and local criteria). Indeed, one can argue here that one requires the advent of hierarchy in order to safeguard the initial, unprompted "imposition" of the gift as the very condition of its generosity (even if the return gesture tends to invert this hierarchy)—whereas pure equality inexorably tends to cause gift to deteriorate simultaneously toward both predatory conflict and fixable contract. But all these functions of monarchy—as biblical and earlier Near Eastern texts make clear—were most certainly regarded as sacral ones.

(4) This would suggest that the axial shifts cannot be regarded as secularizations either. For they indeed assumed a certain "retribalization" and blending of the primitively "compact" with the imperially expansive, especially in what are really the paradigmatic cases of Greece and Israel. In the case of Greece, the oriental fertility cults of the Mother Goddess and her son as reflected in the personage of the king became merged with hyperborean, warlike and shamanic cults of more predominantly male and celestial deities. The Saturnian and the astral returned to consort with the sedentary obeisances to the moon and the sun, which may be why Plato constantly invokes the normativity of the age of Cronos and direct astral guardianship. The political version of this fusion was the unique *polis*, or city-state, which merged a sacral temple focus with a military clan-gathering and encampment (Dawson 1933: 311–84). In the case of Fist Temple Israel, the focus on the temple remained in tension with a more dispersed, pastoral, and wandering focus on the domestic worship conducted by every patriarch. The political result was again a city-state with its circumambient rural *commune* (for the temple aspect, see Barker 2008).

This retribalization brought with it not only a certain return of primitive gift-exchange—if now universalization and defetishization of the reciprocally face-to-face—but also some return of a more democratically and densely enchanted cosmos, even if this became blended in many societies with the king-and-temple versions. Consequent tensions within all the axial faiths tended to result either in a sustaining of this mix or in a democratization of the lone, royal mediating function to every individual soul, with a consequent relative playing down of external cosmic mediation.

Here one has to question Halbertal's (2012) overly voluntarist and positivistic construal of Hebrew monotheism. Because he assumes an initial "separation" of a remote and capricious deity, he also sees sacrifice as the primary religious action which, although it is a mode of gift, is a mode of anxiety-ridden gift since a gift to a superior, unlike one to an equal, cannot expect an automatic return as a reciprocal duty. According to Halbertal, ritual is a secondary phenomenon, designed to ensure acceptable modes of sacrifice and so to avoid the fate both of Cain, who made the wrong choice of offering, and of Aaron's sons, who made the mistake of offering an unspecified "alien fire." Yet this begs the question of how God is known as present in the first place, which is surely through ritual mediation that manifestly had many other normative functions for ancient Israel than merely guaranteeing placatory success. Indeed, it was rather the sine qua non of any just, ordered action. And in this instance also, such a primacy is shown more clearly when one considers the entire cosmic dimension of human relationship to nonhumans, the categories of pure and impure, and so forth, as discussed for the Hebrew Bible by Robert Murray and Mary Douglas. Given the primacy of ritual, a normative assumption of covenant with God and so an expectation of a return from him, even as a superior, if one obeys the cosmic law, tends to follow.

Given his reverse assumption of sacrifice as a primordial site of existential anxiety, Halbertal reads the sacrifice of Isaac as augmenting this scenario to the ultimate degree. Beyond even ritual guarantee, God can only be assured of our respect and personal love if we offer absolutely everything to him—Isaac, the miracle promise of Israel's entire future on earth—in such a way that a return from God becomes impossible since we have committed self-obliteration. Yet this reading omits the whole point of the story as always emphasized within Christianity from St. Paul to Kierkegaard that this is not a test of fealty or of pure disinterested love for the other but rather of faith: trust in God, as the source of everything and of all life can run to the absurd length of giving all up in the surety that all will somehow return. In this way, the apparent obliteration of ritual covenant becomes the ground of its confident renewal and from thenceforwards even foundation. There is a unilateral gift offered to God only because we trust him for the giving of the one absolute unilateral gift which is also the gift of the giving of our very dependent existence and so of the first ground of reciprocity as our existing at all through the worship and praise of our creator.

In this Hebrew instance, therefore, beyond the mega-state, the state itself, in the person of Isaac, is given up before it has come to be but given up in order to be established in such a way that resumes but sublimates the local agricultural scene of sacrifice and approximates the imperial ritual of human sacrifice of king or enemy after all to the relatively peaceful pastoral idyll. This becomes once more fully peaceful, in an almost neo-tribal manner, with the Christian Eucharist—albeit in consequence of the repetition of the *Akedah* as real sacrificial death and miraculous return rather than substitution. This, though, is theologically understood as the cancellation through absorption (a reverse predation) of human wickedness and only needs to be read as a "requirement" of an innocent victim, as by Halbertal, on the false assumption that every sacrifice was anciently seen as a murderous crime—an assumption that supremely cannot apply when the killing is toward the source of life itself, which is just why the divine command to Abraham is not a command to murder his son, but indeed to *sacrifice* him.

To return again to Gauchet: the key issue with regard to his meta-history is, what precisely forbids one from erecting an alternate framing contrast in which the axial or analogical mediation between tribal dogmatism and apophatic agnosticism is the real mark of Giambattista Vico's *acme* at once of religion and civilization (Vico 1984: §§ 1097–1112) as endorsed by Eric Voegelin (1998: 82–148, esp. 123)—which avoids on the one hand the *selvaggio* of idolatry and on the other hand the new urban wilderness of excessive skepticism that must dissolve all human along with all sacral bonds? Nothing would seem to critically rule out the idea of the axial rather than the primitive as "the most religious." Indeed, there is much to argue for it since it resorts less to the, as it were, "secular" bracketings of the physical as diverse made by animism, or to the univocal and linguistifying "rationalization" rendered by Totemism which interrelates in a rigid symbolic order a series of physical-spiritual correlates that compose segmentary tribal groupings. Only analogy leaves everything punctuatedly fluid and totally sacral and sustains also a nature-culture unity prior to the onset of the voluntaristic-rationalistic construal of monotheism during the course of the Islamic and Latin Middle Ages.

(5) Without warrant, Gauchet reads "real" Christianity in terms of this latter "Protestant" model. On his view, one should regard the Christian redefinition (by Tertullian) of the Roman *religio*, which probably meant the "re-reading"

(*re-legere*) crucial to the character of ritual tradition, as now "binding to the true God" (*re-ligio*) as a secularization, since it seems to define "religion" as a matter of belief apart from culture in a way that is alien to almost all human societies (Tarot 2008: 130–35). Yet in point of fact, the Latin Christian grasp of "religion" by no means abandoned the Roman ritual dimension (so that collective liturgy came to enjoy a much more important para-liturgical extension in the Christian west than in the Christian east). Indeed, it tended to imply already that "other" religious practices are false or distorted discernments of an "elsewhere" that now only the *ecclesia* brings clearly into view (Sachot 2001: 167–225).

In one sense then, Christianity is the first and only "religion," but in a second sense, it validly recognizes the "founded in an elsewhere" dimension of all human cultures. In yet a third sense, as Giorgio Agamben (2011, 2013) has implied, one can objectively regard Christianity as "the most religious religion" because if every "religion" links norms of action with the nature of reality, then Christianity takes this to an extreme degree by first identifying (in the wake of the Jewish philosopher Philo) metaphysically theoretical norms of being with politically active ones of governance of action at the very highest transcendent level (where many cultures leave this level as either unknown or depoliticized, not directly relevant to human society). Christianity then seeks to reflect this dual normativity in a pattern of life that shatters any distance between norm and nature (by living according to the "naturalness" of love). From this perspective, Christianity offers no secularization save of the political, which is in any case measured in its validity by its ecclesial surpassing according to Augustine (*De civitate Dei*, book 19, which every individual Christian must integrally reflect) but rather a kind of immanent supernatural saturation.

(6) Yet Gauchet adamantly opposes this more Catholic reading of the Christian religion. For he claims that Christianity happened, contingently, to be the religion that removed the sway of religion. To substantiate this claim, he must give an interpretation of Christianity, indeed endeavor to circumscribe its "essence."

In Gauchet's treatment of Christianity, his handling of the medieval era is crucial since for him, this is supposedly the time of Catholic concealment of Christianity's real essence. Thus, sacral cosmology, analogical hierarchy, and sacramental participation are all regarded by Gauchet as unstable "hybrids" of archaic religion with a purified monotheism which would render God an utterly remote, unknowable, and absolute power. Yet in actual fact, later voluntarist theology makes God more "distant" because this is the only way to preserve transcendence once God, after Duns Scotus and others, became *more immanently* understood as merely "a being," albeit supremely infinite, in just the way that we are beings. That is, once God became no longer being as such, as in Aquinas's version of monotheism, which one could argue was thereby at least as "pure" and biblical. Likewise, medieval villages and town guilds are regarded by Gauchet as unstable compromises between individualism and collectivism. But to speak of hybrid and compromise here is to assume that "the religious" is antithetic to change and individual diversity because it is paradigmatically tribal rather than paradigmatically axial and synthesizing.

Conclusion

All of the above points leave secularization as a contingent event in Western history, not an inevitable one on the assumption of the transcendental primacy of the political. Instead, the evidence, rather than any *a priori* transcendentalist reasoning, suggests that most if not all primitive human societies exhibit a priority of the religious over the political and a grounding of a fundamental reciprocity, trust, and vulnerability in a ritual relation to transcendent forces, cosmically underwriting the human circle.

The historical evidence also suggests that the shift to the monarchical beyond the tribal was not a shift to the political and secular but rather a mutation within a religious, gift-exchanging vision and practice—a mutation that allowed for more individual variation and a coordinating, distributive justice. Against this background, the Christian irruption, as shown especially in the ruminations of St. Paul, looks like a kind of return to the tribal as a universal logic beyond the state: an insistence—in excess of law and justice but not in denial of them as not in denial of the old covenant—on the ultimacy of the interpersonal and the vulnerable exchange of love as defining both human society and humanity itself (Milbank 2008). In a sense, this renders not just the social but the economic more primary than the political in an ultimately divine *oikonomia* of distributive care adapted to the minutiae of circumstances and person. A pastoral economy, then, could later mutate into a social or civil economy, as opposed to a political one (Milbank 2017).

Within this perspective, sacrifice retains what I have here argued was its primordial subordination to gift, although within this subordination it marked a hyperbolic extremity of gift that confirmed its sway: the offering of life itself in emergencies or to divine powers. In the Hebraic context, such an offering is still more retained within gift-circulation to the degree offerings are made in trust of divine return even if the hour and mode of this return remains unknown. Of course, "return" is really the wrong word—it is rather that the most extreme offerings express a trust in God's original generosity and unlimited capacity to renew this.

In the Christian instance, the contingent and politically occasioned offering of a human victim who is also God himself further exacerbates both the extremity of sacrifice and the extremity of confirmation of return and renewal. Yet in either case, once more, the passage of gift through loss and death that characterizes sacrifice only serves to suggest an *unlimited* sway of gift and of gift-exchange. For no abyss interrupts this, or rather the abyss itself proves to be but the transit of generosity—the transit of gift being across a void witnesses to the coincidence of gift with all of reality.

References

Agamben, G. (2011), *The Kingdom and the Glory: For a Theological Genealogy of Economy and Government*, trans. L. Chiesa, Stanford: Stanford University Press.

Agamben, G. (2013), *The Highest Poverty: Monastic Rules and Form-of-Life*, trans. A. Kotsko, Stanford: Stanford University Press.

Barker, M. (2008), *The Gate of Heaven: The History and Symbolism of the Temple of Jerusalem*, Sheffield: Phoenix.

Bellah, R. (2011), *Religion in Human Evolution: From the Paleolithic to the Axial Age*, Cambridge: The Belknap Press.

Caillé, A. (2007), *Anthropologie de Don: Le Tiers Paradigme*, Paris: La Découverte.

Dawson, C. (1933), *The Age of the Gods: A Study in the Origins of Culture in Prehistoric Europe and the Ancient East*, London: Sheed and Ward.

Descola, P. (2005), *Beyond Nature and Culture*, trans. J. Lloyd, Chicago: Chicago University Press.

Gauchet, M. (1997), *The Disenchantment of the World: A Political History of Religion*, trans. O. Burge, Princeton: Princeton University Press.

Gauchet, M. (2005), *La Condition Politique*, Paris: Gallimard.

Godbout, J. (2007), *Ce qui Circule entre Nous: Donner, Recevoir, Rendre*, Paris: Seuil.

Halbertal, M. (2012), *On Sacrifice*, Princeton: Princeton University Press.

Hénaff, M. (2002), *Le Prix de la Verité: le don, l'argent, la philosophie*, Paris: Seuil.

Mauss, M. (1990), *The Gift: The Form and Reason for Exchange in Archaic Societies*, trans. W. Halls, New York: W.W. Norton.

Milbank, J. (2008), "Paul against Biopolitics," *Theory, Culture & Society* 25 (7–8): 125–72.

Milbank, J. (2017), "Oikonomia Leaves Home: Theology, Politics, and Governance in the History of the West," *Telos* 178: 77–99.

Sachot, M. (2011), *L'Invention du Christ: Genèse d'une religion*, Paris: Odile Jacob.
Tarot, C. (2008), *Le symbolique et le sacré: théories de la religion*, Paris: La Découverte.
Vico, G. (1984), *The New Science of Giambattista Vico*, trans. T. Bergin and M. Fisch, Ithaca: Cornell University Press.
Voegelin, E. (1998), *History of Political Ideas, Vol. VI: Revolution and the New Science*, Columbia: University of Missouri Press.

12

Strategy, Spectacle, or Self-emptying?
Sacrifice and the Search for Business Ethics

Philip Roscoe

Philip Roscoe takes the Girardian model of mimetic competition and sacrifice into the business world. The current iteration of capitalism, he holds, yields an ethos of sacrifice-all-for-the-firm. This ethos is to be internalized by individual employees and structures the business environment, from hirings, firings, and production schedules to the "masculinized" agonistic atmosphere that works against female employees. Roscoe adds to the Girardian model the observation that the present business version demands the sacrifice of not only others for the sake of profits (as businesses lay off workers and close factories in response to automation or the lure of low-wage countries) but also oneself, from entry-level workers to CEOs. This is not the sacrifice of the cross, which aims at ending sacrificial violence, but self-donation that keeps the sacrificial cogs going. Yet Roscoe is critical also of a naïve Levinasian counter-model that proposes unending, unstructured, and "unquestioning self-abandonment to a proliferation of demanding Others and forbids a rational settlement of those demands."

—editor's note

Introduction

Sacrifice is integral to the myth of contemporary business. Consider American businessman Lee Iacocca, celebrated for his self-sacrifice in saving the struggling automotive giant Chrysler on a salary of $1 a year. Though Chrysler received a vast government bailout—some $1.5 billion in loan guarantees and huge military orders of trucks—Iacocca attributed the company's turnaround to his own sacrifice and its inspiring effects on those around him. Or Mark Zuckerberg, who has publicly committed to give away 99 percent of his holdings in Facebook stock—worth $45 billion dollars, in his lifetime. Steve Jobs, who needs no introduction, achieved a semi-sanctified status as an entrepreneurial superman whose conspicuous brilliance symbolically doomed him to an early passing. Sacrifice—self-sacrifice in particular—is essential to the striving that constitutes a business life lived well. A more cynical view, common among "progressive" management scholars, sees sacrificial narratives as part of a broader regime of governance and exploitation; self-sacrifice becomes a legitimizing device by which charismatic leaders demonstrate their bona fides while simultaneously necessitating the sacrifice of employees' livelihood or security on the altar of business principles. Sacrifice is wedded to the economy, inherent in the excessive, spectacular, even self-destructive nature of capitalism. At the same time, those same progressive management scholars embrace a vision of ethics based on reckless and chaotic sacrifice to the other.

What can we say about such differing but convergent notions? This chapter reads Girard's (2011) account of sacrifice into the economy. In conclusion, I optimistically hope for a move to non-sacrificial imitation—"mimesis" in Girard's terms—in the economy.

Sacrificial management

The emphasis on sacrifice in management thinking is a relatively new occurrence, driven by the vast expansion of capitalism's horizons at the end of the twentieth century. In the face of the opportunity and challenge offered by the globalization of the market economy, a succession of management gurus (Peters and Waterman 1982; Peters 1992; Child 2005) transformed popular ideas about management. Older staples of industrial production, bureaucratic management, Fordist strategies, and time-and-motion gurus such as Frederick Taylor found themselves banished to the outer darkness of unfashionable concepts. In their place came a swathe of new working practices emphasizing flexibility, autonomy, and knowledge. Offices came to look like homes, providing such rich facilities that employees need leave only to sleep, if that. New technology allowed employees to be constantly available and endlessly supervised. With these working practices came buzz-words and oxymorons, talk of flat hierarchies or creative labor, and a blurring of the semiotics of work and leisure. Fashionable business school academics claimed that Marx had been right all along and that now, the means of production had finally been returned to a new breed of knowledge workers whose "talent makes capital dance" (Nordström and Ridderstråle 2002).

This movement became known as "post-bureaucratic" management, and it turned out that Marx *was* right all along, for the deliberate dismantling of the boundaries of organization simply gave rise to further mechanisms of exploitation and new forms of discipline. Post-bureaucratic managers helped workers police their own conduct, achieving superior productivity without the expense of bureaucratic watchmen (Sewell and Wilkinson 1992), while novel strategies of discursive control allowed employers to deal with the threatening autonomy of knowledge workers (Poulter and Land 2008). By the simple expedient of making employees their own custodians, these new mechanisms of control triumph—as Marx might have said—in the battle of capital over labor, chipping away at the tiny advantages in time or work processes that workers had managed to negotiate or put into place.

The theory of the firm as a self-contained productive unit, investing to generate future rents, deserving all rewards, and bearing all responsibilities, has slipped into policy and popular discourse as the appropriate model for *individual* conduct not only within commercial relationships but also in personal ones (Roscoe 2014); this fusing of categories further prods employees to discipline themselves into working hard for the firm. Self-supervisory motifs as "Me Ltd" pervade the labor market and help organizations achieve transaction economies beyond their walls in an arrangement that Elisabeth Anderson terms "private government" (Anderson 2017). These transaction economies, needless to say, come at the cost of diminished protection and increased insecurity and precarity among those needing to work for a living. In sum, the new world of work emphasized not only flexibility and autonomy but also commitment and self-sacrifice.

At the heart of this movement stands the sacrificial persona of the charismatic leader, fusing the roles of manager and the Schumpeterian entrepreneur: preternaturally gifted, all seeing, spectacular harbinger of creative destruction (Schumpeter 1934). Du Gay (2000: 70) highlights the apocalyptic, millennial imagery and language behind charismatic management, as its new leaders seek to lead employees to a world free of alienating distinctions between work and leisure. Charismatic management, he writes, "repudiates the past in favor of the eschatological future time of the new man"; it promises workers liberation and emancipation from the iron cage of bureaucracy, a system of organization unfit to cope with the threatening chaos of globalization. And if self-sacrifice is a distinguishing characteristic of this charismatic leadership, it is instrumental in intent: strategic, calculative, and self-aware.

The mainstream management literature has been quick to identify the usefulness of self-sacrifice as a leadership tool. Typical findings include claims that self-sacrifice leads to the attribution of charisma, the establishment of legitimacy, the encouragement of follower reciprocity, an increase in organizational commitment and team efficiency, and a decrease in perceived autocracy (the literature on sacrificial leadership in management is extensively reviewed by Śliwa et al. 2013). Grint's (2010) analysis of leadership suggests that sacrifice, with its three constituent parts—setting the leader apart, sacralizing the leader, and settling fears and dissent among followers—is crucial to leadership activities.

Expectations of sacrifice are not confined to the chief executive, however, and discourses of sacrifice trickle down through organizations, pervading organizational structures. Would-be senior managers are expected to sacrifice themselves to the good of the firm, sacrificing friendships and local roots for the sake of geographical mobility, sacrificing leisure and relationships to comply with the norm of extensive availability, even sacrificing a spouse's career. Such self-sacrificial norms give rise to a masculine image of the manager and play a role in excluding women from more senior roles in the organization (Guillaume and Pochic 2009). Across the entire workforce, compliance with organizational norms requires a certain sacrifice of the self—a self-alienation or dis-identification with one's "authentic" persona to become the corporate individual (Costas and Fleming 2009).

Self-sacrifice plays another role in the post-bureaucratic organization. Absent the organizational norms implicit in bureaucracy and the associated ethics of office, it is hard to tell the benevolent charismatic leader from the tyrant-in-making. Self-sacrifice can be seen as a marker of benevolence; the ethical charismatic leader, write Howell and Avolio (1992), uses power to serve others. For advocates of post-bureaucratic management, the act of self-abandonment distinguishes the truly moral leader and makes possible explicit comparisons with figures such as Gandhi, Socrates, and even Jesus. At times, the claims made shift from the hyperbolic to the plain ludicrous, as in this (again courtesy of Śliwa et al. 2013: 863) from leadership guru Koestenbaum (2002), who claims that for any truly committed leader "the bottom line is the willingness to die." Having invoked the ultimate sacrifice, Koestenbaum clarifies: "To risk death is to risk oneself, even sacrifice oneself, for the sake of the company or the customer, the partnership or the client—for what is right." The self-sacrificial charismatic leader is motivated more than nothing by her own moral compass (Howell and Avolio 1992).

It is not only chief executives who are exhorted to self-immolation. Employees are expected to sacrifice themselves as well, whether through accepting redundancy—accepting that the needs of the firm transcend their rights to a stable wage—or through unbounded, limitless exertion on behalf of the company. The expansion of competitive systems of supervision and appraisal within firms—of which Welch's "rank and yank" is just one example—leads directly to strife *within* the organization and in the labor market around it. Employees are pitted against each other in pursuit of a secure job, a bonus, or a promotion. Du Gay does not dwell on the sacrificial content of such a move, but Brown (2016: 3) does so explicitly, commenting that "the conduct, ends and valuation of citizens construed as firms . . . inverts the freedom originally promised by neoliberalism . . . this promise becomes its opposite: a subject governed by extensive normative dicta, vulnerable to life imperilment and available to legitimate sacrifice."

These images of (self-) sacrifice draw from the rich cultural resources available within an audience that is largely white, Anglo-Saxon, and Protestant and to those who have been educated to work well in a culture heavily informed by north European Protestantism. The language of inspirational management writing is tinged with religious metaphor: Jack Welch, the former CEO of General Electric, has been called a visionary "prophet," and a "modern saint" whose "miracles" have inspired a host of "apostles" (Dyck, Starke, and Dueck 2009). Management theory, especially popular management theory, is embedded in the Protestant work ethic, a secularized version of Calvinist Christianity with focus on self-sacrifice as a means of demonstrating one's place among the elect (Weber 1930).

An ethics of sacrifice?

Progressive management scholars object to the calculative aspects of managerial self-sacrifice. For those management scholars tracing one recent turn in business ethics, true sacrifice is by definition free of business "strategy," and a calculative sacrifice is no sacrifice at all. Bureaucratic management falls short of the moral ideal because its sole purpose is to organize others with respect to achieving particular outcomes, a focus on persons as means rather than ends. No less a thinker than Alasdair MacIntyre (1981) offers a sustained critique of the manager as one of the central characters in the moral collapse of the late twentieth century, instrumentally rational and committed only to achieving technical dominance over others. Zygmunt Bauman, meanwhile, offers a stinging critique of bureaucracy as a reservoir of "moral sleeping pills" capable of organizing the Holocaust (Bauman 1989). Bauman's historiography has not stood up to scrutiny, but his claims about the mechanisms of moral distancing at bureaucracy's disposal have given organizational theorists much to think about (ten Bos 1997).

Bauman's *Postmodern Ethics* is deeply suspicious of reason as the source of moral judgment (Jones 2003). He locates the good in terms of utter self-sacrifice to the other. The horrors of the Holocaust have, for Bauman, so tainted any kind of calculative organization that the only true morality can be a self-emptying transcendence of being: the moral agent confronts the Other in a state of defenselessness and finds only the Face. He quotes Levinas, writing, "The Face is what resists me by its opposition and not what is opposed to me by its resistance . . . the absolute nakedness of a face, the absolutely defenseless face, without covering clothing or mask, is what opposes my power over it, my violence, and opposes it in absolute way, with an opposition which is positioning itself" (Bauman 1993: 73). In the end, driven by radical commitment to others and transcending any rational principle, Bauman's morality is contradictory and chaotic precisely because it demands unquestioning self-abandonment to a proliferation of demanding Others and forbids a rational settlement of those demands. There can, for Bauman, be "no self before the moral self, morality being the ultimate, non-determined presence" (Bauman 1993: 13).

Jones (2003) has explored the ramifications of such alterity for business ethics, via Levinas and Derrida: "For Levinas, the ethical relation involves more than simply seeing the Other. It involves a recognition and openness to the face of the Other, which entails, as Derrida puts it, 'a total question, a distress and denuding, a supplication, a demanding prayer'" (Jones 2003: 227). The Other lays claim to Jones, and he must act generously and without expectation of return, for ethical action ceases to be ethical as soon as it is calculative or expectant. In the same way, hospitality, the fundamental ethical act, ceases to be genuine if it is conditional. "Absolute hospitality," Jones (2003: 233) quotes from Derrida,

> requires that open up my home and that I give not only to the foreigner . . . but to the absolute, unknown, anonymous other, and that I give place to them, that I let them come, and that I let them arrive and take place in the place I offer them, without asking of them either reciprocity or even their names.

For Jones any ethical action conducted by a business and driven by strategic self-interest or adherence to legal codes constitutes an abnegation of genuine ethics. He has a particular disdain for corporate ethics that claim to support profitable business—the doing well by doing good theory—and for the claims of management science that issues of fairness may eventually become a matter of calculation, or even law. "The law," he writes, "is not equal to ethics or justice.

Ethics involves the break with good conscience that results from clear knowledge of how to act in obedience to the law" (Jones 2003: 239).

Ironically, the postmodern ethicists and the post-bureaucrats find much in common, both offering a critique of bureaucratic management on the basis that its underlying formal-rational authority sunders the pristine unity of human existence (du Gay 2000). The first group hears humanity calling out for a civic order underwritten by utter self-sacrifice; the second sees the civic order as needing to be completed by the unbounded expansion of economic logics to all domains of life, with all the sacrifices that entails. This motley crew of thinkers hailing from politically and intellectually diverse traditions has settled upon sacrifice as the road to utopia. One might sacrifice one's leisure to the great God of work, sacrifice one's employees on the altar of productivity, or sacrifice one's salary for a place in the afterlife of management heaven with all its lucrative possibilities. Or one might offer oneself as hostage to a strange and overwhelming alterity, in the face of which one cannot judge, calculate, or hesitate. One cannot even seek to *articulate* this responsibility without removing from the Other that strange quiddity—the *Otherness*—by which we are so obliged (Mansell 2008). In these Others, the practical manager might see monsters as much as angels and find herself wishing once again for a simple bureaucratic order. What is the well-meaning manager to do?

Rethinking sacrifice?

The writings of René Girard help us to decode the role of sacrifice in the economic world. Girard sees desire as a social phenomenon originating in an already existing desire, where we want what another has or what another wants. Mimetic desire leads inevitably to competition, and the closer the object of desire, the fiercer and more frustrated the rivalry. Our consumer society thrives on a process of acquisition that is largely positional (Veblen 1994), meaning that the value of goods depends upon their uniqueness, and satisfaction comes from owning what one's neighbor does not. But consumer goods are broadly available, and this positional desire can never be satisfied, at least not for long (Anspach 2004).

Moreover, available "goods" are no longer constrained to the realm of the commodity. Consider Facebook, the archetypal twenty-first-century business, transacting in presentations of the self. We recognize that envy is the engine powering Facebook: that people want, as the essayist John Lanchester writes, to "look at what other people like them [are] doing, to see their social networks, to compare, to boast and show off, to give full rein to every moment of longing and envy, to keep their noses pressed against the sweet-shop window of others' lives" (Lanchester 2017). If envy is the omnipresent motivator of everyday life (Palaver 2005: 1), Facebook expands that desire into digital infinity. This is not simply an academic observation: in 2004, internet billionaire Peter Thiel—cofounder of PayPal—invested $500,000 for some 10 percent of the company. Lanchester tells us that Thiel had come under the spell of Girard's writings studying philosophy at Stanford, and in Facebook he saw a business that was Girardian to the core.

It is not just customers that compete for goods. Businesses struggle for customers, and employees tussle for promotions and bonuses. Firms in capitalism operate in a war of all-against-all, and organizations become containers for violence as they mimetically seek legitimacy and competitive advantage (Desmond and Kavanagh 2003). Such conflict is societally destructive, and Girard understands sacrifice as the means by which the strife of imitative competition is dissipated. An innocent, identified as the source of social ills, is sacrificed as scapegoat to placate the angry God, who is ostensibly punishing society for whatever ill the scapegoat is guilt of. Through the ritual of scapegoating, tensions are dissipated, at least in the short term. In business, we might trace this cycle through competitive expansion, mimetic rivalry, overcapacity, and crisis leading to the closure of factories, offices, or even whole firms. The sacrifice of livelihoods of those identified as the source of crisis—unproductive workers and incompetent managers—is necessary for the settling of destructive economic tensions. Peace is restored, for a while, until the whole competitive cycle begins again.

Girard sees human society as fundamentally religious in character, and the economy is no different. Rivalry for goods that the neighbors do not own, for customers, for opportunities—scarce resources—drives the economy, and sacrifice is the means to forestall competitive self-destruction. Markets are conceived of as quasi-naturalistic orderings dependent upon competition, which itself needs sacrifice to function. To take an example from our own profession: How can a funding call find the best few percent of applicants, if others are not to sacrifice time and energy as the unsuccessful? This order of the market is underpinned by notions of nature and the divine (Foucault 2008; Lubasz 1992), while economic competition evokes ideas of evolutionary selection and survival of the toughest (Mirowski 1994). Brown (2016: 4) once again makes the connection to sacrifice explicit when she speaks of an unfolding logic that "blends the hard-headed approach to human capital of any successful firm with a national-theological discourse of moralized sacrifice, a sacrifice required for the health and survival of the whole."

There are consequences: such sacrifice, she argues, disproportionately affects the most vulnerable members of society by simultaneously entrusting them with responsibility for their destinies yet stripping away mechanisms for collectively shaping those futures—mandating individual responsibility turns attention away from public provision of basic necessities and from collective action as a source of remedy and self-protection. The result is a society of "intensely isolated and unprotected individuals, persistently in peril of deracination and deprivation of basic life support, wholly vulnerable to capital's vicissitudes." Her argument suggests that the sacrifice made by employees—and the un- or precariously employed—may heighten, rather than dissipate, the societal tensions of which Girard speaks.

But Girard, although he discovers the origins of religious ritual in the slaughter of innocents to appease an angry deity, does not end on such a dismal note. On the contrary, he identifies the sacrifice on the cross as enough to end the sacrifice cycle for perpetuity and sees in the New Testament the promise of nonviolent imitation. As Pally writes elsewhere in this volume, the Old Testament's treatment of strangers paved the way for the understanding of the relationship between man and God as one of covenant. By contrast, it is quite clear that neither the recursive and destructive sacrifice of those on the economic margins nor the unachievable goal of chaotic self-abnegation in the name of ethics offers anything meaningful for the manager in search of an ethic.

How might we seek to frame the narratives of economic action in a positive, covenantal light?

Perhaps another postmodernist, Richard Kearney, might have an answer for us. We must rely upon stories: the rich tradition laid out for us in the biblical narratives and the veracity of apostolic testimony. Like Girard, who reads literature as a guide to the truth of human nature, drawing heavily on Shakespeare and Dostoyevsky to shape his arguments (Kirwan 2004), Kearney finds stories a means of understanding ourselves. He sees stories as open-ended invitations to ethical and practical responsiveness, a guide when confronted with the inexplicable and unthinkable: "Freed from all narrative traditions it is undecidable on Derridean . . . terms whether the voice I hear in my tent is that of the love of God or of some monster" (Kearney 2010: 97). And like Girard, he sees Christ's sacrifice as breaking the cycle of scapegoating (Kirwan 2004), reading the Eucharist as a reminder of divine emptying into society, the end of the metaphysical God beyond, and a hallowing of everyday, secular existence, a crazy, mad love of God pouring itself into the world so that we may witness Him in "dappled things," as the poet Gerald Manley Hopkins wrote.

Managers, as we have seen, are in search of a story, and yet the ones they have at their disposal are stories of self-sacrifice and struggle in pursuit of an apocalyptic, millennial vision. The globalized business world that frames both Peters, the anti-bureaucrat champion of the hyper-entrepreneurial autonomous knowledge worker, and the Derridian ethicist Jones has its own stock of stories. It is a secularization of divine order and nature, an evolutionary engine where competition and sacrifice lead us toward progress. These stories make possible mobilizations and other sacrifices—scapegoatings, industrial, ecological, and political (Palaver 2007). We should find other stories, tools of liberation, for "some stories congeal and incarcerate, others listen and emancipate" (Kearney 2003: 179).

God, who "takes leave of his full being in order to make us partners in achieving the Kingdom" (Kearney 2010: 95) prohibits further sacrifice, guaranteeing the Other as eschaton, refusing to let us position her as telos, as a predictable, foreseeable goal. It is no longer, he argues, the sacrifice of the individual that is required to achieve a promised kingdom but a far greater sacrifice already made on the Cross, opening up moments of possibility in the everyday. As Pally (2016) argues, we take our being from the source of God's being, yet remain ontologically, permanently distinct. Our creation in the image of God means that we are, at the core of our being, unable to avoid our relation to the divine and to one another. There is no escape from this "gift." We need better stories and better accounts of economic life.

Globalization scholar Francis Fukuyama might have written of the "end of history" as capitalism triumphed in the 1980s, but the eschaton reminds us that history is not yet done. There are stories about the purpose of the economy being written and still to come: visions of "prosperity without growth" (Jackson 2009) or covenantally grounded political and economic associations (Pally 2016). Both seek to reposition economic activity as meaningful in a world confronting the challenges of global environmental depredation and injustice. They seek to counter the anomie too often inherent in economic relations. Unlike the post-bureaucratic, pseudo-entrepreneurial squirrel-cage imagined by Peters, or the futile, directionless self-abnegation of Levinasian business ethics, these stories set economic activity within a participatory social order that emphasizes respect, dignity, and fulfillment. The vocabulary in each differs: Jackson, the economist, seeks to challenge the narrative of growth and rethink the purpose of enterprise; Pally, the theologian, calls for covenantal, agapic relations which might nurture alternatives to the dominant discourse and culture around us and—in her wonderful phrase—"puncture the numbness of the status quo" (Pally 2016: 317). Kearney himself (2002) shows how stories can draw borders and equally erase them. As we squabble over what to do with the Other (the refugee, the ocean, the iceberg, or the rough-sleeper), new stories can help us undo the boundaries that inculcate such otherness in the first place.

For the moment, however, those stories are consumed by a capitalism that trades in affect and experience as much as concrete goods. We struggle to move beyond a cycle of sacrifice, as yet unbroken. Facebook thrives: Thiel later sold his stake in the firm for roughly $1 billion, and his foundation now supports research into mimetic theory. A new economic covenant still seems far away, and the unity we face is one of endless, self-sacrificial striving, precarious labor, and uncertainty. Alas, it seems Girard is a fine commentator.

References

Anderson, E. (2017), *Private Government: How Employers Rule Our Lives (and Why We Don't Talk About It)*, Princeton: Princeton University Press.
Anspach, M. R. (2004), "Desired Possessions: Karl Polanyi, Rene Girard, and the Critique of the Market Economy," *Contagion: Journal of Violence, Mimesis, and Culture* 11 (1): 181–88.
Bauman, Z. (1989), *Modernity and the Holocaust*, Cambridge: Polity Press.
Bauman, Z. (1993), *Postmodern Ethics*, Oxford: Blackwell.
Brown, W. (2016), "Sacrificial Citizenship: Neoliberalism, Human Capital, and Austerity Politics," *Constellations* 23 (1): 3–14.
Child, J. (2005), *Organization*, Oxford: Blackwell.
Costas, J., and P. Fleming (2009), "Beyond Dis-Identification: A Discursive Approach to Self-Alienation in Contemporary Organizations," *Human Relations* 62 (3): 353–78.
Desmond, J., and D. Kavanagh (2003), "Organization as Containment of Acquisitive Mimetic Rivalry: The Contribution of René Girard," *Culture and Organization* 9 (4): 239–51.
du Gay, P. (2000), *In Praise of Bureaucracy*, London: Sage.
Dyck, B., F. A. Starke, and C. Dueck (2009), "Management, Prophets, and Self-Fulfilling Prophecies," *Journal of Management Inquiry* 18 (3): 184–96.
Foucault, M. (2008), *The Birth of Biopolitics*, trans. G. Burchell, ed. A. I. Davidson, Basingstoke: Palgrave Macmillan.
Girard, R. (2011), *Sacrifice*, East Lansing: Michigan State University Press.
Grint, K. (2010), "The Sacred in Leadership: Separation, Sacrifice and Silence," *Organization Studies* 31 (1): 89–107.

Guillaume, C., and S. Pochic (2009), "What Would You Sacrifice? Access to Top Management and the Work–Life Balance," *Gender, Work & Organization* 16 (1): 14–36.
Howell, J. M., and B. J. Avolio (1992), "The Ethics of Charismatic Leadership: Submission or Liberation?" *The Executive* 6 (2): 43–54.
Jackson, T. (2009), *Prosperity without Growth*, London: Earthscan Routledge.
Jones, C. (2003), "As If Business Ethics Were Possible, 'within Such Limits,'" *Organization* 10 (2): 223–48.
Kearney, R. (2002), *On Stories*, Abingdon: Routledge.
Kearney, R. (2003), *Strangers, Gods and Monsters*, Abingdon: Routledge.
Kearney, R. (2010), *Anatheism*, New York: Columbia University Press.
Kirwan, M. (2004), *Discovering Girard*, London: Darton, Longman and Todd.
Koestenbaum, P. (2002), *Leadership: The Inner Side of Greatness: A Philosophy for Leaders*, San Francisco: Jossey-Bass.
Lanchester, J. (2017), "You Are the Product," *London Review of Books* 39 (16): 3–10.
Lubasz, H. (1992), "Adam Smith and the Invisible Hand — of the Market?" in R. Dilley (ed.), *Contesting Markets*, 37–56, Edinburgh: Edinburgh University Press.
MacIntyre, A. (1981), *After Virtue: A Study in Moral Theory*, London: Duckworth.
Mansell, S. (2008), "Proximity and Rationalisation: The Limits of a Levinasian Ethics in the Context of Corporate Governance and Regulation," *Journal of Business Ethics* 83 (3): 565–77.
Mirowski, P. (1994), *Natural Images in Economic Thought: Markets Read in Tooth and Claw*, Cambridge: Cambridge University Press.
Nordström, K. A., and J. Ridderstråle (2002), *Funky Business: Talent Makes Capital Dance*, Hoboken: Pearson Education.
Palaver, W. (2005), "Envy or Emulation: A Christian Understanding of Economic Passions," in W. Palaver and P. Steinmar-Pösel (eds.), *Passions in Economy, Politics, and the Media*, 139–62, Vienna: Lit Verlag.
Palaver, W. (2007), "Challenging Capitalism as Religion: Hans G. Ulrich's Theological and Ethical Reflections on the Economy," *Studies in Christian Ethics* 20 (2): 215–30.
Pally, M. (2016), *Commonwealth and Covenant: Economics, Politics and Theologies of Relationality*, Grand Rapids: William B. Eerdmans.
Peters, T. (1992), *Liberation Management*, Basingstoke: Macmillan.
Peters, T., and R. Waterman (1982), *In Search of Excellence*, New York: Harper and Row.
Poulter, D., and C. Land (2008), "Preparing to Work: Dramaturgy, Cynicism and Normative 'Remote' Control in the Socialization of Graduate Recruits in Management Consulting," *Culture and Organization* 14 (1): 65–78.
Roscoe, P. (2014), *I Spend Therefore I Am*, London: Penguin Viking.
Schumpeter, J. A. (1934), *The Theory of Economic Development*, Oxford: Oxford University Press.
Sewell, G. and B. Wilkinson (1992), "'Someone to Watch over Me': Surveillance, Discipline and the Just-in-Time Labour Process," *Sociology* 26 (2): 271–89.

Śliwa, M., S. Spoelstra, B. M. Sørensen, and C. Land (2013), "Profaning the Sacred in Leadership Studies: A Reading of Murakami's a Wild Sheep Chase," *Organization* 20 (6): 860–80.
ten Bos, R. (1997), "Essai: Business Ethics and Bauman Ethics," *Organization Studies* 18 (6): 997–1014.
Veblen, T. (1994), *The Theory of the Leisure Class*. Available online: https://www.gutenberg.org/files/833/833-h/833-h.htm (accessed October 1, 2018).
Weber, M. (1930), *The Protestant Ethic and the Spirit of Capitalism*, trans. T. Parsons, London: Routledge.

13

Common Good Economy
Capitalism, Sacrifice, and Humanity

Adrian Pabst

Adrian Pabst takes issue with what he sees as two presuppositions of Rene Girard's thought: one, that resources are scarce so that people must compete for them and two, that humanity is by nature competitive. Pabst finds instead, referring to work done in the humanities and natural sciences, that the most important aspects of life, friendship and beauty, are not scarce commodities for which people must compete. Moreover, human beings are not naturally competitive but seek mutual recognition for their contribution to the common good. This endeavor requires not the sacrifice of others but "self-sacrifice and a commitment to reciprocity, relationships of give and receive." Pabst contrasts this society-building, donative effort with the sorts of sacrifice of "useless" people that is endemic to neoliberal capitalism, with its "globalization of indifference" and neo-Promethean marriage of market and technological change without regard to the aims and relationships people actually live for. On Pabst's account, it is not nature but this culture of indifference to all but greed that teaches competitiveness and which must be opposed.

—editor's note

On the nature of contemporary capitalism

Barely a quarter of a century ago, the Western economic model was seen by many elites around the world as hegemonic. After the end of the Cold War, capitalism had seemingly triumphed over communism, and a global convergence toward liberal market democracy appeared to be underway. Twenty-five years later the reality is largely one of monopoly markets in the West and state capitalism in the East (Lynn 2010; Kurlantzick 2016). The 2008 crash and the ensuing recession cast doubt on the capacity of Western liberal democracy to tame the forces of global capitalism. In response to the "credit crunch," Western states bailed out banks by taking over their debts in a manner that locks democracy itself yet more into a financial logic. Elected government has less and less regard for the political ends (in the sense of *telos*) of its citizens while the long-term needs of national society are subordinate to the short-term interests of a worldwide oligarchy (Kay 2015: 80–140). Instead of a democratic capitalism that distributes power, agency, and wealth to all, we have a capitalist democracy that favors the fortunes of a few.

Western liberal capitalism, especially in its Anglo-Saxon variety, maintains the illusion of open, competitive markets that generate prosperity for the people, whereas in reality they enforce monopoly and enrich a new oligarchic class of "professionals" led by financiers (Pabst 2019). The result is an economy that is characterized for most people by low labor productivity and low real wage growth, in which maximizing financial profit leads to the destruction of productive value (except perhaps in certain high-tech sectors) and the commodification of everyday existence. In turn, all this undermines "the everyday economy, which is made up of the services, production, consumption and social goods that sustain people in their daily life at home and at work" (Reeves 2018: 65). Contemporary capitalism is an engine that not only concentrates wealth and centralizes power but also commodifies labor, land, and life. Building on the notion of "the culture industry" (Adorno and Horkheimer 1947), Fredric Jameson (1991, 1992) has shown how neoliberalism, underpinning the dominant model of globalization, is grounded in a certain cultural logic. This logic tends to "spatialize" culture in such a way that the differentiation between spheres of life (politics, society, education) is dissolved and different social classes and roles in each sphere are increasingly absorbed into a single process of commodification. Accordingly, goods and services, as well as labor and land, are treated as commodities that can be endlessly exchanged within and across territory.

Crucially, commodification sunders material meaning from symbolic significance through a parallel process of abstraction and materialization. Everything and everyone are stripped of their holistic reality and reduced to mere matter or abstract number (Milbank and Pabst 2016: 93–127). Either way, this violates a universal ethical principle that has governed most cultures and societies in history: nature and human life have almost always been recognized as having a sacred dimension beyond power and wealth (Polanyi 1968, 1977). By contrast, capitalist commodification undermines both the dignity of the person and what Pope Francis (2015) calls in *Laudato Si'* "integral ecology"—care for our common home of nature.

Francis's development of "integral humanism" is at the heart of his defense of a moral economy and ecology. Already in *Evangelii Gaudium*, he made the crucial point that the global economic system rests on a neo-pagan form of sacrifice, sacrificing those who are economically "useless" on the altar of capitalist markets. Contemporary capitalism treats human beings as commodities that have some use value or can be disposed of but in any case, lack intrinsic worth:

> Human beings are themselves considered consumer goods to be used and then discarded. We have created a "throw away" culture which is now spreading. It is no longer simply about exploitation and oppression, but something new. Exclusion ultimately has to do with what it means to be a part of the society in which we live; . . . The excluded are not the "exploited" but the outcast, the "leftovers." (Pope Francis 2013b: §53)

Perhaps more so than other Christian leader today, Francis recognizes that capitalism reinforces a culture of greed and selfishness on which interdependency, technology, and statism all thrive—the forces underpinning the "globalization of indifference." In other remarks, the pope denounced a "culture of waste" that involves idolatrous sacrifice:

> Man is not in charge today, money is in charge, money rules. God our Father did not give the task of caring for the earth to money, but to us, to men and women. . . . Instead, men and women are sacrificed to the idols of profit and consumption. (Pope Francis 2013a)

The logic underpinning capitalism, which locks supposedly greedy and selfish individuals in a perpetual "war of all against all" over scarce resources, gets reality wrong, doubly so. Human beings are naturally neither egotistic nor altruist but are rather characterized by "common decency" (George Orwell) and by the pursuit of reciprocal recognition and mutual flourishing (Michéa 2017). It is also the case that over the medium term—rather than at any one point in time—resources tend toward infinity thanks to human labor, ingenuity, and technological tools.

Here one can say with René Girard (1966, 1977) that the fantasy of scarcity supposes a purely natural contagion of mimetic desiring, which denies any hierarchical ordering of values or any sense that the most valuable things, such as friendship and beauty, are not naturally in short supply but culturally either valued or derided. There is no question that Girard's work uniquely captures the various pathologies involved in mimetic desire, but where I differ is on the primacy of competition over cooperation: human beings are not by nature more mimetically competitive than cooperative, precisely because they seek mutual recognition of their talents and roles in society more than they desire competition or conflict. This conception accords with the emphasis on relationality in the humanities (Pabst 2012) and the natural sciences (Pally 2016). Therefore, I would question the tendency in Girard's thought of separating our natural condition of mimetic desire from a culture that either nurtures or denies our natural desire for the good, true, and beautiful. For this reason, Girardian philosophy is caught in the nature-culture divide that—with cognate binaries such as immanence and transcendence, self and other—defines much of modern thinking (Sahlins 2008).

Similarly, capitalist ontology rests on this dualistic logic insofar as it assumes an externally given nature, which humanity can exploit at will, and an artificially constructed culture, which mirrors individual and collective volition. *Really existing* capitalism brings about a social reality in which infinite greed and *scarce* natural resources leave human beings perpetually unfulfilled. Desire becomes debased to mean permanent lust for the (culturally constructed) ephemeral based on a denial of nature's plenitudinous abundance and on the self-fulfilling prophecy of diminishing marginal returns. Just as the capitalist system turns humans *qua* social animals into greedy apes with bigger brains (soon to be superseded by AI-enabled robots), so too it artificially engineers scarcity through a culturally constructed and maintained combination of monopoly control and the extraction of economic rent (Pabst 2019).

The fusion of the liberal tradition with capitalism is grounded in a triple perversion of the classical and Christian heritage: first, the ontological violence of perpetual "war of all against all" replaces an originally peaceful ordering of reality (which nevertheless accommodates the Fall and human sinfulness, as St. Augustine developed). Second, the anthropological pessimism of natural selfishness overrides the natural desire for mutual recognition and cooperation (Pally 2016: 33–35). Third, the profanation of the sacred displaces the sanctity of labor, land, and life in favor of a sacralization of the profane. Thus, capitalism engenders the sacrifice of humanity that renders the underlying liberal logic "the realm of lesser evil"—the best of all possible realities in a world of necessary perversion (Michéa 2007).

Reinforced by globalization and technology, liberal capitalism unleashes the forces of domestication and dispossession of human beings and their intrinsic worth. Instead of a greater degree of self-government, capitalism involves the administration of people and nature as commodities circulating in an unmediated space. It is also grounded in the oscillation between the individual—who is disembedded from history, institutions, and relationships (Polanyi 2001)—and the collective, based upon a positivist legal system.

In sum, this liberal order is inherently unstable and prone to periodic crises because liberalism erodes the very foundations on which it rests (Milbank and Pabst 2016). It brings about economic injustice and divisions in society that are threatening the social contract between the people and their representatives, which is the bedrock of the liberal tradition since Hobbes and Locke. Even on its own terms, liberal capitalism oscillates between the illusion of infinite progress (ever-greater economic growth and social liberation) and the reality of sacrificing our humanity to the idol of commodifying capital.

The anti-humanism of post-capitalist politics

Post-capitalism and kindred movements that purport to resist liberal globalization are no less anti-humanist than the advocates of liberalism. At the hands of the radical Right and the revolutionary left, politics has joined forces with technological determinism and anti-humanism that rest on the same ontology—a conception of being that fuses the idea of "infinite possibility" with the notion of a "closed immanence." This ontology assumes, first of all, that real actuality in some manner derives from possibility, for example, through an act of will or power; second, that the realm of natural immanence is separate from the realm of supernatural transcendence such that the immanent is self-explanatory and self-governing, without any transcendent origin or outlook. As Charles Taylor has argued, "One of the great inventions of the West was that of an immanent order in Nature, whose working could be systematically understood and explained on its own terms" (Taylor 2007: 15). Such an ontology rejects any conception of natural law (in the sense of perennial principles of nature that are given by a transcendent source), fetishizes the transgression of natural limits and embraces the nihilism of "dark enlightenment" (Land 1992, 2013). By this Land means a philosophy that denies the equal worth of all human beings and instead proposes an ontology of Social Darwinism whereby the strong dominate the weak and pursue a machinic desire, the desire of fusing humanity with technology. Humans are now enslaved to technology and operate under the illusion that they can be released from all natural or historical constraints, which mistakes human finitude for divine infinity. This represents a surrender of universal human nature, of the dignity of the person and of the quest for the common good anchored in mutual flourishing and the building of a just society.

Against liberal capitalism, the resurgent extremes seek to invent an alternative modernity that is anti-liberal but in reality is an intensification of certain modern liberal ideas, such as the cult of the individual (the strongman, the libertarian self) along with an invocation of the "will of the people," the unmediated power of techno-science and a non-teleological cosmos in which both nature and humanity will be replaced. Or rather, to use the deceptive "accelerationist" language, "enhanced" by a new Promethean spirit (Brassier 2014).

Prometheanism combines a naturalist philosophy in which reality has no purpose and a materialist politics driven by techno-economic forces—a belief it shares with the accelerationist Marxism that underpins post-capitalist thinking (Srnicek and Williams 2015; Mason 2015; Bastani 2019): "Existence is worthless . . . and nihilism is . . . the unavoidable corollary of the realist conviction that there is a mind-independent reality which . . . is indifferent to our existence and oblivious to the 'values' and 'meanings' which we would drape over it in order to make it more hospitable" (Brassier 2007: ix). Accelerationism rejects transcendental idealism in favor of an empty materialism that is monist or dualist but either way nihilistic.

Just as Prometheus's theft of fire sought to subvert the power of the gods in an attempt to elevate humans from their supposed humiliation, so too the new Prometheanism attempts to remake humanity through the unmediated power of technology. The convergence of nanotech, biotech, infotech, and cognitive science serves to create a "plane of immanence" (building on the immanentist ontology from Duns Scotus via Spinoza to Gilles Deleuze) that transcends our human condition of interpersonal relations in the direction of a "new singularity." This singularity is based upon a flat ontology of equivalence between all subjects that make up the "multitude" (Hardt and Negri 2005). The objective is to liberate the individual and the masses not simply from the trap of contemporary capitalism but above all from any limits of nature or history. Both the natural order and inherited traditions are seen as arbitrary, irrational boundaries on our free mind that artificially creates reality from nothing. Technologically enhanced humanity replaces the Creator God as the immanentized supernatural source of being. Instead of coming into existence ex nihilo, humans are now revealed to have a "will to nothingness" as paradoxically the ground of everything. The nihilist core of Promethean thinking reduces the realm of "closed immanence" to the unmediated power of the individual that seeks nothing other than a self-aggrandizement—an empty ontology of pure will without any relationship to others or to nature. Transhumanism is a nihilism that sacrifices our created human nature to the neo-pagan gods of technology based on an immanentist ontology.

By positing that human nature is in total flux, modern transhumanists from Aldous Huxley's brother Julian Huxley (1960) to Max More (1990, 2013) view the possibilities of science and technology as more fundamental than the actuality of life—to the point where everything from antiaging genetic research, robotics, AI, and cybernetics to life extension, "mind-uploading," and cryonics ends up producing new forms of existence that engender ever more advanced versions of themselves. This "singularity moment" of equivalence among all is portrayed as the new frontier of reason and science when in fact it constitutes the meeting point of closed immanence, "new age" fanaticism and science fiction. "If you love life, extend it into the vanishing ether of cyber-reality" seems to be the transhumanists' oddly life-denying motto.

The Promethean spirit promises to release us from our affections and attachments to relationships and institutions that make us more fully human as social, political beings. Brassier's "nihil unbound" is a release, which is not the same as liberation from oppression and exploitation combined with a promotion of human self-government. Rather, Brassier and his fellow accelerationists have in mind "a Promethean politics of maximal mastery over society" (§21) that fuses "the command of The Plan" (a top-down diktat of administration) with "the improvised order of The Network" (a horizontal plane of individual transactions) (§14) (Williams and Srnicek 2014). Here, libertarian freedom meets totalitarian control, rendering technology the master of human beings rather than an aid.

This means not resisting or transforming capitalism but instead realizing the capitalist utopia of infinite possibility outside of the bounds of history and nature: "Expansion beyond the limitations of the earth and our immediate bodily forms" (§22) "... towards the universal possibilities of the Outside" (§24) (Williams and Srnicek 2014). Only accelerationism can fulfill the promise of the Enlightenment to "shift beyond the world of minimal technical upgrades towards all encompassing change" (§22) because humanity and the universe are by nature deficient and therefore require technological completion. The individual, released from all constraints, can be whatever she wants—an idolatrous illusion that replaces God or some notion of divine transcendence with the closed immanence of the individual.

Based on a similarly Promethean anti-humanism, liberals have passed laws permitting euthanasia and sex changes for minors without parental agreement, as in Belgium, the Netherlands, and Norway. To allow people to die as they wish or to change their gender is to subordinate the intrinsic value of human life in its givenness to individual freedom of choice and the pursuit of happiness, itself construed in merely *utilitarian* terms as maximizing pleasure and avoiding pain—not a richer sense of happiness that combines personal fulfillment with mutual flourishing. Since we are born into specific bodies and cultures at particular moments in history, the idea that our whole life is or should be purely a function of our own volition is misguided. To make it a matter of choice would be to encourage the wider liberal-capitalist illusion that the human subject is an uncharacterized empty will, detached from her body of which she is the mere proprietor (Milbank and Pabst 2016: 247–82). There are very few people who feel neither male nor female, and while their difference should be recognized, exceptions tend to prove the rule that gender occurs exhaustively as male or female. Moreover, to accept historical and natural limits on our bodies includes the acceptance that life involves suffering and dying. Liberals who claim we have a right to happiness abhor the thought of human frailty because it gets in the way of feeling good about yourself. But no person enjoys full sovereign jurisdiction over her own possession of life and her body.

Even self-ownership requires protection by the state because some collective power has to uphold the individual right to property. Therefore, liberalism effectively grants government power over life itself. That is why liberals have not hesitated to liberalize euthanasia, the latest stage in sacrificing our humanity. This hands over life to the forces of the state and the market, treating it as a commodity that can be traded or dispensed with without regard to its intrinsic worth. If this were true, we would have to conclude that we really are isolated individuals, disembedded from relationships with other embodied beings and reducible to biological-chemical processes. To adopt this perspective is to abandon the entire basis of humanism. It is to replace the idea of dignity with private liberty and comfort, which are now the only constraints on individual choice as they stop people from harming others but not from engaging in self-harm. Paradoxically, liberalism promises liberation from any constraint not chosen by consenting adults while at the same time being subordinate to the liberal world order based on an overweening state and the expanding global market (Deneen 2018). Yet behind the negatively self-choosing individual stands the state, which can either permit anti-humanism or, on the contrary, uphold principles in line with natural law that grants human existence a unique status and promotes life over death.

Renewing integral humanism

Faced with the new biological totalitarianism of capitalist and post-capitalist thinking, Pope Francis seeks to renew integral humanism. Building on the writings of Saint John Paul II and Pope Emeritus Benedict XVI, he is developing Catholic social teaching with its principles for reflection and guidance for action. In *Laudato Si'*, Francis (2015) accentuates the importance of natural law and a divinely created cosmic order that are not reducible to human will but instead require careful judgment and prudence. We need to be wary of claims about measureless acquisition and endless growth in a finite world in which humankind transgresses all manner of physical and moral boundaries at its own peril. As Rowan Williams (2015) suggests in his reading of *Laudato Si'*,

> The plain thereness of the physical word we inhabit tells us from our first emergence into consciousness that our will is not the foundation of everything— and so its proper working is essentially about creative adjustment to an agenda set not by our fantasy but by the qualities and complexities of what we encounter. The material world tells us that to be human is to be in dialogue with what is other: what is physically other, what is humanly other in the solid three-dimensionality of other persons, ultimately what is divinely other.

According to Pope Francis's diagnosis of the contemporary world, the fundamental issue is the loss of meaning—the intrinsic worth and purpose of human beings, other animals, and the entire biosphere. This is what lies behind the new culture of "disposability" in which everyone and everything that does not satisfy our immediate desires can so readily be dispensed with precisely because it has already been turned into a commodity. Ultimately, "When the culture itself is corrupt and objective truth and universally valid principles are no longer upheld, then laws can only be seen as arbitrary impositions or obstacles to be avoided" (Pope Francis 2015: §123).

Against the extremes of statist collectivization and capitalist commodification, Catholic Social Thought charts an alternative economics that emphasizes the common good. Legislation and regulation are pointless unless we can move politics and the economy beyond the sole pursuit of private profit or public utility (again, in the utilitarian calculation) toward a plural search for goods in common that are open to all. In the tradition of Catholic humanism, the common good combines individual fulfillment with mutual flourishing. It neither imposes a single conception of goodness on all nor does it represent the utilitarian "greatest good of the greatest number," for both concepts would exclude certain persons or even whole groups.

In *Caritas in veritate*, Pope Benedict XVI (2009: §7) defines the common good as,

> the good of "all of us," made up of individuals, families and intermediate groups who together constitute society. It is a good that is sought not for its own sake,

but for the people who belong to the social community and who can only really and effectively pursue their good within it.

Therefore, the common good is *not* the total mathematically measurable good—the sum total of individual utilitarian happiness in some artificial aggregate average like national output (Zamagni 2010). For national output counts people one by one, not in their real relationships. By contrast, the common good is concerned with the truest goods that we share together as human beings and members of society.

Likewise, against the extremes of egoism and abstract altruism, Catholic Social Thought charts an alternative ethics that focuses on human virtue that itself a just middle between the vice of excess and the vice of deficiency. To speak of virtue does not mean a pious new demand for more morality in public life, as if morality were something alien to the economy or politics (Milbank and Pabst 2016). Instead, the crucial point is that there can be no human practice, which is always shared and communal, unless we are aiming for the good in some sense and have some idea how to recognize and successfully pursue it. Morality is not a kind of optional extra for either the economic or the political process. Instead, ethics is always already in continuity with all human activities, including finance and business. Pope Francis (2013b) puts this succinctly: "Ethics—a non-ideological ethics—would make it possible to bring about balance [in the marketplace] and a more humane social order."

Such an order requires self-sacrifice and a commitment to reciprocity, relationships of give and receive. Catholic Christian notions of self-sacrifice in society and the economy emanate ultimately from Jesus Christ's supreme act of self-sacrifice in the crucifixion. Jesus, by his suffering and death, has become "the mediator of a new covenant" (Hebrew 9:15). These words refract into the acts that instituted the Eucharist as the sacrament of the Lord's own body and blood, given up for all humankind. Self-sacrifice is inextricably intertwined with the saving sacrifice for the redemption of the world. In the practice of the Eucharistic sacrament, our own sacrifices, sufferings, needs, and hopes are united to Christ's supreme sacrifice.

Catholic Social Thought is grounded in this understanding of (self-)sacrifice. Based on the idea of a civil market economy, the task is to tackle the economic injustice common to both free-market capitalism in the West and state capitalism in the East by reconciling estranged interests. Pope Francis links the preferential option for the poor to reciprocal obligations and the value of work in a way that combines proper contribution with just desert. The emphasis on reciprocal obligations means that that the rich have a duty to "help, respect, and promote the poor" (Francis 2013b: 58) and that this "is an ethical imperative essential for effectively attaining the common good" (Pope Francis 2015: §158). At the same time, Catholic Social Thought rejects a passive state of dependency and a mentality of individual entitlements and state handouts, which characterize the modern welfare state. Instead, the aim is to uphold the dignity of the human person by emphasizing contribution to society and the importance of work. That is why, in the words of the Holy Father, financial help for the poor "must always be a provisional solution in the face of pressing needs. The broader objective should always be to allow them a *dignified life through work*" (Pope Francis 2015: §128 [added emphasis]).

"Love and labor, these two things only," as the Christian socialist William Morris said. By contrast, today liberal capitalism promotes lust and leisure. The historical concern of politics with nurturing citizenship and forming character was lost through a slide into moralism, on the "conservative" side, and an obsession with the idea of an "unencumbered self," on the liberal side, which Michael Sandel (1984: 94) describes as "more entangled, but less attached, than ever before." This captures a key characteristic of contemporary society: an increase in interdependence, combined with a sharp decline in attachment to public institutions and civic associations. As the bonds of family, community, work, church, and nation are eroding, the scale of loneliness and isolation is growing. At the same time, individuals are increasingly connected with each other through the global economy and media, but often we lack real relationships in the places we inhabit.

The social theorist Sherry Turkle (2011) calls this phenomenon "alone together." It is not just addiction to the web and the sheer time we spend in cyberspace rather than the real world. The even more worrying trend is the demand for robot companions that are seen as more desirable than fellow human beings. We embrace robots as teachers, caregivers, and even lovers just as we keep humans at a distance. Relationships with embodied beings are mediated by machines that allow us to escape any unwanted human contact with a simple click. Fear of reality unmediated by technology goes hand in hand with a preference for simulations of life over life itself. As interaction with machines becomes a substitute for relationships with flesh-and-blood people, we put our faith in technology as a panacea for human frailty when acceptance of frailty is what makes us human. The defense of humanism is the new pivot in politics.

References

Adorno, T., and M. Horkheimer (1947), *Dialektik der Aufklärung*, Amsterdam: Querido (*Dialectic of Enlightenment*, trans. E. Jephcott, Stanford: Stanford University Press, 2002).

Bastani, A. (2019), *Fully Automated Luxury Communism: A Manifesto*, London: Verso.

Brassier, R. (2007), *Nihil Unbound: Enlightenment and Extinction*, London: Palgrave.

Brassier, R. (2014), "Prometheanism and Its Critics," in R. Mackaey and A. Avenessian (eds.), *#Accelerate: The Accelerationist Reader*, 467–88, Falmouth: Urbanomic.

Deneen, P. J. (2018), *Why Liberalism Failed*, New Haven: Yale University Press.

Girard, R. (1966), *Deceit, Desire and the Novel: Self and Other in Literary Structure*, trans. P. Gregory, Baltimore: Johns Hopkins University Press.

Girard, R. (1977), *Violence and the Sacred*, trans. P. Gregory, Baltimore: Johns Hopkins University Press.

Hardt, M., and A. Negri (2005), *Multitude: War and Democracy in the Age of Empire*, London: Penguin.

Huxley, J. (1960), *Knowledge, Morality and Destiny*, New York: New American Library.

Jameson, F. (1991), *Postmodernism, or, the Cultural Logic of Late Capitalism*, Durham: Duke University Press.

Jameson, F. (1992), *The Geopolitical Aesthetic: Cinema and Space in the World System*, Bloomington: Indiana University Press.

Kay, J. (2015), *Other People's Money: Masters of the Universe or Servants of the People?* London: Profile Books.

Kurlantzick, J. (2016), *State Capitalism: How the Return of Statism Is Transforming the World*, Oxford: Oxford University Press.

Land, N. (1992), *The Thirst for Annihilation: Georges Bataille and Virulent Nihilism*, London: Routledge.

Land, N. (2013), "The Dark Enlightenment." Available online: http://www.thedarken lightenment.com/the-dark-enlightenment-by-nick-land (accessed February 1, 2018).

Lynn, B. C. (2010), *Cornered: The New Monopoly Capitalism and the Economics of Destruction*, Oxford: Wiley.

Mason, P. (2015), *Postcapitalism: A Guide to our Future*, London: Allen Lane.

Michéa, J.-C. (2007), *L'empire du moindre mal. Essai sur la civilisation libérale*, Paris: Editions Climats (*The Realm of Lesser Evil: An Essay on Liberal Civilisation*, trans. D. Fernbach, Cambridge: Polity, 2009).

Michéa, J.-C. (2017), *Notre ennemi, le capital*, Paris: Ed. Climats.

Milbank, J., and A. Pabst (2016), *The Politics of Virtue: Post-Liberalism and the Human Future*, London: Rowman & Littlefield International.

More, M. (1990), "Transhumanism: Towards a Futurist Philosophy," *Extropy* 6: 6–12.

More, M. (2013), "The Philosophy of Transhumanism," in M. More and N. Vita-More (eds.), *The Transhumanist Reader: Classical and Contemporary Essays on the Science, Technology, and Philosophy of the Human Future*, 3–17, Oxford: Wiley.

Pabst, A. (2012), *Metaphysics: The Creation of Hierarchy*, Grand Rapids: Eerdmans.

Pabst, A. (2019), *The Demons of Liberal Democracy*, Cambridge: Polity, in press.

Pally, M. (2016), *Commonwealth and Covenant: Economics, Politics, and Theologies of Relationality*, Grand Rapids: Eerdmans.

Polanyi, K. (1968), *Primitive, Archaic and Modern Economies: Essays of Karl Polanyi*, ed. G. Dalton, New York: Anchor Books.

Polanyi, K. (1977), *The Livelihood of Man*, New York: Academic Press.

Polanyi, K. ([1944] 2001), *The Great Transformation: The Political and Economic Origins of Our Time*, Boston: Beacon Press.

Pope Francis (2013a), General Audience, June 5, 2013. Available online: http://w2.vatican.va/content/francesco/en/audiences/2013/documents/papa-francesco_20130605_udienza-generale.html (accessed February 3, 2018).

Pope Francis (2013b), *Evangelii Gaudium*, Rome, November 24, 2013. Available online: http://www.vatican.va/holy_father/francesco/apost_exhortations/documents/papa-francesco_esortazione-ap_20131124_evangelii-gaudium_en.html (accessed February 6, 2018).

Pope Francis (2015), Laudato Si', May 24, 2015. Available online: http://w2.vatican.va/content/francesco/en/encyclicals/documents/papa-francesco_20150524_enciclica-laudato-si.html (accessed February 10, 2018).

Reeves, R. (2018), "The Everyday Economy." Available online: https://www.scribd.com/document/374425087/Rachel-Reeves-The-Everyday-Economy (accessed February 15, 2018).

Sahlins, M. (2008), *The Western Illusion of Human Nature* (Chicago: Prickly Paradigm)

Sandel, M. J. (1984), "The Procedural Republic and the Unencumbered Self," *Political Theory* 12 (1): 81–96.

Srnicek, N. and A. Williams (2015), *Inventing the Future: Postcapitalism and a World Without Work*, London: Verso.

Taylor, C. (2007), *A Secular Age*. Cambridge: Harvard University Press.

Turkle, S. (2011), *Alone Together: Why We Expect More from Technology and Less from Each Other*, London: Hachette.

Williams, A., and N. Srnicek (2014), "Accelerate: Manifesto for an Accelerationist Politics," in R. Mackaey and A. Avenessian (eds.), *Accelerate: The Accelerationist Reader*, 347–62, Falmouth: Urbanomic.

Williams, R. (2015), "Embracing Our Limits: The Lessons of *Laudato Si'*," *Commonweal*, September 23, 2015. Available online: https://www.commonwealmagazine.org/embracing-our-limits (accessed February 12, 2018).

Zamagni, S. (2010), "Catholic Social Teaching, Civil Economy, and the Spirit of Capitalism," in D. K. Finn (ed.), *The True Wealth of Nations. Catholic Social Thought and Economic Life*, 63–93, Oxford: Oxford University Press.

14

Suffering and Sacrifice in an Unfinished Universe

Ilia Delio, OSF

Distinguishing between sacrifice ex carentia *(from loss) and* ex abundantia *(from abundance of love for the other), Ilia Delio explores the role of sacrifice and suffering in "an incomplete world." Drawing on the work of the Jesuit Pierre Teilhard de Chardin, she describes our incomplete world as evolving continuously to greater forms of intelligence, love, and understanding. As "our fastest evolver is artificial intelligence, . . . We are heading toward a new techno sapien species and thus need values and principles, including the role of suffering and sacrifice, to both understand and guide our evolution." Delio argues that sacrifice* ex abundantia *is not a societal problem but necessary and vital to developing a future of reciprocal concern and commitment. Here, she echoes Girard's emphasis on ending violence by following the cross's lesson of donative self-sacrifice, giving for the sake of others. Though Delio somewhat startlingly posits a new "techno sapiens," this creature is not so very different from our past and present as cooperative sacrifice is precisely what is critical to its future evolution as well.*

—editor's note

Introduction

The book of Genesis tells us that Adam and Eve were created for life in paradise but disobeyed God's command and fell into sin, bringing with them suffering and death (Genesis 3:14-19). Western culture is essentially based on the Judeo-Christian tradition and thus continues to maintain that pain and suffering oppose life. The word "suffering" in this context connotes a "lack of" or "need" (*ex carentia*) in an individual existent. We suffer because we are personally vulnerable and experience loss. However, there is another type of suffering rooted in relationality. Our hearts may be torn because our family members of friends have lost something that belongs to their integrity. We suffer with them because we reach beyond ourselves and identify ourselves with them. In this respect, suffering is not out of need or lack but out of abundance (*ex abundantia*).

Interestingly, both types of suffering are found in the New Testament: suffering *ex carentia* is apropos to the Synoptic Gospels while suffering *ex abundantia* reflects the Gospel of John where Jesus offers up his life to the Father out of an abundance of love. Rene Girard's mimetic theory is based on suffering in the Synoptic Gospels. Jesus is the innocent victim who assumes suffering and becomes the symbol of all those who suffer *ex carentia*, especially in his excruciating cry on the cross (Matthew 26:46). Here, I will build on Girard's insight that humanity may escape the violence we cause each other by embracing the extraordinary love shown on the cross. I will argue that suffering *ex abundantia* is creative suffering in so far as it is grounded in relationality and linked to sacrifice, by which isolated existence is relinquished for the sake of greater union.

The Jesuit Pierre Teilhard de Chardin spoke of suffering as part of creative evolution. Although Teilhard used science to ground his insights, we can find the root of his ideas in John's Gospel where the sacrifice of Jesus's life flows from his unity with the Father, summed up in the prayer "that all may be one" (John 17:21). Although Girard's mimetic theory can help explain the crisis of violence in contemporary culture, Teilhard's insights on creative evolution allows a wider framework for understanding sacrifice and suffering in an unfinished universe. Teilhard held that evolution is moving toward greater personalization and socialization insofar as individual existents must sacrifice isolation for the sake of more union. Union here connotes degrees of relationality and is the basis of personalization, as he wrote: "Love is the only energy in the world that is capable of personalizing by totalizing, of promoting synthesis without destroying personality. It alone unites human beings in such a way as to complete and fulfill them" (Teilhard 1959: 154).

To put this more aptly, modern science discloses a dynamic, unfinished universe in which the fundamental incompleteness of created reality requires openness to new levels of relationship. Life flourishes when sacrifice and suffering are integral to emerging life in evolution. How we approach sacrifice and suffering, therefore, is how we see our role in an unfinished universe. Are we failed creatures who suffer the opposition of one another or we a developing planetary community with an infinite future before us? Despite the tragedies of our world, profound and sorrowful as they are, they do not have the last word.

We are invited into a new future where suffering and sacrifice make a difference in how we live together and envision a new world emerging up ahead.

A dynamic universe

Evolution is usually associated with Charles Darwin, who disclosed mechanisms of change in evolution, such as natural selection and adaptation, challenging the notion of a divine design or plan of nature. Darwin posited evolution within a mechanistic framework and struggled with nature's profound levels of suffering. He could not reconcile the hardness of nature with a loving God. It would take another century for science to reveal a new cosmology and an entirely new understanding of nature as an open process of dynamic life.

In 1905 Albert Einstein published a paper on relativity which changed our understanding of the physical world. Contrary to notions of absolute space and time, Einstein posited that space and time are not fixed but relative to the speed of light and that energy and matter are equivalent. His ideas gave birth to a new understanding of the universe in which space and time are interrelated and unfolding. In 1916 the Dutch physicist Willem de Sitter constructed a universe that could stretch in different directions "like taffy," a theoretical insight that received experimental support in 1928 when the astronomer Edwin Hubble "using the most powerful telescope of his day, found that every galaxy in the sky was moving away from us" (Frank 2009: 146). These discoveries gave birth to the Big Bang and the realization that our universe is about 13.8 billion years old with a future of billions of years before us.

On the micro level, quantum physics disclosed a new role for the human mind in relation to matter. The relationship between energy and matter allowed scientists to revisit causal mechanisms in nature. Whereas Darwin conceived of evolution in terms of natural selection, adaptation, and survival, scientists began to see nature as cooperative and organized into self-sustaining systems. Austrian biologist Ludwig Bertalanffy described living organisms as open systems, meaning that systems feed on a continual flux of matter and energy from their environment. He set out to replace the mechanistic foundations of science with a holistic vision based on general systems (Capra 1996: 48).

Evolution can be described as a movement toward more complexified life forms in which, at critical points in the evolutionary process, qualitative differences emerge. It discloses nature as creative and transcendent. Nature is characterized by genuinely new and dynamic physical reality marked by the term "emergence" which marks nature as *"more than but not altogether other than . . .* a recurrent pattern of novelty and irreducibility" (Clayton 2006: 39; emphasis in original). At some point, evolution reaches a reflexive state in the human person, in whom the idea of evolution comes to explicit expression. Today, our fastest evolver is artificial intelligence, in and through which human nature is transcending itself at an exponential rate. We are heading toward a new *techno sapien* species and thus need values and principles, including the role of suffering and sacrifice, to both understand and guide our evolution. Absent such understanding, we are likely to become increasingly atomized and disconnected from one another and from the realm of nature, especially if we seek to use technology to overcome suffering and death in the pursuit of optimal life.

God in evolution

While natural selection and adaptation may account for diversity, they do not account for the continued emergence of novelty in nature. Henri Bergson said that nature seems to resist the inner evolutionary tendency to change unless there is something different at the heart of nature that challenges nature to change (Bergson 1935: 263). Teilhard de Chardin posited a principle of Omega, something in nature that is wholly other than nature; distinct yet intrinsic, autonomous, and independent, yet deeply influential on the nature's propensity toward complexity and consciousness (Teilhard 1959: 257–60). Omega is the incarnate presence of God.

Teilhard felt that the static God-world relationship described by Thomas Aquinas did not fit the world now described by evolution. He insisted there exists a genuine "complementarity" between God and the world. That is, God and the world form a naturally interrelated and complementary pair, which led him to reject the metaphysics of *being*, proposing instead an alternative metaphysics of *union* (De Chardin 1968: 182). God is different from the world in nature but personally linked to it in a relationship of mutual complementarity (Panikkar 2010: 191). He claimed that the traditional view of God and creation, the "metaphysics of the eternally present," was inadequate for the reality of evolution. Evolution, he claimed, requires a divine source located not in the past or "up above" in a timeless present but "up ahead" in the future. He described the God of the future as the ultimate force of universal attraction, drawing the universe toward intensification of complexity and new creation (Haught 2003: 174).

Teilhard did not hold to a doctrine of creation separate from evolution but saw creative union as the way God acts in evolution by uniting Godself to matter. A Thomistic understanding of creation views creation as a free act of God, but Teilhard focused on the divine love of God. Since God is intrinsically relational, relationality lies at the root of all reality. In this respect, there is no other God than the God of self-involving love, which is the heart of creative union. Creation is a kenosis of divine love, an emptying of divine self into other. God becomes "element" and thus draws all things through love into the fullness of being. We take hold of God in the finite; God is sensed as "rising" or "emerging" from the depths of creation, born not in the heart of matter but *as* the heart of matter (King 1981: 103). Without creation, something would be absolutely lacking to God, considered in the fullness not of his being but of his act of union.

Sacrificial evolution?

God's presence in nature impels nature toward sacrificial love. If God is self-giving love, then so too is nature. Zachary Hayes writes, "Isolated, independent existence must be given up in order to enter into broader and potentially deeper levels of existence" (1997: 91). Sacrifice and suffering are integral to a world grounded in love (Einum and Fleming 2000: 565–67). This pattern of sacrifice and new life can be found from the smallest cellular levels of life to the level of human persons. Holmes Rolston writes, "In the flesh and blood creatures, each is a blood sacrifice perishing that others might live.... In their lives, beautiful, tragic and perpetually incomplete, they speak for God; they prophesy as they participate in the divine pathos.... They share the labor of the divinity" (2001: 57).

While sacrifice may be integral to nature, it is more difficult to reconcile suffering and evil as part of the evolutionary process. In Thomistic philosophy, evil is considered as a privation of being. Teilhard saw evil as an incompleteness of the creature insofar as the creature is oriented toward a higher state of unity (Faricy 1966: 555). "He thought that at every level—preliving, living, reflectively conscious—it is impossible that there not be some disorder or lack of organization in a multiplicity that is progressively moving toward a higher degree of organization" (1966: 556). Evil is the very expression of a state of plurality that is not yet completely organized. It is "the shadow that God raises by His very decision to create" (1966: 557). A universe in evolution is unfinished and therefore labors and suffers (De Chardin 1959: 313). In Teilhard's view evil is, in a sense, inevitable, "bound to the very structure of the cosmos . . . and part of the very law of becoming" (Faricy 1966: 558). Hence, "everything that is not yet finished and is being organized must inevitably suffer in its residual lack of organization and in its possible disorganization" (1966: 559). This is the human condition and the condition of the universe.

Teilhard held that an evolving world is an unfinished and imperfect world. He thought that suffering and sacrifice played a role in helping to fulfill God's project for the world, primarily because they can be transformed into creativity. From the point of faith, he held that the life, death, and resurrection of Jesus Christ recapitulate the process of evolution as cruciform in nature. He envisioned the evolutionary process as one moving toward evolution of consciousness and, ultimately, toward evolution of spirit, from the birth of mind to the birth of the whole Christ. He called this process "Christogenesis" (De Chardin 1964: 309). As such, the universe is in formation and requires the energy of pain, suffering, and sacrificial love. Death is not an erratic disjointed aspect of life; rather it is integral to the evolving fullness of life. Rolston states that "ninety-eight percent of all species that have every existed have gone extinct . . . [yet] the death of the organism feeds into the nondeath of the species . . . on the average, there have been more arrivals than extinctions—resulting in the increase of both diversity and complexity over evolutionary history" (2001: 57).

Metaphorically, the Earth is as much like a womb in its gestation of life rather than like a lion on the prowl. Biological nature is always giving birth (hence, the meaning of *physis*), regenerating itself and thus always in travail. Something is always dying, and something is always living on: "The whole creation has been groaning in travail until now" (Romans 8:22). Death arrives but new life is constantly generated in the effort to pass life on from one generation to the next (Rolston 2001: 58). Death, therefore, must be meaningfully integrated into the biological processes as a necessary counterpart to the emergence of life. Rolston writes, "This whole evolutionary upslope is a calling in which renewed life comes by blasting the old. Life is gathered up in the midst of its throes, a blessed tragedy, lived in grace through a besetting storm. . . . Things perish with a passing over in which the sacrificed individual also flows in the river of life" (2001: 59). Without the sacrifice and death of isolated existences, no new life can emerge.

Does God suffer?

Teilhard's theology is based on the idea that God is involved in creation. The name "God" reflects the incomprehensible wellspring of love at the heart of an expanding universe. The Christian understanding of God's relational nature begins with the Father who vitalizes and engenders, the fontal source of all that is, including the personal center of the Trinity, who is Son and Word. The Spirit is the personal energy of divine love unifying the Father and Son. To ask if God suffers is to ask, how does God love? The Kabbalistic notion of *zimzum* or divine withdrawal means that God makes a space within Godself for creation to exist. This self-limitation suggests that God suffers with or compassions the pain and suffering of creation's new birth. God bends low in love to embrace and accompany fragile created life, as it develops toward freedom in love. God suffers in, with, and through creation so that we do not suffer alone. This compassionate loving presence of God is the hope and source of nature's becoming. Thus, while suffering causes pain it does not necessarily diminish life. For the pain in suffering, Jürgen Moltmann states, "is the lack of love, and the wounds in wounds are the abandonment, and the powerlessness in pain is unbelief" (1991: 46). Where we suffer and give of ourselves in sacrifice because we love, God suffers in us, and it is because of God's suffering in us that light can break through the darkness of our pain. If God was incapable of suffering, then God would also be incapable of love. Love bears the weight of suffering in relation to another. The one who is capable of love is also capable of sacrifice, for he or she is also open to the suffering which is involved in love and yet remains superior to it by virtue of love (Moltmann 1991: 230).

Chaos, cross, and the wages of love

If we seek a God who will save us from suffering and sacrifice, we shall not find such a God to be the Christian God. For centuries Christianity held that God cannot suffer; patripassianism was considered a heresy in the early church. In the twentieth century, a renewal of trinitarian theology based on personhood and relationship argued otherwise. In the mystery of the cross, Jürgen Moltmann wrote, that is, the mystery of the Trinity incarnate and crucified, we find God deeply immersed in suffering. The Trinity connotes an inner dynamic of conflict in God: the Father suffers the death of the Son and, on the cross, the Son suffers the abandonment of the Father. The letting go of the Father and the surrender of Son give rise to the Spirit who is the bond of love between them and thus the breath of God open to the future. God's letting go out of love for the sake of the other reflects both the nature and freedom of God. In the historical event of Jesus, the cross reveals the vulnerability of God's love: "It is God's going forth into the danger and the nothingness of the creation that reveals [God's] heart to be at its origin vulnerable" (Von Balthasar 1984: 356). The cross, therefore, signifies a God who is radically in love with the world, and this love bears within it the ultimate sacrifice of God's Son for the world. The cross reveals God as absolute being-in-love. Love is not what God does; love is what God is. Love is the Godness of God. That is why the cross is the most revealing statement about God, as Moltmann wrote:

> When the Crucified Jesus is called the image of the invisible God, the meaning is that *this* is God, and God is *like this*. God is not greater than he is in his humiliation. God is not more glorious than he is in this self-surrender. God is not more powerful than he is in this helplessness. God is not more divine than he is in this humanity. All that can be said about God is said in the cross. (1991: 205)

God enters into history and assumes death and the abyss of godforsakenness. Hence, "There is no suffering that is not God's suffering; no death which has not been God's death in the history on Golgotha" (Moltmann 1991: 246). The *power* of divine love is shown in the *powerlessness* of the cross, as Cardinal Walter Kasper writes: "On the cross God's self-renouncing love is embodied with ultimate radicalness.... God need not strip himself of his omnipotence in order to reveal his love.... Only an almighty love can give itself wholly to the other and be a helpless love" (1999: 194–95).

But when *we* suffer and sacrifice, does God suffer in us? While God cannot suffer *ex carentia* since God cannot lose what pertains to God's integrity, God can (and does) suffer *ex abundantia*: out of the divine plenitude God suffers out of love for us. God shares our pain and bears our burdens (Baum 2000: 235–36) out of the divine fountain fullness of love. This is a God who gets so "foolishly close" that the boundaries between what is human and what is sacred become blurry (Malone 2000: 22).

Suffering is a door through which God can enter and love us in our human weakness, misery, and loneliness. As we sacrifice and suffer loss, so too God personally experiences loss with us and in us. I can experience God's suffering as desolation or absence of God's comfort, and yet God is deeply present as Spirit and thus sustaining me in love. It is my act of surrender that brings God's indwelling Spirit to life within me because I am now joined to God on a new level that is open to the future. My act of surrender is an act of trust by which Saint Paul writes, "now it is not I who live but Christ who lives in me" (Galatians 2:20). In this mystery of love and surrender is my hope that I will not die because God's love is pulling me forward into a new future. Hence, my suffering and sacrifice for others is, at the same time, God's own suffering and sacrifice in me. My commitment to love is God's commitment to love; my willingness to surrender in love is God's willingness to surrender in love; my pain or sorrow is God's pain as well. My hope comes precisely in the act of relinquishing control of my pain or sorrow, recognizing that I am not alone: that God suffers with me. By surrendering to God I am one with the Son in his obedience to the Father and I am one with the Father in his surrender of the Son and thus I am caught up in the breath of God's love, and this love is always new; hence despite my loss, I live on the cusp of the new because God's love is the power of the future. As Rolston writes, "Things perish with a passing over in which the sacrificed individual also flows in the river of life" (2001: 59).

This deeper truth of suffering must lead us beyond a sense of loss to compassionate suffering, that is, a willingness to be sacrificial love for others. Suffering and sacrifice are intertwined. Suffering *ex abundantia* can lead to sacrifice when love for another impels one to give oneself entirely to the other. One has only to reflect, for example, on the lives of Oscar Romero and Maximilian Kolbe, who were themselves victims of violence and yet sacrificed their lives out of justice (Romero) and compassion (Kolbe). We have the capacity to love others in the face of suffering. The key to sacrificial suffering is a consciousness of belonging to another, an awareness of "Thou" at the heart of "I." Only when we know that we belong to another can we be with others in *their* suffering.

An unfinished universe

To suffer *ex abundantia* does not diminish the level of pain one experiences but it reorients pain within a wider context of purpose. Pain without love can leave one feeling isolated and desolate, cut off from the stream of life. Such pain makes sacrifice for another impossible. However, pain does not necessarily preempt compassion or loving another. That is, the pain of another can evoke in me a horizontal transcendence in love, if there is a deeper reality that binds us together. Here I am thinking of the young Jewish writer Etty Hillesum. Imprisoned and confined to a life of violence and misery, Etty began to talk to God. Her conversations opened up into prayer, and despite her deplorable surroundings, she found herself in the presence of God. In a small diary, she left us profound insights on living joyfully in the midst of suffering. She wrote:

> Dear God, these are anxious times. Tonight, for the first time I lay in the dark with burning eyes as scene after scene of human suffering passed before

me. . . . But one thing is becoming increasingly clear to me: *that You cannot help us, that we help You to help ourselves* . . . that we safeguard that little of You, God, in ourselves. And perhaps in others as well. Alas, there doesn't seem to be much You Yourself can do about our circumstances, about our lives. Neither do I hold You responsible. *You cannot help us, but we must help You and defend Your dwelling place inside us to the last.* (Kidder 2009: 59 [added emphasis])

God is not an object of power we accept or reject. God is the ground of our existence (see 2 Timothy 2:13). Thomas Merton wrote that "if I find God I will find myself, and if I find myself I will find God" because the essence of who I am lies in God (1961: 36). God is born from within when we come to know ourselves in God.

> It is because of God's indwelling presence that the ubiquity of pain in the world is not an argument against the love or goodness of God. Rather, it is the key to understanding our higher calling of love. Every action can be sacred action if it is rooted in love. Our lives affect God's own relational life. When we contribute to building the world in love by giving of ourselves in love for the sake of others, we make a positive difference to God's life. However, when our pain isolates us, and we react with violence, hate, or revenge, our capacity for love turns to evil, and God is erased.

Suffering into a higher love despite our human frailties is the only way to evolve to a more unified world. It means loving by way of sacrifice and letting go of our precious need to control. This higher calling to love requires openness to forgiveness. Forgiveness, Beatrice Bruteau wrote, is an act of the future. It is the gift of goodness *given in abundance* to another where love has been distorted or annihilated. Forgiveness means loving another in the face of unresolved differences or what Miroslav Volf called a "phenomenology of embrace," opening one's arms and embracing the other despite unresolved questions (1996: 141). Albert Haase recounts the story of Corrie ten Boom who, accused of sheltering Jews, was sent along with her family to the concentration camp at Ravensbruck. Only Corrie survived. After the war she committed herself to lecturing on the topic of forgiveness and reconciliation. Haase writes:

> One day after giving her talk in Munich, Germany, a man came forward to thank her for her talk. Corrie couldn't believe her eyes. He was one of the Nazi guards who used to stand duty in the women's shower room at Ravensbruck. The man reached for her hand in friendship. Her physical body remembered too sharply the horror of the camp and the death of her beloved sister. Corrie was blocked emotionally, stuck in the crippling and debilitating rut of resentment, bitterness,

hatred. As Corrie stood there, frozen with shock, the battle raged inside of her. She was torn between the seductive desire to balance the scales of justice with violence and revenge and to heed Jesus' challenge of forgiveness which she herself had preached so often. So, she prayed silently to herself, "Jesus, I cannot forgive this man. Give me your forgiveness." As she prayed that prayer and as her mind's eye reviewed the years of brutality, suffering, humiliation and death, her hand suddenly lifted from her side! This former prisoner found herself offering the former shower guard the one thing she thought she did not know how to give. "I forgive you, brother, with all my heart!" (1993: 162-63)

The German theologian Dietrich Bonhoeffer once said that forgiveness is a form of suffering and sacrifice because it means denying the gratifying desire for revenge (1963: 100). Forgiveness is "the energetic radiation of a good will for the sake of the future" (Bruteau 2001: 129); thus, in the act of forgiveness, we become cocreators of an evolving universe. We love another on the point of *coming into existence* so that "this 'instant,' the moment to moment continuity of living—as the primary reality—is essential to the future of life" (2001: 142).

We are challenged to move beyond suffering and pain that isolates and detaches us toward suffering *ex abundantia*, in which an excess of love stands behind sacrifice as self-gift. Just as eons of cosmic and biological life have undergone extreme violence and mass extinctions, providing the conditions for new life to emerge, so too we must realize that suffering and sacrifice are necessary for the ongoing evolution of life. To resist sacrifice or ignore pain is to suppress the vitality of life and its impulse to evolve. When we are beaten down and defeated, our tendency is to give up and declare life a failure. But if we search within, we will find divine love quietly present, challenging us to get up and awaken to the sounds of a new future because the power of new life is the power of love, and God's love is the power of the future.

References

Von Balthasar, H. U. (1984), *The Glory of the Lord: Theological Aesthetics*, trans. Andrew Louth, Francis McDonagh, and Brian McNeil. Vol. 2, in S. J. Joseph Fessio (ed.), *Studies in Theological Style: Clerical Styles*, San Francisco: Ignatius Press.

Baum, G. (2000), "Meister Eckhart and Dorothee Soëlle on Suffering and the Experience of God," in Mary Heather MacKinnon, Moni McIntyre, and Mary Ellen Sheehan (eds.), *Light Burdens, Heavy Blessings*, 227–29, Quincy: Franciscan Press.

Bergson, H. (1935), *The Two Sources of Morality and Religion*, trans. R. Ashley Audra and Cloudesley Brereton, New York: Henry Holt and Company.

Bonhoeffer, D. (1963), *The Cost of Discipleship*, trans. R. H. Fuller, New York: Macmillan Co.

Bruteau, B. (2001), *The Grand Option: Personal Transformation and a New Creation*, Notre Dame: University of Notre Dame Press.

Capra, F. (1996), *The Web of Life: A New Scientific Understanding of Living Systems*, New York: Doubleday.

Clayton, P. (2006), *Mind and Emergence: From Quantum to Consciousness*, New York: Oxford University Press.

Einum, S., and I. Fleming (2000), "Highly Fecund Mothers Sacrifice Offspring Survival to Maximize Fitness," *Nature* 405: 565–67.

Faricy, R. (1966), "Teilhard de Chardin's Theology of Redemption," *Theological Studies* 27: 553–79.

Frank, A. (2009), *The Constant Fire: Beyond the Science vs. Religion Debate*, Berkeley: University of California.

Haase, A. (1993), *Swimming in the Sun: Discovering the Lord's Prayer with Francis of Assisi and Thomas Merton*, Cincinnati: St. Anthony Messenger.

Haught, J. (2003), *Deeper Than Darwin*, Cambridge: Westview.

Hayes, Z. (1997), *A Window to the Divine*, Quincy: Franciscan.

Kasper, W. (1999), *The God of Jesus Christ*, trans. Matthew J. O'Connell, New York: Crossroad.

Kidder, Annemarie S., ed. (2009), *Etty Hillsum: Essential Writings*, Maryknoll: Orbis.

King, Thomas M. (1981), *Teilhard's Mysticism of Knowing*, New York: Seabury.

Malone, P. (2000), "A God Who Gets Foolishly Close," *America*, May 27: 22–23.

Merton, T. (1961), *New Seeds of Contemplation*, New York: Basic Books.

Moltmann, J. (1991), *The Crucified God*, trans. R. A. Wilson and J. Bowden, New York: HarperCollins.

Panikkar, R. (2010), *The Rhythm of Being*, Maryknoll: Orbis.

Rolston, H. (2001), "Kenosis and Nature," in J. Polkinghorne (ed.), *The Work of Love: Creation as Kenosis*, 43–65, Grand Rapids: Wm B. Eerdmans.

Teilhard de Chardin, P. (1959), *The Phenomenon of Man*, trans. Bernard Wall, New York: Harper & Row.

Teilhard de Chardin, P. (1964), *The Future of Man*, trans. Norman Denny, New York: Harper & Row.

Teilhard de Chardin, P. (1968), *Science and Christ*, trans. René Hague, New York: Harper & Row.

Concluding Thoughts

Marcia Pally

Introduction

In this volume, we have attempted to explore the role of sacrifice in arenas from business and the military to gender relations and the changes brought about by artificial intelligence. We have also sought to address questions that occupied the great theorist of sacrifice, Rene Girard:

- How did the practice of sacrifice begin?
- How and why does it motivate us and to do what?
- Under what conditions is sacrifice productive and when, abusive?

In exploring these questions, contributors to this volume agree with Girard on humanity's social and mimetic nature—that we learn from our surroundings what things are to consider valuable. There is further probing, however, of the idea that shared values—because of their very *shared-ness*, because they are learned through acculturation and mimesis within societies—inevitably bring on society-rending competition and aggression. In short, does mimesis unavoidably lead to competition or are they, under certain conditions of human development, uncoupled? Thus, additional questions emerging in this volume are:

- Were we always mimetic, internalizing, and taking on the values of our neighbors?
- Was mimesis always a source of competition (for things valued in common) and thus of aggression?
- Might mimesis, this close relationship with others, lead to different ends, even to reciprocal concern and to what the biologists call "cooperativity" (giving for the sake of others and the common good)?
- Might competition and aggression be brought about by something other than mimesis and shared values?

These questions inform one of philosophy and theology's most foundational matters: our understanding of human nature. Just how violent are we (created) to be? If it is our nature to be not mimetic and competitive but mimetic and *cooperative*—if not perfectly but at least to substantial extent—cooperativity might be more ready-to-hand today than if we never have lived under norms of fairness.

We are far from having a definitive view of human evolution, and Girardian studies is well-positioned to make a significant contribution in this area: Under which conditions does mimesis lend itself to competitive violence and under which is something else afoot? Girard had a sense for this in his interest in the second lesson of the cross: that Christ's self-giving teaches us about the donative nature or structure of world and humanity. That's the way the world flourishes; we are made for reciprocal giving and have the capacity for it. That is, the premise of Girard's interest in the cross is that humanity is able to learn from it. Something of the goodness of humanity at creation—in evolutionary terms, humanity's mimetic yet cooperative nature—gives us "receptors" so to speak for Christ's lessons. Had we no capacity within human nature to grasp the lessons of the cross, there would be little point in it.

This at any rate is a somewhat hopeful proposal for future Girardian research. We have three. One, that it is not social living or mimesis per se that prods competitive aggression but mimesis under conditions of close quarters (sedentarism), inequality, and the abandonment of the shared or common good—that is, conditions where some have greater access to what's valued than others do and seek to maintain it. This suggestion *uncouples* competition from mimesis, which evolutionary biologists tell us is very old, reaching back to the formation of hominids and other mammals. It posits mimesis and relative cooperativity as a possible early human life form. It further posits that competitive aggression, as a *predominant* feature of society, may have been a later development associated with the shift from hunter-gathering to sedentarism, agrarianism (more goods to value and want), unequal property concentrations, and thus envy and a sense that our *cooperativity—the way we are after long evolution—is being violated*. If people's sense of "the way things should go"—an idea of what's "fair" evolved over a million years—was violated by new agrarian economic and residence patterns, little wonder that resentment, greed, competition, and anger developed.

Our second hypothesis is that ritual emerged, at least at first, from mimesis in relatively cooperative groups as it promotes *play* activities (repeatable activities, ritualized reenactments of the past, and projections into the future). This mimesis-based play/ritual may have served to build solidarity among early humans owing to a three-part outcome of evolution: we are a relational species; our "deeply enculturated" (Donald 2001: 264) relationality emerges at least in part from the long period of childhood mimesis; so that *the activity of mimetically performing together ritual patterns that are fair and shared by all gives Homo sapiens the feelings of relatedness, belonging, and being cared for that we evolved to want and need* (see the Introduction for a more detailed account).

Our third hypothesis is that the cooperativity of our long evolution, the nearly one million years preceding the Girardian archaic, is not lost but remains with us as potential. Our cooperativity-evolved species is not suited for conditions of gross inequities (Schaik and Michel 2016). Our long experience of fairness and sharing protests against them (today still, in forms ranging from riots against elites to political movements and community efforts for more equitable distribution of societal resources). Girard himself suggests such a distant, relatively cooperative past in saying that mimetic competition is as old as "Cain" but not as old as Adam, not as old as humanity itself. There was a time before. The Abrahamic religions share this view insofar as they hold that we retain something of the goodness of creation even after the Fall. Each of these will be discussed below.

Our propositions in greater detail

In looking at human society prior to Girard's archaic—that is, at the evolutionary biology on hunter-gatherer societies that comprise 95 percent of our evolutionary development—there is reason to propose that early humans were indeed mimetic but show relatively low levels of competitive aggression. Hundreds and thousands of years of evolutionary pressures were selected—for reasons of group protection, successful hunts, and care of offspring with long vulnerable childhoods—for "cooperativity" (the Introduction and Chapter 1, this volume). If, in a simple example, persons either within a hunter-gatherer band or from separate bands battle each other to be the only ones to hunt a certain animal, the winner may in the end have more food. But many will be killed in the battle, the capacity to overpower the animal will be diminished, and chances increase of becoming the animal's meal rather than making it one's own. Cooperation may be the better survival strategy as more people live (and may later reproduce) and chances of succeeding in the hunt rise.

This does not suggest a simplistic panacea of generosity among hunter-gatherers but only reasonable evolutionary pressures toward the development of a "sensibility" of cooperativity (Hodge 2019). This cooperativity may turn out to have been the case, as even before *Homo sapiens*, the *Homo erectus*—for success in hunting, group protection, and offspring care—evolved "an entirely new level of social organization beyond anything seen in nonhuman primates" (Bellah 2011: Kindle Location 2019). This social organization relied on communal property and the fair, roughly equitable sharing of resources for the common good of both the primary group and, to significant degrees, "outside" groups.

Importantly, such hunter-gatherer groups were comprised not of foundationally competitive persons who, with evolution, became more aware of their competitive natures that their neighbors value and seek what they do. Under such conditions, cooperativity might have to be imposed top-down, by sagacious leaders who for some reason were unlike their competitive bandmates and saw the societal value of cooperativity. (These leaders would have little personal benefit from enforcing cooperativity as it required communal property and fairly equal access to resources, including women. Thus, they would have little private or "alpha-male" motive to enforce it.) Rather, the idea of an evolved cooperativity suggests a process by which people develop a sense of cooperativity for survival reasons and, as time proceeds, are cooperative by long-evolved sensibility.

Thus, in some sense, exploring the idea of mimesis and cooperativity, rather than the more familiar mimesis and competitive aggression, is a project of cross-cultural investigation: an open and receptive pondering of people who are in many ways similar to ourselves yet with significant differences, among them, differences in cooperativity.

This is not inconsistent with Girard. Mimetic theory itself suggests that there likely were forms of human living that preceded the archaic period—ways of living with significant cooperativity and less violence. After all, Girard's archaic societies *already* had inherited the value of containing competitive aggression—though they need not have. Such pacific values and practices are by no means an evolutionary inevitability, and our closest relatives, the chimpanzees, do not share them (Schmid-Hempel 2015). It was precisely because archaic societies had the idea of limiting aggression that they began the practice of sacrificing a scapegoat, an effort, however, misguided to preserve peace among the many by forfeiting—sacrificing—the few (Girard 1986, 2004: 13). Had archaic societies not already had such a peace-preserving priority, they could well have let competitive mayhem reign. Girard understood that pressures for relatively harmonious living had been part of the human experience before the archaic period, which inherited them.

Moreover, not only Girard but the Christianity he took seriously posit a time before our time, of Adam, Eve, and Eden. Girard held that the competitive aggression of the archaic was as "old as Cain" but not as old as Adam, not as old as humanity itself. There was a time before the competitive violence of Cain. As we note Girard's description of earliest humanity, we recall also that the Abrahamic traditions too recognize, through the Eden narrative, a way of living that is no longer our own but where fruit was gathered up and shared and peace reigned. Modern notions of the "selfish gene"—and their recruitment to advance economic systems of high-competition and low concern for the common good—may have become our normative trope. But this obscures the earlier life forms that Girard and our wisdom traditions point to.

Evolutionary biology now seems to be catching up to them, with important work positing a long earlier period of relative cooperativity and a later shift to greater competitive aggression. As much about this period is unknown, this remains an open question with more research needed and being done. At present, the shift from greater cooperativity to competitive aggression seems to begin with sedentarism and city-clusters, agrarianism (more resources to want), property concentrations and thus inequality, envy and the hoarding and grabbing of wealth that are characteristic of the period Girard called archaic (see the Introduction for a fuller account). Joel Hodge (2019) has fruitfully noted that sedentarism, city-clusters, and agrarianism bring with them the domestication of animals and settlement of large tracts of land, within which people were somewhat safer than in hunter-gatherer bands, where they were exposed to the surrounding terrain and predation from wild animals. While the hunter-gatherer concern with predation was a factor in promoting intra- and intergroup cooperativity, the shift to relative safety decreased concern with predator animals and increased concern about nearby humans who had motive to compete over goods. Moreover, these were no longer owned communally but privately and unequally, giving people greater motive to compete, hoard, and grab.

It is under such inequitable conditions that hierarchies may have become prominent societal features. Though they had *diminished* in the evolution from our hierarchical ("alpha-male") prehuman ancestors to the relatively flat hierarchies of hunter-gathering, the new sedentarism and unequal wealth may have set the conditions for their reemergence. The purpose of hierarchies, Robert Bellah and others suggest, was not to ensure the cooperativity of hunter-gatherer society as this was already fading. It was rather to bolster the new inequitable status quo and control the have-nots (see Bellah 2011: chapters 3–5). To be sure, hierarchies maintained order, and order needed to be maintained—imposed—

under the newly unequal conditions that prodded envy and attempts by those on the lower societal rungs to gain more. Moreover, order may be preferable to chaos, and many throughout society accept hierarchies for this reason. But a societal order that preserves substantial inequities will engender resentment—especially if those living under inequalities evolved to have a sensibility and expectation of more equitable distribution of resources. Such a substrate of potential unrest requires both imposed control by hierarchical elites *and* periodic release, as Girard suggests, by a mechanism such as the identification of a scapegoat whose ritual sacrifice allows people to let off steam and society, to re-bond.

We note that in investigating a shift from more cooperative hunter-gathering to the more inequitable, violent archaic, evolutionary biologists do not propose that hunter-gatherers were choirs of perfect altruism. They propose only that the lower amount of violence characteristic of these early societies is anthropologically and historically meaningful.

On the view of Sarah Hrdy, Merlin Donald, and others, mimesis, unlike competition, began very early in human development with the repetition of facial expressions and gestures between caretakers and offspring during the long period of nurturing relatively unformed infants. As childcare was performed not only by mothers but by many (even nonkin) adults, this back-and-forth exchange of expression and gesture eventually yielded what Hrdy calls "emotional modernity," the human capacities to "read" and relate to the emotions of others, even of strangers (Hrdy 2009: 204–06, 282). Hrdy's work is supported by developmental psychology, which too notes the importance of relationship to human development (Gilligan and Snider 2018) and of mimesis to our relationality (Gallagher 2005: 244–45; Gallese 2005: 105, 111; Reddy 2008: 19–21).

Mimesis under conditions of relative cooperativity was among the prime factors enabling the more advanced communication that allows for the transmission of complex knowledge, toolmaking, and cooperative work. It also enabled the development of play activities such as repeatable games, reenactments of past events, and projections of future events (Donald 2001: 263–65). Other animals may be able to copy actions that are shown to them for immediate use. But a different level of mimesis, information-retention, and transmission is needed to teach and learn a task for later application, under conditions of *absence and an imagined/projected* future (for instance, to make an arrow head in the absence of immediate need but for use in the undetermined future). An even more sophisticated level of mimesis and cognition is needed to teach third parties, other animals, to perform it also in the absence of immediate application. On this view, play—as it conjures the not-now, the imaginary, and develops into repeating activity-patterns with agreed upon goals and procedures—may be the origin of society-bonding ritual, which too repeats action-patterns referring to past or future with agreed upon goals and procedures. Indeed, the very "fairness" requirement of play positions it (and any religious, political, or other rituals emerging from it) as solidarity-building (Bellah 2011: Kindle Location 1579, 1602).

In sum, the bonds forged in mimesis and the evolutionary-survival pressures for cooperativity yielded what Bellah calls "the strong pull of social solidarity" and "community morality" (Bellah 2011: Kindle Location 2783), where desire for affection and belonging are the primary human motivators. To be sure, the situation between hunter-gatherer groups is more complex than within groups, featuring both cooperativity and competition. Yet there is some question of whether preference for the in-group, "parochial altruism" (Bowles 2008: 326; Palaver 2015: 153–56), of necessity brings along hostility toward others, especially among hunter-gatherers. First, competition among groups is more likely among sedentary, agricultural societies with city-clusters, where nearby tribes/nations were often in competition for resources. It is less likely in roving hunter-gatherer bands, where contact with outsiders was intermittent and bands were less frequently in resource competition as they continually moved around. Clare, Dietrich, Gresky, Notroff, Peters, and Pöllath (2019, 101) note, "There is presently no conclusive evidence for intergroup fighting in the early Pre-Pottery Neolithic," and though they warn against ignoring evidence of violence where it did occur, they conclude, "caution should nevertheless be exercised if we wish to avoid a situation which sees the 'bellicosification' of prehistory (2019, 101)." Second, evidence for "*reciprocal* altruism" (Trivers 1971; emphasis mine)—fairness and sharing—is not inconsiderable, as noted by Bowles and Gintis (2013); Churchland (2012); Pfaff (2014); Roca and Helbing (2012); Seyfarth and Cheney (2012: 170); Silk and House (2011); among others (see the Introduction for a longer discussion).

Importantly, however complex the situation may have been across groups, there is good evidence for cooperativity *within groups*, precisely where Girardian theory posits mimesis and high competitive aggression. This suggests a tension between evolutionary biology and mimetic theory. But the apparent incompatibility may be resolved by understanding them as describing different moments in human development. The evolutionary biology may offer insights into an earlier, long hunter-gatherer period of relative but not insignificant cooperativity. Mimetic theory may offer insights into the more recent period of agrarianism, sedentarism, population, and property concentrations, and greater competition and violence. Thus, *it may be not social living or mimesis per se that prod competitive aggression but mimesis under conditions of inequality and the abandonment of the shared or common good—that is, when some have far greater access to what's valued than others do.*

At any rate, this is one of the open questions of this book, one where Girardian studies may make substantial contribution. If we attend to Girard's insight that competitive aggression is as old as "Cain" but not as old as Adam, the biblical Fall from Adam to Cain may be understood as a metaphor for the shift from the Eden of relatively fair resource distribution to the harsher world of subsistence farming, private property, envy, and violence. In such a world, sacrifice may have indeed functioned as a steam valve for intragroup aggression. Earlier, where communal property and long-evolved fairness made competition/aggression less prominent, we face conditions where there might have been less need for such a ritual steam valve.

Ritual among hunter-gatherers thus may have developed from mimesis-based play, as suggested by Hrdy, Donald, and Whitehouse and Lanman (2014). Our second hypothesis for further study, then, is that mimesis-based ritual may have served to build solidarity owing to a three-part outcome of evolution: we are a relational species; our "deeply enculturated" (Donald 2001: 264) relationality emerges at least in part from the long period of childhood mimesis; so that *the activity of mimetically performing together ritual patterns that are fair and shared by all gives Homo sapiens the feelings of relatedness, belonging, and being cared for that we evolved to want and need.* Clare, Dietrich, Gresky, Notroff, Peters, and Pöllath (2019) describe Göbekli Tepe, a ritual site shared by small, roaming groups (9000–7000 BCE), as just such a "play" arena. The architecture and ornaments expressed "shared moral values, the documentation of group memories and histories, the formation of identities and the promotion of intergroup cooperation and altruism" (2019, 105). Moreover, the gathering of many groups at the site "would have fostered strong between-group bonds." There is no evidence, they add, of human or animal sacrifice—as release for accumulating competitive aggression or other reasons. In short, Göbekli Tepe was a site of ritual but not necessarily of violent sacrifice.

Evolutionary biology also notes that tensions may have arisen in hunter-gatherer societies as certain members might have transgressed group norms of sharing and cooperativity. These groups developed ways of sanctioning such lack of fairness, usually shaming or temporary exclusion from group activities; occasionally, more aggressive sanctions may have been needed. One might even argue that shaming was the first "othering" and sacrifice, which would make

Girardian theory pertinent not only to the archaic period but to earlier hunter-gatherer societies. This would make sacrifice indeed as old as Adam.

Yet shaming-as-first-sacrifice may be a difficult argument to sustain. Temporary shaming served to uphold the sensibility of sharing and equitable distribution of resources, which archaic sacrifice was not developed to do and did not do. These are two, quite different phenomena. Indeed, Girard's point is that after sacrifice releases intragroup competitive tensions, they start to accumulate again as sacrifice is not a mechanism capable of addressing their underlying causes. Rather, mimetic competition continues as it had before, and tensions accumulate once again. Sacrifice, as Girard wrote, is a steam valve not a *solution*.

Importantly, temporary shaming and archaic sacrifice have opposite aims. While in temporary shaming, the purpose is to reintegrate the offender into the community, the purpose of archaic sacrifice is to "other" and eject the victim, so that he may be murdered or exiled. Moreover, the long evolution toward hunter-gatherer cooperativity made both its violation and violent punishments *un*usual because *these societies were not harboring foundationally competitive individuals straining to break free of cooperative norms but rather were comprised of people who had over hundreds of thousands of years evolved into just this cooperative sensibility*. While the logic of shaming leading to "othering" leading to exile or sacrifice might have been assumed or "unmarked" in the later archaic period, to hunter-gatherers evolved for cooperativity, such a chain may well have appeared incoherent. It violates the very purpose and design of shaming, which is not a linear process out of the group, leading straight to exclusion, but a loop, leading to re-inclusion.

In the archaic, Girard held, the original scapegoating act was "crystallized" and repeated sub rosa in later myth and rituals, preserving societal bonds yet obscuring the original violent act from memory. If this is the case for the heirs of archaic societies, a similar crystallization may have occurred with the heirs of earlier hunter-gatherer societies. Their cooperativity and forgoing-for-the-commons would have, *on Girardian theory*, been submerged during the transition from hunter-gatherer to agrarian living. In short, it is not only violent sacrifice that may be retained as a trace in later periods but also other important societal features, such as cooperativity.

Here we come to our third hypothesis: the submerged cooperativity of early human living would remain as a palimpsest under the layers of hierarchy since the archaic period. It peers through our art and religious faiths, which are replete with both the violence of the archaic and acts of great generosity and donation, perhaps the remnant of more cooperative living. We have already remarked on the Eden narrative recalling a paradise of peace and plenty before the Fall. The Hebrew Bible covenant may be another remnant of reciprocal giving as it marks just such a relationship between God and humanity and among persons (see Blanchard and Pally, this volume). The crucifixion narrative, as Girard emphasizes, begins with violence yet turns to the donative sacrifice of Jesus, fully human, giving his life for the common good of humanity.

The (relatively) cooperative past as hope

If relative cooperativity is the longue durée of human nature, it is perhaps not surprising that it comes through also in this volume. Of the fourteen chapters, only two focus on sacrifice in its abusive forms (Brunotte, Roscoe), though much investigation of sacrifice over the last several decades has involved a postcolonial, gender, and minority critique of sacrifice's abuses. Nonetheless, twelve chapters here focus on sacrifice's productive potential, a practice of sacrifice where each party reciprocally gives for others and the common good.

One might understand this as exploring a reconfiguration of early human cooperativity for present conditions. This common theme emerged though the authors live on different continents, work in various fields (in the academy and not), and each wrote her chapter independently of the others and editorial *telos*. The original project to which all authors responded called broadly for explorations of the role of sacrifice in present societal arenas. From this wide terrain, twelve contributors landed upon the problem of self-absorption, withdrawal from the commons for private benefit, and reciprocal giving for the common good as solution.

Evolutionary biologist Peter Kappeler notes the strong cooperativity in human development. Tsvi Blanchard describes the use of sacrifice in the Hebrew Bible to create sanctified spaces and times that enable one to near God and others in covenantal reciprocity. My own chapter looks at sacrifice as a symbolic, dialogic act in the covenantal conversation with the transcendent and other persons—covenant itself being a bond that sustains relationship and reciprocal giving. Hassan Rachik explores sacrifice as symbolic act in societal/community relationships.

David Pan, in his exploration of the Kantian sublime, notes that what's moral about (self-) sacrifice for a higher good is not one's internal capacity to sacrifice but the good itself as it benefits the world and thus becomes a value around which societal life is organized. Anna Mercedes cautions us to note this benefit even in cases of injustice: the sacrifice made by the downtrodden is not pathetic—a label that would minimize if not blame the victim—but may be powerful and transformative. Francisco Canzani, while noting the abusive sacrifice of the poor for the wealthy and powerful, finds the solution in precisely the sort of sacrifice that characterized early *Homo sapiens*: giving to others and common good. Rolf von Uslar makes a parallel argument for the military: argument for the military, where abuse there is often rampant as Brunotte impressively shows in her research on the Weimar and Nazi periods. But the antidote is not *no* military, not no sacrifice, but a military as *Katéchon*, the readiness to sacrifice to *restrain* violence.

Adrian Pabst, like Canzani, Roscoe, and Brunotte, critiques the sacrifice of people deemed "useless" and the "globalization of indifference." Yet like Blanchard, Canzani, von Uslar, and me, Pabst calls for the reinvigoration of the relational networks in which people actually live and of the practices of contributing to the commons. We are not, he holds, by nature competitive but seek friendship and mutual recognition for our contribution to the common good. John Milbank argues that the political is not secular—a move away from religion, as is the popular contemporary argument—but religiously grounded in gift-giving and reciprocity, which is our *prevailing* way of living. Ilia Delio closes the book by noting the need for an ethics of donation, of reciprocal giving, for the world now being brought about by artificial intelligence.

This sort of sacrifice is societally productive and needed, as Girard held. Thus, our contributors call not for the *end* of sacrifice but rather buttressing forms of sacrifice, giving, that contribute to the well-being of society through fair distribution of resources among its members. To guide us, we have our wisdom traditions—the donative lessons of the cross (a Girardian emphasis) and the Hebrew Bible covenant, among other wisdom traditions (see Palaver, this volume)—*and* we have the traces of our past as evolved or created by the God who gave us our wisdom traditions.

Our evolution toward cooperativity remains with us, making us unsuited to conditions of gross unfairness and inequality. As Schaik and Michel (2016) point out, the last 10,000 years of agriculture and property concentrations are too short a time to have substantial influence on the cooperative creatures humans evolved to be. Resistance to significant inequality was visible already in the archaic world, shortly after the shift to sedentarism and agriculture. Those on lower societal strata sought a fairer share of resources and attempted to take it, if necessary, from elites, who in turn, sought to put down such usurpation, often violently. This third hypothesis of the book, that traces of earlier times inform later living, is what Girard described as the process of human civilization: earlier experience is "crystallized" and passed along in traces to future generations. The idea of *trace as potential for future* is addressed in different ways in chapters by Blanchard, Delio, Mercedes, Milbank, Pabst, Rachik, von Uslar, and me.

This idea may be seen in Augustine, who, while certain of the devastation of the Fall into sin, was also sure of humanity's prelapsarian goodness, which remains with us as a "relic." Upon creation, he wrote, God held humanity to be "very good," a goodness which is not entirely lost (Augustine 390/1953: 11.21). It is a palimpsest and human potential. To be sure, we may now, post-Fall, need God's grace to access it, but it is there to be accessed. One might say, we have receptors for it.

As Augustine describes, as we are finite, live in time, and require language to communicate (we do not live in "union" with the divine), we are not in a state of grace (Smith 2000: 141). Yet, humanity was not sinful at creation but became so only upon Adam and Eve's decision to ignore God's principles. Prior to that, humanity was sinless although we were finite, material, and language-using. Thus, humanity's materiality cannot be per se sinful. "Matter," Augustine writes, "participates in something of the ideal world, otherwise it would not be matter.... All existence as such is good" (Augustine 390/1953: 11.21).

We were created good, partaking of God's perfect goodness in order to exist "as matter" at all. We retain a "relic" of this goodness and the *imago* even after the Fall and though we are radically different from God. This is Augustine's *maior dissimilitudo* (God's alterity) together with *tanta similitudo* (of-a-kind-ness). It is the partaking of God and the "relic" of him in each of us—even post-Fall—that gives each person the capacity to love in a (limited, imperfect) human iteration of God's love.

Moreover, the *imago* means that we can know something of God, however, limitedly and imperfectly. On Augustine's view, the human mind, in God's image, knows something of the world's undergirding principles that God has created (numbers, ratio, beauty). So too the mind, because it is of God, may understand something of God himself. The Trinity, for instance, is a divine community where each Trinitarian person is foundationally different from, yet in union with, the other Trinitarian persons. Each gives identity to and for the sake of the others. It is a community of donation and peace amid difference. As humanity is of this triune divine (to be "matter" at all), we can know something about it, something of donation amid difference. The mind, Augustine writes, is "able to remember and understand and love him by whom it was made"

(Augustine 400–417: 15.4.15). And we are able to love others, whom God has also made. "Whoever, then, thinks," Augustine writes, "that he understands the Holy Scriptures, or any part of them, but puts such an interpretation upon them as does not tend to build up this twofold love of God and our neighbor, does not yet understand them as he ought" (Augustine 397/426: Ch. 36, par. 40).

Like the Bible, which speaks of the time before the Fall, Augustine recognizes a prelapsarian Edenic life as potential for future living based on reciprocal giving, indeed, on love. In parallel discourse, modern biology suggests a past time of fairer distribution that is yet available to us as it is part of our long evolution. The evolutionary biology and theology point to the same ontology of giving, which is not suited for conditions of gross inequities. Our long-evolved cooperativity protests against them in both societally productive forms (political movements for greater equity in access to resources) and unproductive ones (rioting, crime, and "deaths of despair" such as alcohol and drug abuse).

Aquinas's perspective might also be helpful here. He, along with Maimonides, understood God as the source of all things and thus as inhering in all things. As causes, on Aquinas's understanding, yield resembling outcomes (resembling not at the surface but at the underlying level), humanity, caused by the source of all being God, has an underlying resemblance to him. "Nothing created," Aquinas held, "is so far from God as not to have Him in itself" (*Summa Theologica*, I, q. 8).

As existence results from the source of all, Aquinas writes, God "is properly the cause of universal being which is innermost in all things ... in all things God works intimately" (*Summa Theologica*, 1948/1265–1274, Ia, q. 105, art. 5). All things, in turn, partake of the divine in order to exist. Though persons are radically different from God, echoing Augustine's *maior dissimilitudo* (differences in materiality/immateriality and finitude/infinitude), something of God inheres in us, and we intimately partake of God to exist at all—as with Augustine's *tanta similitudo*. The Jewish tradition gets at this nicely in holding to the paradox of *tselem Elohim*: we are in the image (underlying similarity) of an imageless God (radical difference). In his theory of the *analogia entis* (analogy of being), Aquinas holds that we do not partake of God identically or proportionally but analogically. We are to God what an analogy is to its referent: holding an underlying of-a-kind-ness yet profound difference in particulars.

Thus, humanity, as a condition of its existence, analogously retains something of the good of the divine even post-Fall. Continuing the Augustinian understanding of mind as the human feature nearest God, Aquinas held that, of the three ways in which God's image inheres in each person, reason is primary. Reason is given by God to direct each person toward him. It makes us able to know something of God and thus able to act in correspondence with his vision for world. God has bound himself "to the created intellect, as an object made intelligible to it" (Thomas Aquinas, *Summa Theologica*, I, q. 12, art. 4; 1:52). Aquinas explains that, just as sense impressions take on meaning when interpreted by human intellect, God's sacred books ("prophetic visions") take on meaning when interpreted by human intellect supported by grace, God intimate within us. Thus, with God within us, we may reach some understanding of him and of his loving principles for the world (*Summa Theologica* 1.12.13).

Much of the *imago/similitudo*, on Aquinas's view, was lost in the Fall, but not all (Gardoski 2007). We retain the capacity, with God's grace, to gain (limited) understanding of him and to cooperate with him to further the world. God's grace, Aquinas held, is operative; it makes things happen. But we possess a cooperative aspect, wherein we willingly cooperate with God. We bring something of our (free) will and abilities to it. In his doctrine of secondary causality, Aquinas notes that God creates the primary conditions of the world. But we, in God's image and analogously partaking of him, act "secondarily" to make particular things from these basic principles. In the classic example, God creates oxygen, moisture, and the principles of germination while we plant seeds and make grains grow.

A parallel idea in the Jewish tradition is "cocreatorship": as we are *b'tselem Elohim* (image of God), we may contribute to the development of God's covenantal vision for world. In the Islamic tradition, the medieval philosophers al-Ash'ari and al-Ghazali understood humanity as "performing" what God creates. Indeed, the point of being in God's image is that we have the capacity to so contribute—we have the ability to act in "moral correspondence" (*dmuth Elohim*) with the divine. "The creative activity of the human, in particular," Terence Fretheim writes, "has the potential of significantly enhancing the ongoing life of the world and every creature therein" (Fretheim 2005: Kindle Location 460–62; Pally 2016: 132, 186–88).

In sum, these traditions are important for our discussion in understanding humanity as retaining something of its foundational goodness, its likeness to God, even after banishment from paradise to the tough world of agricultural labor. More than that, humanity may access this foundational goodness for the way we organize life, present and future. We may recognize its palimpsest throughout our faith traditions, art, and in political and economic notions of the common good.

If this is the case, we in some sense know why things go awry in the world. As we develop worldviews and economies of the "selfish gene," we find ourselves in Girard's archaic: a world "unequal in power, wealth, and social prestige," governed by "a tiny ruling group that used coercive powers to augment its authority" and suffering from substantial violence (Bellah 2011: Kindle Locations 3279–80). The non-powerful may accede to this structuring of society because they lack the means to oppose it, because it maintains social order against a worse chaos, or for still other reasons. Yet, it may be that gross inequities and rigid or rigidifying hierarchies—today, as ten thousand years ago in the shift to agrarianism—are a violation of our natural "baseline" (Narvaez 2014: 438). Thus, it is not surprising that many of this book's contributors call for greater (self-) sacrifice for the common good.

If we are living under material and symbolic inequalities for which we have not evolved, we are going against (created/evolved) human nature, which predictably would stress body, mind, and social fabric. Girard taught us much about the competitiveness and violence of gross inequality. We would do well to take seriously also Girard's attention to the donative lessons of the cross and his tutelage in the traces of the past that remain yet with us so that we may learn from the palimpsest of cooperativity. These are resources of hope.

References

Aquinas, T. (1948; original 1265–1274), *Summa Theologica*, trans. Fathers of the Dominican English Province, vols. 1–5, Westminster: Christian Classics.

Augustine (390/1953), "De vera religione," in *Augustine: Earlier Writings*, trans. J. Burleigh, Philadelphia: The Westminster Press.

Augustine (397/426), *On Christian Doctrine*, http://www9.georgetown.edu/faculty/jod/augustine/ddc1.html (accessed February 3, 2019).

Augustine (400–417), *De Trinitate*, in *Patrologia Latina* 42, Vo. 1, pt. 5.

Bellah, R. (2011), *Religion in Human Evolution*, Cambridge: Belknap/Harvard University Press.

Bowles, S. (2008), "Being Human: Conflict: Altruism's Midwife," *Nature* 456 (7220): 326–27.

Bowles S., and H. Gintis (2013), *A Cooperative Species: Human Reciprocity and Its Evolution*, Princeton: Princeton University Press.

Churchland, P. (2012), *Braintrust: What Neuroscience Tells Us about Morality*, Princeton: Princeton University Press.

Clare, L., O. Dietrich, J. Gresky, J. Notroff, J. Peters, and N. Pöllath (2019), "Ritual Practices and Conflict Mitigation at Early Neolithic Körtik Tepe and Göbekli Tepe,

Upper Mesopotamia: A Mimetic Theoretical Approach," in I. Hodder (ed.), *Violence and the Sacred in the Ancient Near East: Girardian Conversations at Çatalhöyük*, 96–128, New York/London: Cambridge University Press.
Donald, M. (2001), *A Mind So Rare: The Evolution of Human Consciousness*, New York: Norton.
Fretheim T. (2005), *God and World in the Old Testament: A Relational Theology of Creation*, Nashville: Abingdon.
Gallagher, S. (2005), *How the Body Shapes the Mind*, Oxford: Oxford University Press.
Gallese, V. (2005), "'Being Like Me': Self-Other Identity, Mirror Neurons, and Empathy," in S. Hurley and N. Chater (eds.), *Perspectives on Imitation*, 101–18, Cambridge: MIT Press.
Gardoski, K. (2007), "The *Imago Dei* Revisited," *Journal of Ministry and Theology* 11 (2): 5–37.
Gilligan, C., and N. Snider (2018), *Why Does Patriarchy Persist?* Cambridge/Medford: Polity Press.
Girard, R. (1986), *The Scapegoat*, trans. Y. Freccero, Baltimore: Johns Hopkins University Press.
Girard, R. (2004), "Violence and Religion: Cause or Effect?" *The Hedgehog Review* 6 (1): 8–20.
Hodge, J. (February 19, 2019), personal communication.
Hrdy, S. (2009), *Mothers and Others: Evolutionary Origins of Mutual Understanding*, Cambridge: Harvard University Press.
Narvaez, D. (2014), *Neurobiology and the Development of Human Morality: Evolution, Culture, and Wisdom*, New York: W. W. Norton & Company.
Palaver, W. (2015), "Parochial Altruism and Christian Universalism: On the Deep Difficulties of Creating Solidarity Without Outside Enemies," in P. Dumouchel and R. Gotoh (eds.), *Social Bonds as Freedom: Revisiting the Dichotomy of the Universal and the Particular*, 153–73, New York: Berghan.
Pally, M. (2016), *Commonwealth and Covenant: Economics, Politics, and Theologies of Relationality*, Grand Rapids: Eerdmans.
Pfaff, D. (2014), *The Altruistic Brain: How We Are Naturally Good*, New York: Oxford University Press.
Reddy, V. (2008), *How Infants Know Minds*, Cambridge: Harvard University Press.
Roca, C., and C. Helbing (2012), "Emergence of Social Cohesion in a Model Society of Greedy, Mobile Individuals," *Proceedings of the National Academy of Sciences*, http://www.pnas.org/content/108/28/11370.full (accessed October 17, 2018).
Schaik, C. van, and K. Michel (2016), *The Good Book of Human Nature: An Evolutionary Reading of the Bible*, New York: Basic Books.
Schmid-Hempel, P. (May 15, 2015), personal communication.
Seyfarth R., and D. Cheney (2012), "The Evolutionary Origins of Friendship," *Annual Review of Psychology* 63: 153–77.

Silk, J., and B. House (2011), "Evolutionary Foundations of Human Prosocial Sentiments," *Proceedings of the National Academy of Sciences* 108 (suppl. 2): 10910–17.

Smith, J. K. A. (2000), *The Fall of Interpretation: Philosophical Foundations for a Creational Hermeneutic*, Downers Grove: InterVarsity.

Trivers, R. (1971), "The Evolution of Reciprocal Altruism," *Quarterly Review of Biology* 46 (1): 35–57.

Whitehouse, H., and J. A. Lanman (2014), "The Ties that Bind Us," *Current Anthropology* 55 (6): 674–95.

Contributors

Rabbi Tsvi Blanchard is the Meyer Struckmann Professor of Jewish Law at Humboldt University Faculty of Law in Berlin and scholar-in-residence at the Institute for Law, Religion and Lawyer's Work at Fordham Law School. He has taught at Washington, Northwestern, and Loyola Universities. His publications include the 2002 Riesman Award–winning *How to Think About Being Jewish in the Twenty-First Century: A New Model of Jewish Identity Construction*.

Prof. Dr. Ulrike Brunotte is Associate Professor for Gender and Diversity at Maastricht University and adjunct Professor at Humboldt University Berlin. Since 2013, she has been Chair of the International Research Network Rengoo: "Gender in Orientalism, Occidentalism and Antisemitism." Her recent publications include *Helden des Todes. Studien zur Religion, Ästhetik und Politik moderner Männlichkeit* and *Orientalism, Gender, and the Jews. Literary and Artistic Transformations of European National Discourses*.

Dr. Francisco Canzani was, from 2004 to 2014, the head of the Department of Ecumenism at the Theology Faculty of Uruguay, Monsignor Mariano Soler. Since December of 2014, he has been a member of the general council of Focolare Movement in Rome, where he is co-responsible with Dr. Renata Simon for the Department of Culture and Studies of the institution.

Prof. Ilia Delio, OSF, is a Franciscan Sister of Washington, DC, and currently holds the Josephine C. Connelly Endowed Chair in Theology at Villanova University. She is the author of nineteen books including *Care for Creation*, winner of two Catholic Press Book Awards. *The Emergent Christ* and *The Unbearable Wholeness of Being: God, Evolution and the Power of Love* have also received several awards.

Prof. Dr. Peter M. Kappeler holds a chair for Sociobiology/Anthropology at the University of Göttingen and is the head of the Behavioral Ecology and Sociobiology Unit at the German Primate Center. He has authored more than 200 peer-reviewed papers and authored or edited about 15 books and special issues, including *The Lemurs of Madagascar*.

Rev. Dr. Anna Mercedes is Associate Professor of Theology at the College of Saint Benedict and Saint John's University. She teaches at the intersections of Christian theology, gender studies, and peace studies. Her most recent book is *Power For: Feminism and Christ's Self-Giving*. She is ordained in the Evangelical Lutheran Church in America.

Prof. Dr. John Milbank is Professor Emeritus of Religion, Politics and Ethics and President of The Centre of Theology and Philosophy at the University of Nottingham. Additionally, he is Principal of The Methexis Institute in Charlottesville, Virginia, and Visiting Professor at the Edith Stein Institute of Philosophy, Granada. He is the author of many books, of which the most recent are *Beyond Secular Order* and *The Politics of Virtue* (with Adrian Pabst).

Dr. Adrian Pabst is Head of School, Politics & IR, University of Kent; a Reader in Politics at Kent; and Fellow at the National Institute of Economic and Social Research. He is the author of *Metaphysics: The Creation of Hierarchy*, and, with John Milbank, *The Politics of Virtue: Post-Liberalism and the Human Future*. His most recent books are *Liberal World Order and Its Critics: Civilizational States and Cultural Commonwealths* and *The Demons of Liberal Democracy*.

Prof. Dr. Wolfgang Palaver is Professor of Catholic Social Thought at the University of Innsbruck (where he was Dean of the Faculty of Catholic Theology from 2013 to 2017). His most recent books are *René Girard's Mimetic Theory* (2013), *The European Wars of Religion* (2016), *The Palgrave Handbook of Mimetic Theory and Religion* (2017), and *Mimetic Theory and World Religions* (2018).

Prof. Dr. Marcia Pally teaches at New York University and is a regular guest professor at the Theology Faculty of Humboldt University, Berlin. Her most recent book is *Commonwealth and Covenant: Economics, Politics, and Theologies of Relationality* (2016), which was nominated for the Grawemeyer Award in religion and selected by the U.N.'s Committee on Education for Justice to be distributed to "educators, academics, policy-makers . . . throughout the world."

Prof. Dr. David Pan is Professor of German and Chair of the Department of European Language and Studies at the University of California, Irvine. He is editor of the journal *Telos* and is the author of *Primitive Renaissance: Rethinking German Expressionism* and *Sacrifice in the Modern World: On the Particularity and Generality of Nazi Myth*.

Prof. Dr. Hassan Rachik is Professor at the University Hassan II of Casablanca, Director of Paul Pascon Chair for Social Sciences (Rabat). He is the author of numerous articles and books including *Le sultan des autres, rituel et politique dans le Haut Atlas, Symboliser la nation, Essai sur l'usage des identités collectives au Maroc, L'islam au quotidien* (coauthor) and *Le proche et le lointain Un siècle d'anthropologie au Maroc.*

Dr. Philip Roscoe is Reader in Management at the School of Management, University of St Andrews. He has been a Leverhulme Trust research fellow and has published in leading sociology and management journals, including *Organization Studies, Accounting Organizations and Society,* and *Organization,* with monographs published by Oxford University Press and Penguin.

Colonel Dr. Rolf von Uslar is Head of Division Organization, Bundeswehr Medical Service Headquarters. He served, inter alia, as Commander Bundeswehr Medical Training Regiment and as a Staff Officer in ISAF HQ, Kabul/Afghanistan.

Index of Names and Concepts

Akedah 106, 110, 13, 185
ancient Greek 68–70
animal consecration 65–7, 82–3
ANSF (Afghan National Security Forces) 165–6
apes 39–41, 44
Aquinas, Thomas 4, 114–15, 187, 219–20, 239–41
Assmann, Hugo 131–3, 136–7, 141
Augustine 4, 105, 115, 186, 206, 239–40

Barash, David 10
Bauman, Zygmunt 194–5
behaviour
　altruistic 40, 42
　cooperative 42, 45
　mutualistic 40
　selfish 40
　social 40
Bellah, Robert 7–11, 14, 17–19, 105, 111, 182, 231–2, 234, 242
Bhagavad-Gita 51, 54, 56, 56–9
Brunotte, Ulrike 148, 150, 152, 238

capitalism 27–8, 91, 190–1, 197, 199–200, 203–10, 212–13
Catalhöyük 15–16
Cheney, Dorothy 3, 9, 234
chrism 124, 126, 128
Clare, L. 10, 13, 15, 234–5
Coakley, Sarah 25, 118, 120, 127–8
cooperation among kin 39–41
cooperativity 6, 8–11, 14, 17–20, 23, 28–9, 37, 228–38, 240, 242
covenant 3, 19–20, 25, 78–9, 80, 87–8, 103–4, 105–6, 108, 110–15, 184, 187, 198, 200, 212, 237–8, 241
covenantal relations 24, 77, 87–8, 108, 110–15, 198–200
crucifixion (narrative) 19–22, 25–6, 37, 103, 105–6, 109, 113, 130, 137–9, 147, 161, 212, 222–3, 237

Darwin, Charles 39, 218
Descola, Philippe 27, 177, 180–3
Détienne, M. 69–70
Dietrich, O. 10, 13, 15, 234–5
Donald, Merlin 8, 11, 230, 233, 235
donative/second lesson of the cross 25, 29, 216, 229, 238, 242

Evangelium gaudii 139, 205
evolution and evolutionary theory 6–15, 19–20, 29, 37, 39–45, 216–21, 226, 229–30, 232–5, 240

Facebook 190, 196–7, 200
feminist theory 118–22, 127–8
First World War 26, 115, 147, 150, 163, 166
fitness
　direct 40
　inclusive 40, 45
　indirect 40

Gandhi, Mahatma 24, 51–2, 54, 56–60, 193
Gardner, Andy 40–1
Gauchet, Marcel 177–82, 185–7
Genesis, Book of 19–20, 80, 111–12, 127, 216
gift and gift-exchange 177–84, 187–8
gift of self 137, 141–2
Girard, René 2–6, 10–11, 14, 20–5, 52–4, 64, 90, 103–6, 115, 119–28, 137, 140, 191, 196–8, 205, 229, 231–2, 236
Göbekli Tepe 13–14, 235
Goodhart, Sandor 2, 105, 107–8, 112
Gospels, the 55–6, 119, 120–1, 125, 140, 217
Gresky, J. 10, 13, 15, 234–5

Halbertal, Moshe 92–5, 104, 136, 177, 184–5
Hebrew Bible 24, 77–82, 84, 184, 237

Index of Names and Concepts

Hill, Kim   43–4
Hobbes, Thomas   3–4, 20, 90–1, 93, 95, 181, 207
holi(ness)   66, 68, 78–82, 84, 87–8, 124, 126, 128
House, Bailey R.   3, 9, 39, 45, 234
Hrdy, Sarah   7, 11, 233, 235
Hubert, Henri   64–6, 69, 71, 74

intent   84–7, 114
IRA (Irish Republican Army)   165
ISAF (International Security Assistance Force)   165–6
Ishopanishad   56–7, 59

Jones, Campbell   195–6, 199

Kant, Immanuel   4, 25, 90–101, 170, 237
katéchon   170–1, 238
Kearny, Richard   198–200
Kin   41, 45
Kracauer, Siegfried   12–13

Langemark-myth   149–53, 156
Laocoön   149, 156
Latin American Episcopal Council Conferences   135, 137–41
Laudato Si   204, 211
Levinas, Emmanuel   28, 78–9, 190, 195, 199
liberalism and liberal theory   3, 90–2, 194, 204, 207, 210
liberation theology   130, 132–41
Logos   121–3, 125
Lumen Gentium   135–8

Magisterium of the Catholic Church in Latin America   26, 130, 134–40
Männerbund   150, 156
Marx, Karl   191–2
Marxist   132–4, 208
masculinity   26, 147–53, 156
Mauss, Marcel   64–6, 69, 71, 74, 112, 180–1, 183
Michel, Kai   9, 14, 17–18, 230, 238
Mimesis and mimetic theory   2, 4–8, 11–14, 17, 22–3, 52, 60, 120, 126, 130, 140, 191, 196–7, 200, 206, 217, 228–31, 233–5

Mishna, the   79, 82–7
Moltmann, Jürgen   222–3
morality and moral law   25, 92, 94–6, 98–100, 115, 195, 212
moral responsibility   25, 103, 106–8, 114
Morocco   65, 68, 72
Münkler, Herfried   148, 162–4

Narvaez, Darcia   3, 7, 10, 242
Nazi Germany   26, 57, 147
Notroff, J.   10, 13, 15, 234–5
NS-Ordensburg Vogelsang   154, 156

ontology of peace   20, 23–4, 29, 51–2, 54, 77, 104

Palaver, Wolfgang   4, 9, 20–4, 52–4, 77–8, 104–5, 112–13, 137, 161, 197, 199, 234, 238
Peters, J.   10, 13, 15, 234–5
play (fictive world)   8, 11–16, 229, 234–5
Pöllath, N.   10, 13, 15, 234–5
poor laws   109, 112, 115
Pope Benedict XVI   133, 210–12
Pope Francis   136, 139, 204–5, 210–13
post bureaucratic management   192–3, 199
Prometheanism   208–9

rabbinic law   80–5, 108
resistance   22, 24–5, 51, 57, 118, 120–6, 171, 238
rituals   8, 11–13, 14–15, 24, 38, 66, 79, 82–4, 88–9, 113, 124–5, 151, 154, 178, 184, 186, 229–30, 233–5

sacrifice
  archaic   24, 38, 52–3, 104–6, 109–10, 114–15, 147, 236
  of Christ   52–4, 59, 78, 105, 118–20
  civic/political   66–70
  covenantal   105–15
  fruitful   137–40
  heroic   38, 99, 148, 153–5
  humiliating   72–3
  of Isaac (*see Akedah*)
  Islamic/Muslim   65–68
  Judaic conception   78, 82–5, 104–15, 240–1
  military   161–71

self-sacrifice   21, 24–5, 26–9, 38–9, 46, 51, 55, 57, 59, 94, 97, 101, 124, 130, 141, 148–9, 150–1, 155, 161–71, 190–6, 199, 200, 203, 216, 237, 242
  on a slant   124–8
sacrificial rites   24, 65–74, 79, 82–6, 88–9
Saint Paul   60, 124, 170, 184, 187, 223
sanctification   78–81, 84, 88–9
scapegoating   5–6, 8, 12, 17, 20–5, 27, 54, 103–7, 109, 114, 127, 140, 181, 197–8, 212, 231, 233, 236
Schwarz van Berk, Hans   152–3
Second Vatican Council   135–6, 137
Second World War   162–3, 167–8
self-giving and self-donation   19, 24–6, 28, 52, 54, 59–60, 77, 108, 118, 124, 126, 128, 190, 220, 229
self-interest   78, 91–3, 95–6, 100, 136
Sermon on the mount   57–8
Seyfarth, Robert   3, 9, 234
Silk, Joan B.   3, 9, 39, 45, 234
sin(ful)   5, 11, 59, 78, 80–5, 105–6, 108, 113–14, 133–5, 139, 206, 216, 239
Sklar, Robert   13, 15
society
  archaic   6, 17–18, 20, 28, 111, 137, 230–1
  hunter-gatherer   6–20, 42–5, 230–6
  post-heroic   26, 148, 161–3, 167, 170

sublime, the   96–9
suffer ex abundantia   216–17, 223–4, 225–6
suffer ex carentia   216–17, 223

Talmud   79, 80, 85–7
Tanach, the   103–15
Taylor, Charles   4, 164, 207
Teilhard de Chardin, Pierre   216–17, 219
Temple, the   78, 80–4, 183–4

van Schaik, Carel   9, 14, 17–18, 230, 238
victimage mechanism   120–1, 124–6
victim-sacralization   151
victim-survivors   122–3
violence   4–6, 10, 12, 14–19, 20–3, 51, 52–9, 60, 106–8, 115, 119, 120–7, 140–1, 148, 161–2, 168, 181, 217, 224, 226, 232–5, 242
von Clausewitz, Carl   161–2, 164
von Schirach, Baldur   151, 155
von Tresckow, Henning   171

Weil, Simone   54–7
Weimar   26, 147, 150–1, 153, 238
West, Stuart A.   40–1
West, Traci C.   25, 118, 120, 122–4
Westermarck, Edvard   66, 72–3
Winckelmann, Johann Joachim   149, 156

www.ingramcontent.com/pod-product-compliance
Lightning Source LLC
Chambersburg PA
CBHW070030010526
44117CB00011B/1768